Living PEACEFULLY

When the World Won't Leave You Alone

D1128176

Books by J. Allen Blair

Living Patiently—When God Seems Far Away
A Devotional Study of Job

Living Victoriously—When Winning It All Isn't Enough
A Devotional Study of Philippians

Living Peacefully—When the World Won't Leave You Alone
A Devotional Study of 1 Peter

Living
PEACEFULLY

When the World Won't Leave You Alone

A Devotional Study of 1 Peter

J. Allen Blair

Grand Rapids, MI 49501

Published in 1994 by Kregel Publications, a division of Kregel, Inc., P.O. Box 2607, Grand Rapids, MI 49501.

Cover Photograph: Sid Lenger
Cover Design: Don Ellens

Library of Congress Cataloging-in-Publication Data
Blair, J. Allen
  [Living peacefully]
  Living peacefully, when the world won't leave you alone: a devotional study of 1 Peter / J. Allen Blair.
      p. cm.
  Originally published: Living peacefully, 1st ed. New York: Loizeaux Brothers, 1959.
  1. Bible. N.T. Prayer, 1st—Meditations. I. Title.
BS2795.4.B5   1994   227'.9207—dc20   93-41447
                                                CIP

ISBN 0-8254-2183-7 (paperback)

            1 2 3 4 5 Printing / Year 98 97 96 95 94

Printed in the United States of America

CONTENTS

Affectionately dedicated
to our daughters
Sherril
Judith
Cynthia

INTRODUCTION

One of the most interesting and versatile personalities in the Bible is the Apostle Peter. Probably no other person characterized in Sacred Writ appears so impetuous, unstable, and distrustful, and yet at the same time so bold, fearless, and devoted. Until he met the Saviour, he was a plain man of the nets. But when Christ became his Master, he was transformed into a mighty servant for the Lord. Peter was not a man of letters; yet, inspired by the Holy Spirit, his Epistles evidence a literary genius.

The apostle's first Epistle is written to persecuted believers who sought refuge not only from the state, but from fanatical Jews and pagans. Many of them were converts from Judaism and were the targets of extreme hatred by the unconverted members of their families and friends. Their property was destroyed and their bodies tortured in an attempt to force recantation of the newly confessed faith. Peter writes to encourage, comfort, and strengthen them. Though they were suffering severe persecution, the Epistle suggests the possibility and privilege of "living peacefully," regardless of surroundings.

Today also, 1 Peter is a favorite book because of its practical approach to the needs of every believer. The problems of the ominous age in which we live, though they differ in nature, are no less complex than those of the apostolic Church. This little Epistle provides a splendid source of peace and comfort for all God's people who are perplexed and troubled. Truly we can say of 1 Peter, as Paul said of all the Scriptures, "For whatsoever things were written aforetime were written for our learning, that we through patience and comfort of the scriptures might have hope" (Romans 15:4).

J. ALLEN BLAIR

1

SEPARATED UNTO GOD

"Peter, an apostle of Jesus Christ, to the strangers scattered throughout Pontus, Galatia, Cappadocia, Asia, and Bithynia, Elect according to the foreknowledge of God the Father."—1 Peter 1:1-2a.

Peter establishes his authority for writing by describing himself as "an apostle of Jesus Christ." As God's messenger he was divinely appointed to his task. He addresses the letter to "the strangers scattered throughout Pontus, Galatia, Cappadocia, Asia, and Bithynia." Weymouth in his translation speaks of these scattered strangers as "God's own people . . . living as foreigners." How descriptive this should be of every true believer in Jesus Christ. Too often, Christians settle comfortably in this present world as though it were to continue for eternity. The Bible promises no sure dwelling place here. "Our citizenship is in heaven" (Philippians 3:20, ASV). We are "strangers and pilgrims on the earth" (Hebrew 11:13). "For here have we no continuing city, but we seek one to come" (Hebrews 13:14). Believers are to be in the world, but not of it. They are, as Paul said, "Ambassadors for Christ" (2 Corinthians 5:20).

No follower of Christ should become entangled with earthly ties which neither please nor honor God. He should break with worldliness and discard all that gives no time or thought to Christ. By worldliness is meant anything which prevents the believer from exalting Jesus Christ. Our Lord said in John 15:19, "I have chosen you *out* of the world." In 2 Corinthians 6:17 God says, "Wherefore *come out* from among them, and be ye *separate,* saith the Lord." Through Christ we are to be instruments of holiness and virtue, wholly separated for God. Not the kind of separation that says "don't do this" or "don't do that," but positive separation that says "do something for the Lord." A negative type of separation is all too common. This is extremely ineffective and fruitless. Often it is legalistic and even pharisaical.

Dr. Theodore Cuyler gave excellent advice on the subject of worldliness when he said, "Never do what you cannot ask Christ to bless, and never go into any place or any pursuit into which you cannot ask Jesus Christ to go with you." How worthwhile to heed this precept.

As "strangers" in this world, we should follow the example of our Lord in separated living. Jesus said, "I have meat to eat that ye know not of. . . . My meat is to do the will of Him that sent Me, and to finish His work" (John 4:32, 34). Many Christians have never tasted of the sweetness of this meat of which Jesus spoke. Why? Because they are too busy eating of the meat of this world's pleasure, the meat which can never satisfy hungry hearts.

What was the meat of which Jesus ate? The Scriptures tell us it consisted of two things: doing the will of God and finishing His work. Daily we must yield ourselves completely to the Lord Jesus with but a single ambition: to fulfill His absolute will in our lives. In so doing we shall be keenly aware of the needs of the lost, motivated by an impelling compassion to reach them with the gospel of salvation. This is the work God wants us to do. To this end we should pray, give, and sacrifice. As we faithfully honor Christ by seeking to win others to Him, the world and its allurements will grow strangely dim, and the Lord Jesus will become more real to us and occupy the center of our affections.

A young university student, who had plastered the walls of his room with cutouts of scantily clad movie actresses and pin-up girls, received as a gift a copy of Holman Hunt's famous picture of "Christ knocking at the Door." It was handsomely mounted and framed; and the student felt that, out of courtesy to the donor, the picture should be hung. Nonchalantly, he placed it in the midst of his gaudy collection. But something was wrong. He removed a few of the adjacent pin-ups. The improvement was marked. But still, as he looked from it to the surrounding walls, a subtle sense of unrest and incongruity prodded him. Then, one by one, he removed each risqué pin-up of his collection until at last only the picture of Christ remained in quiet pre-eminence.

Should not this be the cleansing and transforming effect of the Lord Jesus in the heart of every true child of God? He desires first place—as King to reign supreme. As long as we occupy ourselves with the pleasures and lusts of this world, we shall never know the joy and peace God has intended. David wrote many years ago, "How shall we sing the Lord's song in a strange land?" (Psalm 137:4) If we follow the world and the flesh, we shall have no song in our hearts. The joy of fruitfulness and Christian victory come only to those who separate themselves and surrender unto the Lord.

Those to whom the Epistle is addressed are described not only as "strangers," but as the "elect." Election has to do with God's solemn truth of predestination. To many, both believers and unbelievers, the subject of predestination has brought much consternation. They seem distressed whenever the word is mentioned. One view of predestination, widely believed and taught, is that God in His will and providence calls certain individuals to salvation and passes over others. How could a God of love predestinate some to be saved and ignore the rest, leaving them to suffer the pangs of hell?

May I submit this question for your consideration? Did God, before the foundation of the world, predestinate *persons*—or *a plan?* Did He ordain certain *individuals* to be saved? Or did He decree that there should be *a plan of redemption* in which

His Son would die for all men—that *whosoever* should call upon Him should be saved? A careful searching of the Scriptures seems to evidence the latter, a God-predestinated *plan*.

In Ephesians 1:5 we read that God "predestinated us *unto . . . adoption . . . by Jesus Christ,*" a plan of redemption whereby we are made children of God through Christ. In the light of this and other passages of Scripture, I am convinced that the important truth is that God predestinated a plan of salvation for all through Jesus Christ. In 2 Peter 3:9 we read that the Lord is "not willing that *any* should perish, but that *all* should come to repentance." I have always found God to mean what He says. This verse is emphatic, and it clearly portrays that God wants all men to be saved.

The Lord foresaw the actions of all His creatures. He knew man would naturally turn from God to Satan, from righteousness to sin. Consequently, God predestinated a plan of salvation whereby sinful man, by believing, might through the Holy Spirit "be conformed to the image of His Son" (Romans 8:29). Everyone is invited in Revelation 22:17 to be the recipient of God's love and grace and to come to the great salvation He has provided: "And the Spirit and the bride say, Come. And let him that heareth say, Come. And let him that is athirst come. And whosoever will, let him take the water of life freely."

The classic illustration used by Dr. Harry Ironside gives a clearer understanding of predestination. Dr. Ironside pictured man as wandering down a broad road leading to destruction. Along the way he comes to a building. Its door is open; and over it, where every passer-by may see, is written: WHOSOEVER WILL, MAY COME. But on its other side, where only those who have believed and entered in may see there is inscribed: CHOSEN IN CHRIST BEFORE THE FOUNDATION OF THE WORLD.

The Door of Salvation is open to all. Those who enter may be certain they were "chosen in Christ before the foundation of the world." D. L. Moody has said, "The *Whosoever Wills* are the elect. The *Whosoever Won'ts* are the nonelect."

Let not one of us pass by the door lest he never approach it again; lest he travel on to destruction. Take God at His Word. Believe Him. Obey Him. "For this is good and acceptable in the sight of God our Saviour; Who will have all men to be saved, and to come unto the knowledge of the truth" (1 Timothy 2:3,4).

2

VICTORY THROUGH CHRIST

"Elect according to the foreknowledge of God the Father, through sanctification of the Spirit, unto obedience and sprinkling of the blood of Jesus Christ: Grace unto you, and peace, be multiplied." —1 Peter 1:2

Continuing in verse 2, we see the *means* by which believers are brought into the family of God—"Through sanctification of the Spirit," that is, through the *sanctifying work* of the Holy Spirit. *To sanctify* means *to set apart*. One important ministry of the Holy Spirit is the setting apart unto salvation of all who receive Christ as Lord. It is impossible to be saved without His work in our hearts. One does not become a Christian by baptism, reciting a creed, memorizing a catechism, attending public worship, contributing to the financial needs of the church, or seeking to maintain a decent, moral character. There is only one way: there must be a new birth by the Holy Spirit. In the new birth, the Spirit of God imparts new life which alone prepares man for eternity. Without this life, there can be no hope.

All human efforts to attain salvation are as useless as planting a stick in the ground with the expectation of growth. Though faithfully watered day by day, it would soon rot and ultimately disintegrate. But plant a living shrub and tend it with the same care. How different the result. Soon it takes root and, impelled by the life principle, grows and bears fruit. So with all mankind. Only those who receive the new life, implanted in the heart through the sanctifying work of the Holy Spirit, are saved and enabled to "abound" for God.

The Holy Spirit not only instills new life in the believer, but He enters to make His abode with us, never to depart. In the Old Testament, David prayed, "Take not Thy Holy Spirit from me" (Psalm 51:11). Since the Ascension of Christ, we need never pray this prayer. For our Lord said in John 14:16, "I will pray the Father, and He shall give you another Comforter, that He may abide with you for ever." The Holy Spirit is our constant friend and companion who will neither leave nor forsake us. The impact of this truth upon the believer, once realized, is tremendous in its effect upon thought and manner of life. There will then be the constant awareness of our joyous privilege in following the guidance of our Master and Friend. "Know ye not that your body is the temple of the Holy Ghost which is in you, which ye have of God, and ye are not your own? For ye are bought with a price: therefore glorify God in your body, and in your spirit, which are God's" (1 Corinthians 6:19-20). Wherever we go, or whatever we do, let us keep in mind that the Holy Spirit dwells within us. Through the shed blood of the Lord Jesus, we have been purchased by God to heed the direction of His Spirit in every endeavor. How important that each Christian surrender to the autocracy of the Spirit of God.

There are three prepositions in this second verse of 1 Peter which carry tremendous meaning: "according to," which suggests *the fact* of our salvation; "through," which presents *the means* of our salvation; and "unto," which expresses the *purpose* for which we are saved.

For what purpose does God save us? Why are we Christians? Why have we been set apart by the sanctifying work of the Holy Spirit? Is it merely to enjoy Christianity, to be happy, to have the assurance of Heaven? Is it an easy way of escape from the complexity of problems which weigh so heavily on all of us? The Scripture is clear. We are set apart by the Spirit of God in salvation "unto obedience." Here is one of the most important purposes of our salvation stated explicitly: that we might obey God. Obedience is one of the foremost requisites in the Christian life. Without it we cannot please the Lord.

Before the foundation of the world God foresaw the disobedient and rebellious spirit that would mark us all. Considering our own inadequacy to overcome it, He predestinated a plan of redemption whereby all who believe in Christ might be saved and have the power to obey. Because of God's grace and mercy in making such a satisfactory provision, we owe Him our strict obedience. "We have received grace and apostleship, *for obedience to the faith*" (Romans 1:5).

Consider Paul as he was before his conversion, arrogant and pompous, hastening along the Damascus highway to persecute Christians still further. Suddenly a great light shone from Heaven. Falling to the ground, Paul listened in fear to the solemn tones of a voice which demanded, "Saul, Saul, why persecutest thou Me?"

"Who art Thou, Lord?" he cried out trembling. And the Lord said, "I am Jesus whom thou persecutest: it is hard for thee to kick against the pricks."

Immediately Paul surrendered to his Master asking, "Lord, what wilt Thou have me to do?"

The import of these words is significant. Paul not only was saved at this very moment, but he voluntarily submitted, completely and obediently, to the will of God for his life. Some Christians would be afraid to ask God what He would have them do. They already know in their hearts what He wants them to do, but they choose to disobey rather than enjoy God's best through a life of implicit obedience. Paul wanted above all else to obey God. It is for this reason that he became such a mighty and useful servant of Christ.

Nothing is more satisfying to the heart of God than the obedient saint. Often we come to the Lord offering our money and talents with a certain sense of sacrifice. But God declares that "to obey is better than sacrifice" (1 Samuel 15:22). He wants nothing before our humble and willing obedience to His will. No gift we might bring could supplant complete obedience to Him; for when we obey, every other essential will follow.

One of the firstfruits of obedience is holiness. God wants us to be like Christ who is the epitome of both obedience and holiness. The world is watching believers to see whether or not Christianity is real. Only as we obey the Lord can we have the holiness of life which will convince unbelievers, without question, of the real and transforming power of Christ.

While out walking one day, Dr. John Jowett observed a display of packets of seeds in the window of a florist's shop. In the center of the display was an exquisitely beautiful plant in full bloom. A small sign was attached which read: GROWN FROM OUR SEEDS. No better advertisement could have been used to sell the seeds.

God says in 1 Peter 1:23, "Being born again, not of corruptible seed, but of incorruptible, by the word of God, which liveth and abideth for ever." The world is ever watching to see what the incorruptible seed of God's Word produces. The most forceful advertisement any Christian can give the world is a life of holiness resulting from sincere obedience. As Christ is seen in us, unbelievers will be more likely to call upon Him for salvation.

As long as we obey God, we dwell high on the mountain top of joy and blessing. Disobedience will pull us down from this lofty estate. All Christians know what it is to be confronted with sudden temptation, and the tragedy of yielding to it. Then the crash from the mountain top of joy to the valley of despondency. Remorse and discouragement follow. All seems lost. But is it? Ah, no. God has yet another word to say in this marvelous second verse. Not only are we set apart unto obedience, but unto the "sprinkling of the blood of Jesus Christ."

The word "sprinkling" means cleansing. Precious truth! Suppose we yield to temptation, commit sin, and fall from victory into defeat. Are we defeated forever? No! Praise His Name! Our God, in His merciful plan of redemption has provided for every need. A defeated Christian should be an anomaly. In Christ, we may be constantly victorious. Through the shed blood of our Lord Jesus, immediate cleansing is possible for the sinning saint. By confessing to the Lord, we may return instantly to the mountain-top experience.

Never hesitate to confess to God. Immediately upon sinning, bow your head in humble repentance and confess the sin. God says, "If we confess our sins, He is faithful and just to forgive us our sins, and to cleanse us from all unrighteousness"(1 John 1:9). You need not plead with the Lord to forgive. He has promised that He will. If you obey, He will fulfill His promise faithfully. If we *confess,* He will *forgive.* Take Him at His word.

But you ask, "Isn't it necessary for me to do something to earn forgiveness?" The Scripture is plain: The "sprinkling of the blood" is the paid price. You can do nothing. "The blood of Jesus Christ His [God's] Son cleanseth us from *all sin*" (1 John 1:7). Is this clear? "All sin." This means *every* sin, large or small. Whatever the sin you have committed, it comes under the category of *all.* Christ paid the whole price, His shed blood. It is this that makes possible immediate and complete forgiveness.

But God has made a yet greater provision for the believer. Where is Christ today? And what is He doing? He is at the right hand of the Father constantly pleading our case on the ground of His shed blood. It is He who makes instant forgiveness possible. "My little children, these things write I unto you, that ye sin not. And if any man sin, *we have an advocate* with the Father, Jesus Christ the righteous: And He is the propitiation for our sins: and not for our's only, but also for the sins of the whole world" (1 John 2:1,2). If we sin, *we have* an *advocate.* He is always willing and ready to forgive. The "sprinkling" of the blood of Jesus is all-sufficient. Oh, how many carry the burden of sin in memory even after confession of it. When it is confessed, forget it! Take God at His Word! Believe Him! Accept the forgiveness He bestows upon you. Be assured you will know anew that victory which can never remain in defeat. For in Christ we are identified with the Victor.

How wonderful is this victory which God has ordained for every truly born-again believer. Victory in Christ is continuous. We are defeated in ourselves; yet as we daily turn our eyes from self to our Lord Jesus, we know the joy of uninterrupted victory.

Some years before the advent of the telephone or the radio, a certain high school football team, which had traveled to a neighboring city to meet a strong opponent on the gridiron, was to return home by train. Long before arrival time, enthusiastic fans thronged the station, eager to welcome the team and to hear the results of the game. Among them was a small boy who managed to push his way through the crowd to a place beside the tracks. When the train roared in and screeched to a stop, and the first team member stepped to the platform, the small boy eagerly asked, "What's the score?" Hearing, he dashed back into the mob, darting here and there and shouting, "We've won. We've won." But how could he say, "We've won"? He was not a member of the triumphant team, nor even a student of the high school. He was victorious because he identified himself with the winning team and claimed its victory as his own.

Is this not also the privilege of every believer in Christ? No merit is ours. But as we are identified with Christ, His cleansing blood makes eternal victory a reality. Oh, praise His name, we've won.

The result of this great plan of redemption at work in the hearts of God's people is further revealed in the words, "Grace unto you, and peace, be multiplied."

When the words "grace" and "peace" appear together in the Bible, "grace" precedes "peace." This is truly God's order. None can know the peace of God without first experiencing a work of grace in the heart. Peter tells of the work of grace "through sanctification of the Spirit," whereby God through salvation transforms our lives. At conversion His peace should become our immediate possession. "Therefore being justified by faith, we have peace with God" (Romans 5:1). Justification by faith is the work of grace which results in the present realization of God's peace.

Many Christians, unfortunately, know little of the reality of this peace. Their hearts are fearful and anxious. Why? Because there is so little of Christ in their lives. Their hearts are crammed and cluttered with worldly lusts. There is no room for the Lord Jesus. How can there be peace?

God wishes His people to depend upon Him for His wonderful peace. We may choose one of two ways when we are confronted with the trials and sorrows of life: the world's way, or God's way. The world says, "Keep smiling! Keep a stiff upper lip! Have courage! Grin and bear it!" This sounds well. But when a loved one is snatched from us by death, or some other sorrow or tragedy befalls us, we need more than a stiff upper lip or a smile on the face. Many a life has cracked under such a strain for lack of abiding peace in the heart. The worldly view of sorrow is empty and shallow. God's way is the only satisfying way. He longs for us to meet our troubles squarely, with an unwavering assurance of faith that "He doeth all things well."

The Lord does not promise the believer freedom from burdens and problems, but He points to deliverance through Christ, in whom there is peace, strength, and guidance. The world's solution crumbles under the crushing troubles and pressures of life. But Jesus said in John 14:27 "Peace I leave with you, My peace I give unto you: not as the world giveth, give I unto you. Let not your heart be troubled, neither let it be afraid." There is no comparison between the peace Christ gives and the pseudo-peace offered by the world. Christ's peace sustains, despite complex and confusing circumstances. Through Him there may be perfect peace within, though turmoil seethes without. Uncertain winds may blow; the storms of life may come; but the peace of Christ in every believer's heart is ever sure.

At one time an award was offered to the artist who could best depict a scene of peace. Among the paintings submitted, one seemed to portray the theme of peace more vividly than the others—a blue sky flecked with clouds above a field of golden grain, heavy and ripe for harvest, cattle quietly grazing on a far hill, and to one side, trees standing stately and serene as though surveying peace. To the surprise of many, however, this painting did not win the award, but rather one which depicted a bleak, forbidding shore where breakers dashed angrily upon sharp rocks, and skies, gray and overcast, suggested biting winds. Jutting from the rocks was a solitary tree branch with a bird's nest resting securely on it. There sat a little bird, snug in its nest, warm and safe above the jagged rocks and raging sea. This was peace!

In Jesus Christ, though surrounded by the tumults of life, the true believer may rest with perfect serenity, oblivious to the storm. Nothing can shake the tranquil heart if Christ is there. The prophet said, "Thou wilt keep him in perfect peace, whose mind is stayed on Thee" (Isaiah 26:3).

Believer in Christ, is His marvelous peace yours? Your loving Father wants you to have it. Appropriate it by faith. Never doubt your wonderful Lord. Trust Him now and forever. He never fails.

3

A LIVING HOPE

"Blessed be the God and Father of our Lord Jesus Christ, which according to His abundant mercy hath begotten us again unto a lively hope by the resurrection of Jesus Christ from the dead."— 1 Peter 1:3

In his opening words Peter has briefly outlined God's great plan of redemption through Jesus Christ. Step by step he has unfolded this glorious truth from election before the foundation of the world, to the believer's present experience of God's marvelous grace and sustaining peace. He then writes in verse 3, "Blessed be the God and Father of our Lord Jesus Christ." This could well be read as an exclamation, *"Thank God!"* The apostle was so awed and overwhelmed by the grace of our Lord in providing a plan of salvation, complete and sufficient for fallen man, that he ejaculated, *"Thank God."*

How important that we, as believers, get on our knees frequently in the quietness of meditation to consider what the Lord has done for each of us. We should be far more thankful than we are. Most of us murmur and grumble but rarely give thanks. Once a year we respect a holiday we call Thanksgiving Day. Every day should be Thanksgiving Day for the true believer in the Lord Jesus. God says in Psalm 107:8, "O that men would praise the Lord for His goodness, and for His wonderful works to the children of men!" How important that we take a daily analysis of the blessings we have received and spend adequate time before the Lord giving thanks. Learn to praise Him for *all* things, the seemingly bad as well as the good. "In *every thing* give thanks: for this is the will of God in Christ Jesus concerning you" (1 Thessalonians 5:18). How marvelous that we who believe can look at life with such assurance that "in every thing" we can give thanks. Such an attitude will rout discouragement and flood our hearts with an overwhelming joy.

Probably the worst pest in the world is the pessimist. The Christian should never be a pessimist. He should be a confirmed optimist. There are many things we may not know, but one is certain: "We know that *all* things work together for good to them that love God" (Romans 8:28). Not some things, but "*all* things work together for good." With such assuring knowledge through Christ why should the believer be pessimistic? There is no basis or foundation for complaint. We may be optimistic in the face of any situation. This "we know" because "all things work together for good." For this reason we can "Thank God."

Years ago a saintly preacher in a small farming community was known for his gracious and thankful spirit. In every public prayer it seemed he had something new for which to express thanks. The worshipers would gather on the Lord's day curious and eager to hear the subject of thanks for the day. Rarely did he repeat himself. His was a heart overflowing with thankfulness. One Lord's day, however, it was unusually stormy. A deep snow had fallen, and a sharp, bitter wind blew from the north. As the little flock trudged many miles from all directions to attend the service, they wondered what the pastor could possibly be thankful for on such a day. But once again he was equal to the occasion. He began his morning prayer by saying, "Our Heavenly Father, we thank Thee that not every day is as bad as this one." Believer in Jesus Christ, let us learn to give thanks to the Lord for all He has done. Life will flow easier and the way will be smoother. "O give thanks unto the

Lord; for He is good: because His mercy endureth for ever" (Psalm 118:1).

Having expressed thanks for the great provision of redemption through Christ, Peter offers praise for God's "abundant mercy." The mercy of God is mentioned in the Bible hundreds of times. Indeed, this is one of the grandiose subjects of the Word. Where would any of us be today were it not for the mercy of God? We deserve hell. But God in His "abundant mercy" offers Heaven to all who believe in Christ. No matter how far one may have drifted from God's grace and love, His "abundant mercy" is sufficient to reconcile the sinner to Himself. One may have degenerated into the lowest depths of sin, but the mercy of God is sufficient to implant the feet of the believing soul upon the solid rock of Christ. "Where sin abounded, grace did much more abound" (Romans 5:20). God's mercy avails for all who commit themselves to Christ. "Let the wicked forsake his way, and the unrighteous man his thoughts: and let him return unto the Lord, and He will have mercy upon him; and to our God, for *He will abundantly pardon*" (Isaiah 55:7). God's "abundant mercy" extends to the deepest dregs of sin to redeem the worst profligate and scoundrel. At the same time it ascends to the loftiest heights to reach the self-righteous and morally self-satisfied. Both are brought to the common ground of redemption and made one in Christ Jesus. Regardless of the sin, God in abundant mercy will forgive.

One of the best-loved characters of the Old Testament is Moses. Early in his life he slew an Egyptian in defense of his own people, and wandered forty years with this sin troubling his conscience and burdening his heart. But one day, the Lord spoke to Moses from the burning bush, and, in His "abundant mercy," forgave him. Immediately Moses was restored to fellowship with the Lord and was divinely appointed to be a leader of his people. The mercy of God was sufficient.

David likewise had a similar experience. In addition to the sin of adultery, he committed murder. Like any believer out of fellowship with the Lord, he was miserable. For an entire year he knew only restless days and sleepless nights. The hand of God was heavy upon him. In Psalm 51:7 David tells us of the blessed turning point. It came when he cried out to God in repentance, "Purge me with hyssop, and I shall be clean: wash me, and I shall be whiter than snow." And with loving mercy the Lord welcomed David back into His fellowship.

Peter also comes to mind. Recall how he denied his Lord three times. He cursed and swore and declared of Christ, "I know not the man." Like Moses and David, Peter was distressed mentally, physically, and spiritually. There seemed to be no release from anguish. But when he repented, once again victory was his. It was God's mercy which made immediate restoration possible. It was then that Peter went forth endued with power, and became a mighty evangel of the message of light, reaching thousands for Christ.

As God's eternal mercy availed for these saints in their extremity, so His wellspring of grace flows for those who turn to Him in true repentance for their sins. Satan would restrain us, whispering, "Give up! You've failed! There is no hope!" But do not be beguiled. The fountain of God's mercy is forever flowing to provide cleansing and forgiveness.

As the result of God's abundant mercy, the Lord has "begotten us again unto a lively [living] hope by the resurrection of Jesus Christ from the dead." The words "begotten us again" could well be translated *created us anew*. When the Lord saved us, we were not merely patched up. We were made new creatures in Christ. He imparted new life to the soul through the miracle of the new birth. Jesus said in his conversation with Nicodemus, "Except a man be born again, he cannot see the kingdom of God. . . . Except a man be born of water and of the Spirit, he cannot enter into the kingdom of God. That which is born of the flesh is flesh; and that which is born of the Spirit is spirit. Marvel not that I said unto thee, Ye must be born again" (John 3:3,5-7). There can be no substitute. Only the divinely-effected new birth can make us new creatures in Christ.

Notice, too, that the new birth is directly dependent upon

"the resurrection of Jesus Christ." The same miraculous power that broke the bands of death and delivered the Lord Jesus from the grave is that which breaks the shackles of the bondage of sin's penalty and power, and forever delivers the believing soul from eternal death. It is for this reason man can never save himself. Only the power that raised Jesus from the dead can transform the sinful hearts of men and women. No human being can generate life in his own heart. Eternal life can be received only as a gift from God through the miracle of the new birth.

Occasionally we have heard some say it is not necessary to believe in the Resurrection of Christ to be a Christian, that it was Christ's life and character which were of greater importance. The critics boldly declare that it matters little whether or not Christ arose from the grave. Such reasoning may appeal to those willing to accept a man-made philosophy of salvation, but certainly this is not the teaching of God's Word. If Jesus Christ did not rise from the dead, we might as well destroy all our Bibles, close and bar the doors of our churches, and never utter another word of prayer. Every eternal truth revealed in the Scriptures depends on the Resurrection of Jesus Christ for its authenticity.

Concerning salvation and eternal life, Paul writes, "And if Christ be not raised, your faith is vain; ye are yet in your sins. Then they also which are fallen asleep in Christ are perished" (1 Corinthians 15:17-18). If Christ did not rise from the dead, we are hopelessly lost and condemned to spiritual death and eternal separation from God. We shall die as beasts of the field which have no life beyond the grave.

But Christ *did* rise from the dead. This is the pinnacle truth of the Bible. It is not simply a beautiful story to be sung or preached about once a year on a day called Easter. This sublime and majestic resurrection truth should not be mentioned so rarely in our churches. The resurrection should be proclaimed every Lord's day. We serve a Christ who *lives* in the flesh.

Off the coast of Chile there is a rocky island about fifty miles square called "Easter Island." It was so named because it was discovered on Easter Sunday in 1772. Restricting treatment of the resurrection message from our pulpits to Easter only, suggests that too many consider it an unimportant island of truth, detached from the shores of Christian doctrine. The Bible, however, presents it as the mainland of truth upon which all else stands or falls. Our hopes are built on the resurrected Saviour who desires to dwell in every heart.

A little Sunday school girl, in conversing with a very learned man, told of her belief in Jesus as her Saviour. He laughed mockingly and said, "My dear girl, don't you know there have been hundreds of saviours in the history of the world? How do you know which one to trust?" The child replied with complacent confidence, "I believe in the one who rose from the dead." He is the only One. The living Christ is God's way to eternal life.

Some years ago the French skeptic, Ernest Renan, sneeringly declared, "Christianity lives on the fragrance of an empty vase." Unwittingly, he was correct. This is unquestionably true. If Christ had remained in the tomb, we should have no hope. The Resurrection of Jesus Christ is God's "Amen" to Christ's victorious cry on the Cross, "It is finished." It is the seal of redemption made complete for all eternity.

Those who have believed in the resurrected Christ should evidence it by resurrection living. A low plane of living is inexcusable. Not only does the resurrection power save us, but it also *enables* us to live for Christ. Through this power the believer can overcome temptation and sin. Victory is ours because of the limitless power that brings life from death.

Paul declares, "We are [God's] workmanship, created in Christ Jesus unto good works" (Ephesians 2:10). Having been recreated by resurrection power, the good works of resurrection living are to be expected. Paul further explains it this way: "What shall we say then? Shall we continue in sin, that grace may abound? God forbid. How shall we, that are dead to sin, live any longer therein? Know ye not, that so many of us as were baptized into Jesus Christ were baptized into His death?

Therefore we are buried with Him by baptism into death: that like as Christ was raised up from the dead by the glory of the Father, *even so we also should walk in newness of life*" (Romans 6:1-4). The new birth identifies the believer with Christ in His death, burial, and resurrection. Christ's living in the sincere believer should result in a holy hatred of sin and an earnest desire to walk in the newness of the resurrection life.

There is an age-old tradition that after Lazarus was raised from the dead, the stench of the grave forever clung to him. I cannot accept this. When the Lord Jesus performs a miracle, He does it thoroughly. Yet it is sadly true that many who claim to have been raised from spiritual death by belief in Christ, still reek with the gravelike stench of the old life and its sinful habits and lusts.

By contrast, he who truly comes to Christ and fully trusts Him for salvation, evidences the immediate and glorious new life of the resurrection. Old things pass away. All things become new. Such a life bears well the scrutiny of God and men, even as Paul declared, "Herein do I exercise myself, to have always a conscience void of offense toward God, and toward men" (Acts 24:16).

We are exhorted to "put on the new man, which after God is created in righteousness and true holiness." Much of the so-called holiness seemingly experienced by many is pseudo and superficial. When one is reborn by the Holy Spirit, he is enabled through the resurrection power to put on the "new man" and to become the recipient of the veritable righteousness and holiness of Christ. At the moment of salvation God imparts His holiness to the sincere, believing soul. The normal consequences of this impartation will be seen in a life of usefulness and holy obedience.

A rather pompous and arrogant Sunday school teacher was endeavoring to explain the importance of Christian living to his class. With head high and chest out, strutting back and forth impressively, he asked, "Now boys, why do people call

me a Christian?" There was a momentary silence. Then one
boy raised his hand.

"Yes?" asked the teacher.

"Probably because they don't know you."

Paul declared in Colossians 3:1-3, "If ye then be risen with
Christ, seek those things which are above, where Christ sitteth
on the right hand of God. Set your affection on things above,
not on things on the earth. For ye are dead, and your life is
hid with Christ in God." If we have experienced resurrection
power in salvation, then this same power should be evidenced
in transformed living. There should be a clean break with all
amusements, habits, and lusts that oppose or hinder resurrection living. As believers in Christ, we should seek the higher
things which honor and exalt our Lord. How many earnest,
seeking souls there are among the unsaved, who become disgusted and are lost to the possibility of salvation, because of
the inconsistencies seen in professing believers living on a low
spiritual plane. A life of holiness is so important.

David Ben-Gurion is a household name in the nation of
Israel, as well as in the world. A Christian had a conference
with him and the opportunity opened to testify to the saving
grace of our Lord Jesus Christ. Mr. Ben-Gurion asked, "Are
there any Christians in the world? I have read the New Testament and am deeply moved by what I read there. I have read
it in the Greek. The teaching and standard is wonderful, but
where are those who live up to it? Are there any living the
Christian life? Can this Book really produce that which it sets
forth?"

"It can, Mr. Ben-Gurion," replied the Christian. He then
gave his own testimony to newness of life through the Lord
Jesus Christ.

"But are there others like you?" asked Mr. Ben-Gurion.

"Yes, millions," the Christian affirmed.

"Where are they, then?"

"There are real Christians all over the world," said the
Christian. "One cannot point to any one church or religious

organization and say, 'These are the real Christians,' but in every group of those who profess Christ as their Saviour, there are some who live up to the standard set forth in the New Testament."

What a shameful rebuke to those who profess to be followers of Christ—"Are there any Christians in the world?" Not one but thousands of Christians should be proving to the world, by transformed living, that they are living according to the Book. Too many of God's people are failing Christ by neglecting to bear a positive Christian testimony through the resurrection power. The Lord Jesus said, "Let your light so shine before men, that they may see your good works, and glorify your Father which is in heaven" (Matthew 5:16).

The apostle further reveals in these opening verses of 1 Peter, three treasures which God has provided for believers as the result of the Resurrection of Christ: a living hope (verse 3); an incorruptible inheritance (verse 4); and an endless security (verse 5).

In Christ, God "hath begotten us again unto a lively hope" —literally, an *ever-living* hope. It should be remembered that 1 Peter is written to comfort God's despairing people who are weary and troubleladen. In the midst of mounting anxiety Peter reaches the high peak of encouragement by declaring, "we have an ever-living hope." The word "hope," as used here, does not mean desire or expectation. It is not that of the student who *hopes* he will pass an examination. It means *confidence*. It is the hope that banishes all doubt and uncertainty. The believer need never be distressed by fears if Christ is his "ever-living hope." The apostle speaks of this "hope" as an "anchor of the soul, both sure and steadfast" (Hebrews 6:19). It does not rest upon the fleeting philosophies of men, but is imbedded in the solid rock of Christ. Years ago the prophet declared, "The Lord will be the hope of His people" (Joel 3:16). The Christian's hope is the Lord "Jesus Christ, the same yesterday, and today, and for ever" (Hebrew 13:8).

Strengthened by such eternal confidence in Christ, no believer should experience the slightest worry since everything should be laid in confidence at the feet of our Lord. David could say, "The Lord is on my side; I will not fear: what can man do unto me?" (Psalm 118:6) Even amidst the sorrows of death, he could assuredly say, "Yea, though I walk through the valley of the shadow of death, I will fear no evil: for Thou art with me" (Psalm 23:4). Should the death of loved ones leave us distraught, our hopes blasted? Ah, no. In Christ, the ever-living hope, we have a light to guide us through the darkest valley, even death itself. "The Lord is my light and my salvation; whom shall I fear? The Lord is the strength of my life; of whom shall I be afraid?" (Psalm 27:1) How often these precious promises of the Word are read, yet never appropriated. We may trust God implicitly, for what He has promised, He will perform. If Christ is your hope, you may rely upon His Word with full assurance that He will not fail. We cannot always trust the word of others, but God's Word will never fail.

There are times when we cannot trust even the preacher's word. A preacher's daughter learned, while talking to their grocery boy, that he liked the sermons of the assistant better than her father's.

"But why?" she asked.

"Well, you see," the boy said, "when the assistant comes to the end of his sermon he usually says, 'And now, in conclusion,' and he concludes. But when your Dad comes toward the end, he says, 'And now, lastly,' and he really lasts."

God not only says what He means, but He means what He says. Unfortunately all of us make promises we do not fulfill; but we may rest assured that God has never made a single one that He has not kept. We can believe Him. One reason for this is found in 1 Samuel 12:22, "For the Lord will not forsake His people *for His great name's sake*: because it hath pleased the Lord to make you His people." God has a great Name. He is Jehovah, the Almighty One, who by a word has called the universe into existence. If He should fail His Name once, our hopes would be eternally shattered. But God cannot fail His great Name. With certainty we know He will never forsake His people. We belong to Him. We are His eternal possession in Christ. "It hath pleased the Lord to make you His people." Then why should we worry or doubt Him?

In the early days of the immigration to the West a traveler approached the banks of the mighty Mississippi. Seeing the river sheeted with ice and not knowing its thickness, he was fearful to trust himself to it. He spent the entire day debating whether or not he should cross. Finally, as the sun was setting, he decided he must reach the other shore before nightfall. So, with much trepidation, he got on his hands and knees, distributed his weight as much as possible, and with painstaking caution crept toward the other side of the river. Halfway across, he heard a rumbling behind him, and turning with care, he saw a wagon loaded with coal, drawn by four horses, crossing the frozen river's vast expanse. The driver's lusty voice rang out across the ice in clear and carefree song.

How like this timorous traveler are they who fail to step out boldly upon the firm and everlasting promises of God. Truly, "The eyes of the Lord are upon the righteous, and His ears are open unto their cry" (Psalm 34:15). Glorious truth! Believe it! Receive it into your heart! And when confronted by problems that would overwhelm, "stand still, and consider the wondrous works of God" (Job 37:14). Look up to the heavens. Consider their height and breadth. God who created them is powerful to save and careful to provide. There is nothing too hard for Him. Then trust Him for today; and leave tomorrow in His hand.

There was once a small boy helping his mother store apples in the cellar to keep them cool and fresh. Trying to show how many he could carry at once, he gathered an armload of them and started down. But in a very few steps, they fell one by one from his arms.

"Son," said his mother, "bring just one at a time, then they'll not be dropped and bruised." So God wants us to live trustfully, one day at a time. "Take therefore no thought for the morrow: for the morrow shall take thought for the things of itself. Sufficient unto the day is the evil thereof" (Matthew 6:34).

Oh, believer in Christ, are you trying to carry tomorrow's load, or the burden of the years to come, with the strength of today? Walk in trust with the Lord today and commit the future's care to Him. So you may say with David, "What time I am afraid, I will trust in Thee" (Psalm 56:3).

4

THE INHERITANCE INCORRUPTIBLE

"To an inheritance incorruptible, and undefiled, and that fadeth not away, reserved in heaven for you."—1 Peter 1:4

Not only does the true believer in the Lord Jesus receive an "ever-living hope" through the new birth, but an "inheritance incorruptible." As to its *quality*, the "inheritance incorruptible" is undefiled"; in its *durability*, "it fadeth not away"; and in its *certainty*, "it is reserved in heaven for you."

The question might be asked, "What is this *inheritance incorruptible?*" It is eternal life through Christ, the Son of God. In the final analysis, it is Christ Himself; for He is life eternal. Apart from Him, there can be no life. Years ago David declared in Psalm 16:5, "The *Lord* is the portion of mine inheritance." The Lord Jesus declared, "I am the resurrection, and the life" (John 11:25), "I am the way, the truth, and the life: no man cometh unto the Father, but by Me" (John 14:6). John tells us that "in Him [Christ] was life; and the life was the light of men" (John 1:4). From these Scriptures and many others throughout the Bible, it is unquestionably clear that when one is in Christ, he is the possessor of eternal life, the "inheritance incorruptible."

First let us consider the "undefiled" quality of the "inheritance incorruptible." This has reference to the spotless and flawless nature Christ commits unto all who believe on His name. Before being born anew by the Holy Spirit, man is the possessor of a sinful nature only. This is the corruptible inheritance committed to all at birth as the result of Adam's sin. David declared in Psalm 51:5, "Behold, I was shapen in iniquity; and in sin did my mother conceive me." He also said in Psalm 58:3, "The wicked are estranged from the womb: they go astray as soon as they be born, speaking lies." Because of this innate sinful condition, there can be no fellowship with God. In fact, all who have not trusted in Christ are the children of the devil. "Ye are of your father the devil," Jesus declared to the unbelieving Pharisees in John 8:44. The corruptible inheritance can lead only to eternal death. Nothing but a divine miracle can alter this condition and provide an incorruptible inheritance.

Walter Beckwith, the famous lion trainer, tried to change the nature of lion cubs by adopting an entirely different method of training. He sought to rear them on milk and train them with kindness. One day while working in a cage, when the cubs were about ten months old, he heard his wife shouting, "Walter, Walter, come here quickly!" Dashing out, he saw his pet burro grazing some fifty feet away. One of the lion cubs was stealthily creeping on his belly toward the burro, and— quick as a flash—leaped at its shoulder, knocking it to the ground, clawing its nose with beastly ferocity. In a matter of seconds the cub was sinking its bared teeth into the helpless creature's jugular vein. Though fed with milk and trained with kindness, the animal instinct remained in the lion. Only a miracle could have changed him. Similarly, only a miracle of God's grace can change human nature.

The corruptible inheritance offers no hopeful prospects for the future. Eternal death, which means endless separation from God, is the sad and calamitous end. "Wherefore, as by one man sin entered into the world, and death by sin; and so death passed upon all men, for that all have sinned" (Romans 5:12). But is there no hope? Need we suffer the consequences of the old nature? Ah, no! God has provided the remedy, the "incorruptible inheritance" received by the new birth.

After hearing the gospel, man reacts in one of two ways: either he attempts to *cover* his sinful state by means of self-justification; or, recognizing his own helplessness and unworthiness, he *confesses* his sins to God. The inevitable result of any human attempt to cover sin is condemnation. A willingness to confess to God produces immediate and lasting consolation. "He that covereth his sins shall not prosper: but whoso confesseth and forsaketh them shall have mercy" (Proverbs 28:13).

It is not unusual for sinful humans to resort to humanistic attempts to cover their sinfulness by such means as morality, philanthropy, or religiosity. How futile are these Satan-inspired substitutes. God still sees the sin; but when sins are confessed to Him and Christ is received as Lord, the repentant believer's sins are covered over immediately with the precious blood of Jesus Christ, which completely blots out all sin from God's sight. All of this is beyond the comprehension of the human mind. It cannot possibly be understood until Christ is invited into the heart as Lord. The experience test is the only proof. "O taste and see that the Lord is good" (Psalm 34:8).

A little boy was sent to the store to buy some honey. While returning home, he repeatedly stuck a finger into the pail and licked the sweet substance from it. A stranger walking close behind noticed the boy's delight and asked, "What do you have in the pail, son?"

"Honey, sir."

"Honey! Is it sweet?"

"Yes, sir."

"How sweet is your honey?"

"It is very sweet, sir."

"I do not understand you. I asked you how sweet your honey is, but you have not told me. How sweet is it?"

"It's very, very sweet, sir."

"Well, you're a funny little fellow. I asked how sweet your honey is and you simply tell me it is very, very sweet. Can you really tell me how sweet your honey is?" Impatiently, the lad dipped his finger into the honey and held it up saying, "Here, sir, taste and see for yourself."

Sermons and literature may aid in giving a limited understanding of Christ, but only as He is received into the heart can He be known. There can be no real satisfaction in life until the "inheritance incorruptible" is possessed. The world with its glitter and glamour may appeal to the eye, but Christ alone can satisfy the heart.

Titus Salt thought his empty heart could find contentment in earthly pleasures, but he discovered the unsoundness of his delusive dream. Later, however, it appeared that good fortune turned his way when he invented alpaca and became a multimillionaire. To add to his attainments, Queen Victoria made him a baron. But none of this brought satisfaction to his restless heart. One day while in church, he listened intently as the preacher told of sitting in his garden and watching a caterpillar climb a painted stick used for decoration.

"After reaching the top," said the preacher, "the caterpillar reared itself, waving its body in search of a juicy twig to feed upon, or some way to continue the climb. Discovering only space, it slowly returned to the ground, crawled along until it found another painted stick and repeated the same futile process. This occurred several times. There are many painted sticks in the world," continued the preacher, "pleasure, wealth, power, and fame. All these call to men, 'Climb me and find the desire of your heart, fulfill the purpose of your existence, taste the fruit of success and find satisfaction.' But alas! They find only painted sticks."

The next day the preacher had a visitor, Titus Salt. He confessed that all his life he had been climbing painted sticks, and that, though materially rich, he was a spiritual pauper and without peace. The minister had the joy of telling him of One who said, "Come unto Me, all ye that labour and are heavy laden, and I will give you rest." Titus Salt yielded to Christ, and for the first time in his life found abiding joy and peace. He received the "inheritance incorruptible and undefiled," and experienced the glory of the Lord.

But does the "inheritance incorruptible" really last? God affirms, "It fadeth not away." Life in Christ, if sincerely received into the heart, can never be lost. But you say, "I am unstable! I say things I should not. I think defiling thoughts. I am tempted to look at things that do not please God. I do unkind things." God realizes our instability far better than we do. But the "inheritance incorruptible" does not depend upon our stability: it is based upon Him, our immutable Lord. It rests upon His unchanging love. "The love of Christ constraineth us" (2 Corinthians 5:14). God's love is all-sufficient and inexhaustible for every wayward child who will lean upon Him.

In the state of Ohio there is a large pool of water called "the Blue Hole." It is fed by an underground stream. Though repeated attempts to measure its depth have been made, it is seemingly bottomless. Day in and day out, its waters well up incessantly to replenish the loss of the overflow. How like the wellspring of God's wondrous love is this fathomless, inexhaustible pool. It matters not how much of God's love is poured out upon His people, there is abundantly more to take its place. Its flow is steady, constant, and dependable. It never fails! "Because the love of God is shed abroad in our hearts by the Holy Ghost" (Romans 5:5). In His great love, God, foreseeing our waywardness, gave us hope. "God commendeth His love toward us, in that, while we were yet sinners, Christ died for us" (Romans 5:8). "Herein is love, not that we loved God, but that He loved us, and sent His Son to be the propitiation for our sins" (1 John 4:10). He first loved us; and for all eternity He will sustain us by His love. "I have loved thee with an everlasting love," He says in Jeremiah 31:3. Having graciously given us this "inheritance incorruptible," He keeps it ever living within our hearts.

What will be the culmination? Peter says the "inheritance incorruptible is reserved in heaven for you." This inspired statement confirms the certainty of eternal life. You cannot lose it because God Himself is reserving it for you.

How gratifying for the weary traveler, after driving hundreds of miles, to find upon reaching the hotel that a room has been reserved. On the other hand, how disappointing to find that by error his reservation has been neglected and that no space is available. No true believer in Jesus Christ will be disappointed. Christ's sacrifice reserves forever the place prepared for him in Heaven. So it is, the child of God may look forward with absolute confidence to the time of meeting Christ face to face, to dwell with Him eternally. We read in Hebrews 11:10 that Abraham "looked for a city which hath foundations, whose builder and maker is God." The believer in Christ looks toward that city with joyful anticipation.

Little is known about Heaven because of our human limitations. It is impossible to perceive that of which we have such scant knowledge. There are also language limitations. No language is comprehensive enough to describe what God has prepared for His redeemed people. But of this we may be certain: Heaven is a place, and Christ is there. Our Lord left no doubt about this, for He said in John 14:1-3: "Let not your heart be troubled: ye believe in God, believe also in Me. In My Father's house are many mansions. if it were not so, I would have told you. I go to prepare a place for you. And if I go and prepare *a place* for you, I will come again, and receive you unto Myself; that *where I am*, there ye may be also." What a wonderful place Heaven will be, forever in the presence of the Lord Jesus. What more could be desired?

> "Think of stepping on shore and finding it Heaven,
>   Of taking hold of a hand and finding it Christ's hand,
>   Of breathing new air and finding it celestial air,
>   Of feeling invigorated and finding it immortality,
>   Of passing from storm and tempest to perfect calm,
>   Of waking up and finding it Home."
> —The Gospel Call

Truly the believer's future is glorious beyond imagination, real beyond our fondest dreams. For we shall see Him as He is. The Lamb of God slain from the foundation of the world shall be everything to us. "Whom have I in heaven but Thee?" we hear the Psalmist cry (Psalm 73:25). And with him we shall join to sing in praise, "Blessing, and honour, and glory, and power, be unto Him that sitteth upon the throne, and unto the Lamb for ever and ever" (Revelation 5:13).

5

ENDLESS SECURITY

"Who are kept by the power of God through faith unto salvation ready to be revealed in the last time."—1 Peter 1:5

The third great treasure Peter suggests, which becomes the possession of the believer through the new birth, is *endless security*. If there were no other statements in the Bible to present this marvelous truth, verse five would be sufficient. The believer is "kept by the power of God." The word "kept" could be translated *guarded* or *garrisoned*. Our salvation is eternally guarded by an indefatigable heavenly militia composed of legions of angels. No enemy, not even the diabolical forces of hell itself, can penetrate the line of defense God has established to protect our salvation. God promises not only to save the repentant believer, but to keep him saved. Jesus said in John 10:27-29: "My sheep hear My voice, and I know them, and they follow Me: And I give unto them eternal life; and *they shall never perish*, neither shall any man pluck them out of My hand. My Father, which gave them Me, is greater than all; and no man is able to pluck them out of My Father's hand." The follower of Christ is safely sheltered in the hands of both the Father and the Son. Who could fall or be snatched from this security?

The Bible makes the fact clear that when one receives Christ as Lord a covenant relationship is established. The transaction is forever sealed by the Holy Spirit. "After that ye believed, ye were sealed with that Holy Spirit of promise, Which is the earnest of our inheritance until the redemption of the purchased possession" (Ephesians 1:13,14). The "sealing" by the Holy Spirit signifies both *ownership* and *completion*. The Spirit of God takes up His abode in the believer as God's possession, never to depart. At the same time complete deliverance from the power of sin is made a present reality. The believer is a child of God, never to be forsaken. The covenant is sealed and cannot be broken. But you ask, "Isn't there a danger of falling away and being finally lost?" Not when you enter into a covenant relationship with God. It is for eternity.

Less than one per cent of the wills that are contested through litigation in the United States are broken. The courts take a very high position with respect to the wishes of those who have died. You may be sure that our God is no less concerned about His covenants. They can never be broken, for they are established and protected by the Lord Himself. When we believe on Christ, we become "heirs of God and joint heirs with Christ." To remind us of His faithfulness in fulfilling His covenant with us, God declares in Psalm 89:34, "My covenant will I not break, nor alter the thing that is gone out of My lips." Our immutable God remains the same yesterday, today, and forever. He who begins a work of grace in our hearts will continue it. "Being confident of this very thing, that He which hath begun a good work in you will perform it until the day of Jesus Christ" (Philippians 1:6).

To assure us of this promise of eternal life in Christ God has given to us His written word, the Bible. "And this is the record, that God hath given to us eternal life, and this life is in His Son. He that hath the Son hath life; and he that hath not the Son of God hath not life. These things have I written unto you that believe on the name of the Son of God; that ye may know that ye have eternal life, and that ye may believe on the name of the Son of God" (1 John 5:11-13). The Bible speaks authoritatively on the subject. There is no room for questions or uncertainties. In fact, the only really reliable source of truth in the world is God's infallible Word.

On April 15, 1912, the mighty "Titanic" went to a watery grave after receiving a mortal wound when she hit an iceberg. The ship, 1,600 miles from the New York harbor, carried 1,500 people to their death in water two miles deep. It is said that when the "Titanic" left the English harbor, someone had scribbled on the hull, "God Almighty could not sink this ship." It was known as the unsinkable vessel. But what man makes must perish. There is little security in that which comes from the hands of men.

But how wonderfully certain is our security in Christ. Even though waves of doubt beat against us and thousands of obstacles infest our course, true believers never sink. Paul asks the question in Romans 8:35: "Who shall separate us from the love of Christ? shall tribulation, or distress, or persecution, or famine, or nakedness, or peril, or sword?" In verses 38 and 39 he answers this question with unshakable confidence: "For I am persuaded, that neither death, nor life, nor angels, nor principalities, nor powers, nor things present, nor things to come, nor height, nor depth, nor any other creature, shall be able to separate us from the love of God, which is in Christ Jesus our Lord." No force is strong enough to sever the Christian from Christ's love. This is an insoluble bond. In spite of all the assurance the Lord gives in His Word, there is a great host of professed believers throughout Christendom who are uncertain as to their salvation. If they would but take the Word at face value, their doubts would disappear.

Ira D. Sankey, the noted evangelistic singer, though a believer, was filled with doubt, fear, and conflict of mind concerning the assurance of his own salvation. He said, "I must find out whether I possess eternal life or not." He went to God in prayer and asked for a word that would settle this definitely and eternally. He then opened his Bible and his eyes fell upon John 20:31: "But these are written, that ye might believe that Jesus is the Christ, the Son of God; and that believing ye might have life through His name." He read and reread this great truth and it came to him with new power. He later declared that the words burned into the depths of his soul as he cried out, "Thank God, I do believe on Jesus Christ and therefore I *have* eternal life." Doubts never entered his mind again. He could say with Paul, "I know whom I have believed, and am persuaded that He is able to keep that which I have committed unto Him against that day" (2 Timothy 1:12). Yes, "we are *garrisoned* by the power of God." There should be no fear of losing our salvation, if we are in Christ. If you have not believed this wonderful truth, claim it for yourself immediately. If you have received Christ, it is God's will for you to know that you are saved.

Peter further states that God's keeping power is "through faith unto salvation." Does he mean that our keeping saved depends on our regular and constant exercise of faith? It would be unutterably sad if this were so. It appears that he is speaking of our present condition in contrast to our future state. During our pilgrimage through this life, we are to "walk by faith, not by sight" (2 Corinthians 5:7). The day is coming when we shall meet Christ face to face. From that time on we shall walk by sight, and not by faith. "It doth not yet appear what we shall be: but we know that, when He shall appear, we shall be like Him; for we shall see Him as He is" (1 John 3:2,3). When we "see Him as He is," we shall at the same time understand all things. Confusion, perplexities, and disturbing questions will be banished forever. But right now we must live by faith rather than sight, trusting God for all things. Our inquisitive minds must wait until we see Him. Charles Haddon Spurgeon said, "Faith is reason at rest in God." If we are to live with the joy of the Lord in our hearts, even reason must be surrendered to the Lord. Then, and only then, will doubts and problems disappear.

Do you have the assurance in your heart that you belong to God? If not, why not? Take Him at His Word, believe and receive His truth as He desires. Have you received Christ and yet are you unsure that you are saved? Many are. It is possible to own some things not possessed. I own a book I do not possess. Some years ago, I loaned a very valuable book to someone. I forgot who borrowed it and it has never been returned. I still own it, but I do not possess it. Possibly you are saved, but you do not possess the assurance of your salvation. God invites us to receive the assurance with the salvation.

Two Scotsmen were traveling to the United States by boat. Endeavoring to keep expenses down as much as possible, they decided to eat cheese and crackers during the entire trip. For breakfast, dinner, and supper on the first day, their diet consisted entirely of cheese and crackers. The same was true of the second and the third days. About the fourth day, however, they began to weaken. Passing the dining room and savoring the aroma of food, they decided to enter and buy at least one good meal. Approached by the steward, they inquired as to the price of a good meal.

"Why, don't you know?" he answered. "All meals are included in your passage."

These two Scotsmen remind us of so many of God's people who have received Christ as Lord, but have not realized that the assurance of eternal life has been included. They are merely existing on the cheese and crackers of uncertainty rather than feasting upon the solid and assured truth of eternal life. "We are kept by the power of God through faith."

God promises to keep us "unto salvation, ready to be revealed in the last time." This refers to the future tense of salvation. The Bible presents salvation in three tenses: past, present, and future. In the past, we were delivered from the penalty of sin when we received Christ as Lord—our justification. At present, we are being delivered daily from the power of sin through the ministry of the Holy Spirit—our sanctification. In the future, we shall be delivered from the presence of sin—our glorification. The future tense of our salvation is ready, but not yet revealed. It will be revealed when Christ returns. Until then,

"Be ye also patient; stablish your hearts; for," God declares, "the coming of the Lord draweth nigh" (James 5:8). Surely this time cannot be far distant. "For yet a little while, and He that shall come will come, and will not tarry" (Hebrews 10:37).

6

SORROW'S PURPOSE

"Wherein ye greatly rejoice, though now for a season, if need be, ye are in heaviness through manifold temptations: That the trial of your faith, being much more precious than of gold that perisheth, though it be tried with fire, might be found unto praise and honour and glory at the appearing of Jesus Christ."— 1 Peter 1:6, 7

The readers to whom Peter wrote this Epistle had been the objects of suspicion, hatred, and severe scourgings. They had suffered untold violence at the hands of their persecutors. But with the assurance of their endless security in Christ, Peter exhorts them in verse 6, "greatly rejoice." What a marvelous consolation! Though surrounded by trials, the true believer in Christ can always rejoice.

In John 16:33, our Lord said, "These things have I spoken unto you, that in Me ye might have peace. In the world ye shall have tribulation: but *be of good cheer;* I have overcome the world." "Be of good cheer" could also be translated, *cheer up.* Tribulation on every hand; yet God says, "cheer up." It should be remembered that our Lord spoke these words at one of the darkest hours in history. Sinful men were about to vent their hatred on Him and perhaps on the disciples as well. Yet He declared, "cheer up." This is the same exhortation Peter has for us. Whatever the circumstances, "rejoice"!

We are to rejoice even though we are suffering "heaviness through manifold temptations." This statement may appear to be paradoxical. How can one both rejoice and suffer at the same time? It is only possible as we wholly rely on Christ. Though the suffering may be severe, there can still be abiding joy. We may not always have happiness, for happiness depends on what happens. If circumstances are adverse, happiness may disappear temporarily. But joy never departs because it is neither circumstantial nor consequential. It is nourished by our unchangeable Christ.

Paul had a practical understanding of this marvelous truth. In writing to the Corinthian Christians he said, "We are troubled on every side, yet not distressed; we are perplexed, but not in despair; Persecuted, but not forsaken; cast down, but not destroyed; Always bearing about in the body the dying of the Lord Jesus, that the life also of Jesus might be made manifest in our body" (2 Corinthians 4:8-10). James also had a practical understanding of the reality of this blessed truth. He wrote, "Count it all joy when ye fall into divers temptations" (James 1:2). What marvelous joy God has provided for every believer in Christ!

Years ago I saw this joy expressed in the life of a consecrated servant of God. It was Christmas day when one of the members of my church came to me at the close of our Christmas morning service and asked if I would drive with her that afternoon to visit a friend whose son had been killed the night before. As we drove out in the country to the home of her friend, I listened to the details of the tragic death. The seventeen-year-old victim was one of the best-liked fellows in his high school class. Both he and his mother had been looking forward to his graduation in June. On Christmas Eve he rode his bicycle as usual to deliver his newspapers. Turning on the highway to return home, he was struck by an automobile and killed instantly.

Naturally, I began to anticipate something of the sorrow and sadness I would find in this home clouded by death. On arrival

I was ushered into the kitchen where the boy's mother was. She was complacent and serene. We then went into the living room to see the remains of the battered body. On a table by the casket was a picture of the boy, a splendid looking chap. Turning from his likeness to the broken body, and considering the mother's sweet spirit, I thought, "How can his mother be so calm?" Then I noticed a motto which hung on the wall above the casket, and immediately my question was answered: "Thou wilt keep him in perfect peace, whose mind is stayed on Thee" (Isaiah 26:3). This mother knew the Lord and completely trusted Him for "perfect peace." As a result, she could "rejoice" though in "heaviness." God yearns for all His people to experience this marvelous joy. It comes through absolute dependence and reliance upon Him.

Trials in the believer's life are temporary, "for a season." Compared to the endless security we possess in Christ, they are short-lived. We may rejoice in the assurance of a far better day to come. "For our light affliction, which is but for a moment, worketh for us a far more exceeding and eternal weight of glory; while we look not at the things which are seen, but at the things which are not seen: for the things which are seen are temporal; but the things which are not seen are eternal" (2 Corinthians 4:17,18). "Light affliction"? Yes, but only "for a moment," God declares. How encouraging! How thrilling! No room for discouragement or defeat.

A certain minister appeared unusually cheerful though suffering severe affliction. One of his parishioners asked the secret of his contentment.

"I make a right use of my eyes," was his serious reply.

"Your eyes? I don't understand."

"It is very simple," replied the minister. "First, I look up to Heaven and remember that is where I am going. Next, I look down upon the earth and realize how small a place I shall occupy when I am dead and buried. Finally, I look around and see the many who are in all respects much worse than I. This brings me to three conclusions," he continued. "First, I learn where true happiness lies. Secondly, I recognize where all our care ends. And thirdly, I realize how little reason I have to complain."

A right attitude toward our trials helps tremendously. Too often we hear the question, "Why?" which suggests a refusal to accept what the Lord sends. Why must these disappointments come to my life? Why must I face unexpected trials and tribulations? Why must my plans and hopes be blasted? Peter assures us trials are necessary. We cannot get along without them. "If need be," could be translated, *It is necessary*. But why? "For the trial of your faith." Actually, *to see if your faith is genuine*. Not that God wants to know, for He knows all things. He wants us to discover how far short we fall of His desire for us. But why does He choose to test our faith? Why not our love, courage, or holiness? Because everything depends on faith. If faith goes, the foundations crumble. All stands or falls with faith.

Only trial can so reveal the deep resources and the reality of one's profession. Fair-weather Christians manifest God's peace so long as all goes well. But when the storm clouds lower and the winds of sorrow blow, they quickly collapse.

Jewelers have a method of determining the genuineness of a diamond.

"Place it in water," they tell us. "If it is real, it will reflect even greater brilliance. If it is an imitation, its lustrous sparkle will grow dull." So the deep waters of trial reveal the believer's genuine beauty. The nominal Christian, when submerged in sorrow and pain, may complain and grumble. The child of God rejoices in the Lord.

In emphasizing further the necessity of trial, Peter says in verse 7, "the trial of your faith" is "much more precious than of gold that perisheth." Gold, together with the earth, will pass away. But the immortal soul will live forever. If perishable gold must be subjected to fire, how much more the believer. Through trials we are cleansed, purified, and strengthened. The present trial prepares us to face the one to come. It is for this reason we should never revolt when suffering comes. Nor should we be surprised that God permits it. Peter tells us later in this Epistle, "Beloved, think it not strange concerning the fiery trial which is to try you, as though some strange thing happened unto you: But rejoice, inasmuch as ye are partakers of Christ's sufferings" (1 Peter 4:12). Christians cannot grow and mature without trial.

A collector of moths found a living chrysalis which he kept in his conservatory throughout the winter. In the spring, upon seeing the tremendous struggle of the moth to escape its prison, he decided to help by making a slight incision in the sheath which enclosed it. Soon it emerged, a beautiful, great emperor moth. Delighted, the collector placed the valuable specimen on a shelf so it might grow strong for flight. But the moth never flew. Denied the struggle to free itself from the cocoon, the muscles of its wings never developed. The intended kindness of the collector had robbed it forever of the power to fly.

If we are in fellowship with the Lord, the afflictions He permits are to develop our spiritual muscles, to tone us up, to give us self-discipline, to crucify the flesh. We must accept them as such. "My son, despise not thou the chastening of the Lord, nor faint when thou art rebuked of Him: For whom the Lord loveth He chasteneth, and scourgeth every son whom He receiveth. . . . Now no chastening for the present seemeth to be joyous, but grievous: nevertheless afterward it yieldeth the peaceable fruit of righteousness unto them which are exercised thereby" (Hebrews 12:5-6,11). From the fire of suffering we emerge stronger in faith than ever before. Therefore, the Lord tells us not to despise His chastenings but rather to accept them as expressions of His love for us. He could easily have placed us in environments free from suffering, but what puny Christians we would be!

When God made the oyster, He guaranteed him absolute economic and social security. The oyster became heir to a house, a shell to protect him from his enemies. When hungry, he simply opens his shell and the food rushes in. But how different when God made the mighty eagle. "The blue sky is the limit," said the Creator. "Go build your nest." So the eagle went out and built his nest in the highest mountain crag, where storms rage daily and where he must battle winds and rain to obtain his food.

In the Bible, the believer is likened to an eagle; never to an oyster. "They that wait upon the Lord shall renew their strength; they shall mount up *with wings as eagles;* they shall run, and not be weary; and they shall walk, and not faint" (Isaiah 40:31). Put on your eagle's wings and "mount up" high above your suffering. Rest in the Lord's promises. Only then will you be "found unto praise and honour and glory at the appearing of Jesus Christ." Face all trial as God has intended. For "Blessed is the man that endureth temptation [trials]: for when he is tried, he shall receive the crown of life, which the Lord hath promised to them that love Him" (James 1:12).

Peter assures us of "the appearing of Jesus Christ." How blessed it will be to see Him when He comes again. While we wait, it is wonderful to know we may enjoy His spiritual presence. Whatever the affliction, we have the glorious assurance: "The eternal God is thy refuge, and underneath are the everlasting arms" (Deuteronomy 33:27). Those great arms of mercy and love are always beneath. However deep we may sink in sorrow's depth, the "everlasting arms" are ever there. How marvelous! Let us not weep and lament, but rejoice and be glad in Him.

7

THE EYE OF FAITH

"Whom having not seen, ye love; in whom, though now ye see Him not, yet believing, ye rejoice with joy unspeakable and full of glory: Receiving the end of your faith, even the salvation of your souls."—1 Peter 1:8, 9

God has endowed us with five senses: hearing, sight, smell, taste, and touch. Psychologists tell us there are more than five. I am convinced, however, that every born-again believer possesses a sixth—the God-given sense of faith. The two verses we are to consider in this chapter seem to present three aspects of the sixth sense: what faith *sees*, what faith *produces*, and what faith *receives*.

"Whom having not seen, ye love." How can you love someone you have not seen? This seems impossible, but it is most reasonable. Though Christ is not seen with the physical eye, the believer sees Him with the eye of faith. How do we see Him? Through His Holy Word, the Bible! The more time we spend searching the Scriptures, the greater will be our love for Him. Every child of God needs this fresh glimpse of the living Christ every morning.

John wrote in his first Epistle, "That which was from the beginning, which we have heard, which we have seen with our eyes, which we have looked upon, and our hands have handled, of the Word of life." John had the opportunity of seeing Christ with the physical eye, but he had no more than we. Our experience can be equally satisfying as we daily fellowship with the Lord Jesus and see Him in the Word with the eye of faith. Looking away from the busy world in which we live, we shall find love for Christ abounding as we look to Him in the Book.

Many Christians neglect the morning watch, rushing into the day without the much-needed fellowship with their Lord. What a tragedy! Failure cannot be averted. Joy and blessing cannot be known. There can be no strength to withstand the temptations that must come. When spiritual food is neglected, the soul will be an easy prey for Satan's subtleties. The tongue will be uncontrolled. The eyes will be easily attracted by lust. The common sins of dishonesty and deceitfulness will seem but easy steps to coveted goals.

Have you no time to see Christ in the Book? Are you too busy to invest the best hour of the day to derive needed strength for your soul? Oh, foolish Christian, you cannot continue long without diligence in the morning watch. Just as the body demands food and water, so the soul must have the bread and water of life. "Man shall not live by bread alone, but by every word that proceedeth out of the mouth of God" (Matthew 4:4). If you were to neglect eating and drinking for a week, your body would be dangerously weakened. The soul is no less in need of nourishment and strength. We must feed on God's Word.

Few of us love Christ as we should. But how can we expect to love Him if we fail to take time to be with Him? Lovers are eager to be together. When young people are in love, they take every opportunity to spend time in each other's company. What can be said about the Christian who professes to love Christ and repeatedly neglects fellowship with Him in the Word? Can we love Him and still fail to take time to be with Him? Those who observe the quiet hour each morning will be less likely to fail in their walk with Christ.

Christ is in the Book. We need to be ever-mindful that, as

one studies the Bible prayerfully and carefully, the Lord Jesus will be visualized. The Lord Jesus said of the Scriptures, "They are they which testify of Me" (John 5:39). Christ is the grand theme of the Bible. "In the volume of the book it is written of me" (Hebrews 10:7). There are no short cuts for fellowship with the Lord Jesus. If we are really to know Him, we must spend time with Him. The words of the hymn writer are most appropriate: "Take time to be holy. Speak oft with thy Lord."

Set between the tracks of a transcontinental railroad, for a quarter of a mile or more at a certain point in Ohio, is a metal trough filled with water. As they rush along, through trains never stop at tanks to take on water. But when they reach the place where the trough lies, the fireman pulls a lever which drops a scoop from the bottom of the train's storage tank. This takes up the needed water while the train rushes on without so much as even slowing up.

Such hasty replenishment may be extremely advantageous for the speeding train; but haste will never suffice to nourish and satisfy the deep spiritual needs of the child of God. We cannot scoop up needed spiritual food on the run; rather we must be willing to wait on the Lord with the open Bible, looking for Jesus.

As you daily study God's precious truth and search its sacred passages, it will become more and more precious. You will say with David: "How sweet are Thy words unto my taste! yea, sweeter than honey to my mouth!" (Psalm 119:103) Unfortunately the Bible is a sadly neglected Book in many homes. Such a condition can only produce weak and emaciated Christians. Someone has said, "A clean Bible denotes a lean Christian." How about you? What place does the Word have in your home? Is it but an ornament, or is it well-worn from frequent use?

There was once a little boy who was assisting his mother in spring housecleaning. Closets and drawers were being put in order. In cleaning out one drawer, the boy found a copy of the Bible. Upon asking his mother what it was, she replied, "Why, that's God's Book."

"Well," he said, "we might just as well give it back to Him. No one ever uses it!"

Is this true of your Bible? Have you been careless in not reserving precious time for the study of God's Word? Can you say as did the Psalmist of old, "O how love I Thy law! it is my meditation all the day" (Psalm 119:97). Give the blessed Book the place it should have in your life.

Someone asked a young Christian girl how to read the Bible to get the most out of it. The young girl replied, "Yesterday I received a letter from one to whom I have given my heart and devoted my life. I freely confess," she said, "that I have read that letter through five times, not because I did not understand it the first time, but because I am devoted to the one who wrote it."

If you are in love with the author of the Bible, you will read His Book over and over. You will love His Word. You will desire to see Him and hear His voice of cheer and comfort amid the many difficulties of this present evil world.

Dr. J. Wilbur Chapman has given us some helpful hints to make Bible study more beneficial. *Study it through.* Never begin a day without mastering at least a verse from its pages. *Pray it in.* Never lay aside your Bible until the verse or passage you have studied has become a part of your being. *Put it down.* Mark the thoughts God gives you in the margin of your Bible or in a notebook. They will have lasting value. *Work it out.* Live the truth you get in the morning through each hour of the day. *Pass it on.* Seek to tell someone else what you have learned. These suggestions are most helpful and, if practiced, will enable us to love Christ more.

If we are to know Christ intimately we must study His Word. "Study to show thyself approved unto God, a workman that needeth not to be ashamed, rightly dividing the word of truth" (2 Timothy 2:15). How important that every believer be a Bible student who faithfully studies the Book. It should be understood, however, that Bible study is more than simply storing up knowledge and facts. God intends that Bible study effect a change in our conduct. As you and I fellowship in the

Word each day and pore over its sacred pages, getting a clearer glimpse of Christ, we shall experience His cleansing and transforming power in our lives, becoming more and more like Him. He has declared, "Now ye are clean through the word which I have spoken unto you" (John 15:3).

How needful then that every believer go to the Word each morning and pray as did David, "Open Thou mine eyes, that I may behold wondrous things out of Thy law" (Psalm 119:18). As we behold the wonderful things God has there for us, our hearts will overflow with love for the Lord Jesus. As we look to Him daily in His Word, we shall rejoice with "joy unspeakable and full of glory." The word "rejoice" as used here is expressive of *leaping,* bounding joy based upon a believing, trusting, faith. Faith produces joy inexpressible, unutterable joy, that comes from the heart of God as we have fellowship with Christ. The more the Scriptures are studied, the greater this faith will become. "Faith cometh by hearing, and hearing by the word of God" (Romans 10:17). The results will be *joy,* ineffable joy!

Robertson McQuilkin tells of witnessing to a classmate during his university days. The classmate boldly declared himself to be an atheist. After a friendly discussion, the self-styled atheist stated, "I have a god."

"Who is your god?" inquired Mr. McQuilkin.

"I am my god," was the hasty reply. Mr. McQuilkin then asked, "Does your god make you happy?" There was a strained silence. "Nobody is happy," the student replied.

How hopelessly blind is unbelief! It knows nothing of the joy of faith. Faith produces "joy unspeakable and full of glory." But unfortunately, not even believers always realize this wonderful joy. Why? They are not taking the time daily to look for Christ in the Word. You cannot sacrifice the quiet hour and yet know this peace-giving joy. If we do not look to Christ, we look to ourselves. Self can only produce misery and failure. The secret of daily blessing is found in *"looking unto Jesus* the author and finisher of our faith; who for the joy that was set before Him endured the cross, despising the shame, and is set down at the right hand of the throne of God" (Hebrews 12:2).

We must look unto Jesus *every* morning if we are to live victoriously. Only then can we know the joy He possessed, even in the face of the sufferings of the Cross. David declared in Psalm 5:11, "Let all those that put their trust in Thee rejoice: let them ever shout for joy." Is your life marked by this keynote of joy? If not, can it be that you are overlooking the importance of a fresh daily experience with Christ in His Word?

Remember the testimony of the disciples on the Emmaus road after Jesus had been with them. "They said one to another, Did not our heart burn within us, while He talked with us by the way, and while He opened to us the scriptures?" (Luke 24:32) As you seek His face in the Book, your heart will burn with joy and overflow with blessing. But you must take time. You must claim the promises of His truth if you are to reap the benefit. "Thou wilt show me the path of life: in Thy presence is fullness of joy; at Thy right hand there are pleasures for evermore" (Psalm 16:11). The pleasures are there, but they must be claimed by the believer in Christ. John tells us he wrote his first Epistle, portraying the truths about Christ, that we might abound with God's joy. "These things write we unto you, that your joy may be full" (1 John 1:4). Yes, there is abounding joy for all who will look to Christ in His Word.

What will be the result of increased faith through the Word? "Receiving the end of your faith, even the salvation of your souls." The word "salvation" here means *healing*. Our souls are often broken by sorrow and disappointment. But there will be complete healing for the soul. We shall be at rest when we meet Christ and see Him not only with the eye of faith, but with the physical eye, and acclaim Him as Lord of Lords and King of Kings. This will truly be a day long anticipated.

But during our pilgrimage here on this earth, we are to seek Him daily in the Book He has given, looking to Him with the eye of faith, believing and loving Him. "Walking by faith," the apostle says, "yet believing." Here is the key. Trusting God for all things with unwavering faith. "Abraham believed God, and it was counted unto him for righteousness" (Romans 4:3). So you and I may believe Him as we are refreshed and strengthened daily by the morning dew of blessed assurance through His Word. Our love for Him will be a never-ending source of praise that overflows from joyous hearts.

8

MAN'S ONLY HOPE

"Of which salvation the prophets have enquired and searched diligently, who prophesied of the grace that should come unto you: Searching what, or what manner of time the Spirit of Christ which was in them did signify, when it testified beforehand the sufferings of Christ, and the glory that should follow. Unto whom it was revealed, that not unto themselves, but unto us they did minister the things, which are now reported unto you by them that have preached the gospel unto you with the Holy Ghost sent down from heaven; which things the angels desire to look into."—1 Peter 1:10-12

The theme of these three verses is expressed in the third word of verse 10, "salvation." Three phases of "salvation" are suggested by the apostle: its prophecies (verse 10); its price (verse 11); and its provisions (verse 12).

In his second Epistle Peter informs us that "holy men of God spake as they were moved by the Holy Ghost" (2 Peter 1:21). Though these men were divinely impelled to record God's communications to them, it is highly improbable that they fully comprehended all they wrote. For Peter tells us they "enquired and searched diligently," thus signifying that those who wrote the Word earnestly sought to understand the revelations they received. Though faithful in preserving God's truth, they were frequently confused as to its meaning.

In Genesis 3:15, the first prophecy of Christ's redemptive work on the Cross is stated. "I will put enmity between thee and the woman, and between thy seed and her seed; it shall bruise thy head, and thou shalt bruise His heel." Thousands of years before the Cross, God made it known that He would provide an eternal victory over Satan and sin. It is quite possible that the one who wrote these inspired words did not completely understand the full significance of this verse.

Years later, Jeremiah gave us another prophetic picture of the Cross. "Is it nothing to you, all ye that pass by? behold, and see if there be any sorrow like unto My sorrow, which is done unto Me, wherewith the Lord hath afflicted Me in the day of His fierce anger" (Lamentations 1:12). The context indicates that this verse has a direct prophetic reference to the indifference of millions to the sufferings of our Lord on the Cross for their sins. We can hear this cry of our Lord even now as teeming multitudes ignore His atoning sacrifice and give little or no thought to His gracious provision of salvation. Undoubtedly, not even Jeremiah himself was fully aware of the import of these pathetic words. He must "have enquired and searched diligently" into their meaning.

Consider another of the descriptive prophetic chapters in the Old Testament. "Surely He hath borne our griefs, and carried our sorrows: yet we did esteem Him stricken, smitten of God, and afflicted. But He was wounded for our transgressions, He was bruised for our iniquities: the chastisement of our peace was upon Him; and with His stripes we are healed. All we like sheep have gone astray; we have turned every one to his own way; and the Lord hath laid on Him the iniquity of us all. He was oppressed, and He was afflicted, yet He opened not His mouth: He is brought as a lamb to the slaughter, and as a sheep before her shearers is dumb, so He openeth not His mouth" (Isaiah 53:4-7). In this portion of God's Word, we have a minutely detailed account of our Lord's crucifixion and its purpose. But like the other Old Testament writers, Isaiah, too, must have been perplexed by some of the things the Spirit of God constrained him to write.

It is not intended to suggest that these inspired servants were not redeemed by God's grace, but merely that they did not wholly understand God's entire scope of truth as we now know it, fully declared in the Bible. Jesus confirmed this fact in Matthew 13:17 when He said, "Verily I say unto you, That many prophets and righteous men have desired to see those things which ye see, and have not seen them; and to hear those things which ye hear, and have not heard them."

Have you ever considered the privilege that is ours to enjoy God's revelation in its entirety? The Old Testament saints looked forward to the Cross by faith. Through the Holy Spirit, we may see God's complete program for man. Because of this privilege, ours is greater responsibility. The greater the knowledge of truth, the more demanding the obligation to obey it.

Regrettably, privilege often leads to neglect and procrastination. There are millions who have heard the gospel and are familiar with God's plan of salvation, yet do nothing about it. Church pews are occupied every week by professors of Christianity who have head knowledge only of the gospel but have never experienced it in their hearts. To such Jesus says, "Remember Lot's wife." Though almost saved, she was eternally lost! Having listened to the Word of God, even starting to obey, she turned back—and perished! Our Lord's admonition is a clarion call of warning to all who are undecided, lest the same judgment befall them.

One day a funeral director phoned and asked me to call on an elderly lady whose eighty-year-old husband had died. After offering words of comfort to the widow, I asked, "Had your husband received Christ into his life?"

"Yes," she replied, "just a few days before he died, he heard a gospel message over the radio and believed on the Lord Jesus."

What assurance this brought to the heart of the bereaved wife. Thank God, Christ will receive us, however late in life we turn to Him. But as I drove home, I thought of what this man had missed by delaying until he was eighty years of age to receive Christ. Though saved a few days before death, he never experienced the joys and blessings of following Christ day by day throughout a lifetime. Like many, he relegated Christ to the bottom of the list and lived only for himself and his own interests, until in the very face of death he turned at last to Christ for refuge. If you, too, have been ignoring the Lord who loves you, come to Him *now*. God has but one time, today! He says in 2 Corinthians 6:2, "Behold, *now* is the accepted time; behold, *now* is the day of salvation."

> "The present only is thine own.
> Then use it well before it be flown."

The price of our great salvation seems to be suggested in verse 11. Peter mentions here "the sufferings of Christ." Considering this in the light of Matthew 16, it is obvious that a wonderful knowledge filled the apostle's heart. As we hear him in the presence of our Lord on the eve of the Transfiguration, he displays little or no understanding of the Cross and its meaning. Jesus began "to show unto His disciples, how that He must go unto Jerusalem, and suffer many things of the elders and chief priests and scribes, and be killed, and be raised again the third day. Then Peter took Him, and began to rebuke Him, saying, Be it far from Thee, Lord: this shall not be unto Thee" (Matthew 16:21-22).

See the apostle rise to his feet, eyes blazing with indignation. Hear him shout, "Be it far from Thee, Lord: this shall not be unto Thee." This was to say, "They will never kill you, Lord! I will see to that!" Jesus answered him in a quiet but firm rebuke: "Get thee behind Me, Satan: thou art an offence unto Me: for thou savourest not the things that be of God, but those that be of men" (Matthew 16:23).

Any attempt to keep Christ from the Cross would be but a plot of Satan; for a crossless Christ could never redeem fallen humanity. The atoning work of Christ is man's only hope. Without it there can be no salvation. So, in a word, our Lord points out to Peter his mistaken conception of the vital things of God. Peter was far from the full realization of God's plan for lost men. Yet after the Cross and Resurrection of our Lord, Peter clearly perceived the truth. He writes of "the sufferings of Christ, and the glory that should follow." At last, he understood that all we have and all we believe depends upon the sacrifice of our Lord and His resurrection.

Despite God's full revelation, there still remains gross misunderstanding of the true meaning of the Cross. The Cross is recognized as a symbol of the Christian faith. For many, unfortunately, this symbolism has degenerated into a mere fetish or charm. To others, the Cross is but a great event in history which changed the course of civilization. Still others consider it an object of religious sentiment to which they are strongly drawn. But the Bible teaches that the Cross symbolizes two things: salvation and submission.

At Calvary, the price for sin was forever paid. Our Lord's cry from the Cross, "It is finished!" was expressed by a Greek word meaning *paid*. The same word is found repeatedly on tax receipts. This is the exact equivalent of the English, *Received Payment*. When Christ died on the Cross, the sin-debt of mankind was completely wiped out. Eternal payment was made so that all who believe on Him might be saved. To this end, God proclaims, "Neither is there salvation in any other: for there is none other name under heaven given among men, whereby we must be saved" (Acts 4:12).

But the Cross means still more than salvation. After our Lord rebuked Peter for trying to prevent His death (Matthew 16:23), He said in verse 24, "If any man will come after Me, let him deny himself, and take up his cross, and follow Me." Oh, do not miss this vital truth! Taking up the cross means complete submission to Christ. It can mean nothing else. It is not enough to say, "I believe." There must be a total submission to the Lord together with belief, if the meaning of the Cross is to be fully realized. Too many have accepted the Christ of the Cross, but not the cross of the Christ. Paul said, "God forbid that I should glory, save in the cross of the Lord Jesus

Christ, by whom the world is crucified unto me, and I unto the world" (Galatians 6:14). His was a complete submission to Christ. This is the need among God's people today.

A Christian father was entertaining his little son one Sunday afternoon by singing with him at the piano. They had sung the chorus children so love to sing: "Praise Him, Praise Him, all ye little children." The father had included, he thought, all the stanzas—"Serve Him, Serve Him—Love Him, Love Him," et cetera. But when he stopped, the boy looked up into his face with surprise and amazement and said, "But Father, you forgot to crown Him!" So they sang, "Crown Him, Crown Him, all ye little children!" Is it not true that many who profess to believe on Christ for salvation have forgotten to crown Him their King by bowing to His will? It is imperative to consider "the sufferings of Christ" for salvation, but "the glory that is to follow" can only be realized through complete submission to Him.

"Unto us they did minister *the things,* which are now reported unto you by them that have preached the gospel" (verse 12). What are "the things" proclaimed by the preachers of the blessed gospel? They are the provisions God has made possible through Christ's sacrifice for all who come to Him for salvation. There appear to be at least seven such provisions mentioned in the Scriptures.

First, eternal salvation for all. No one is excluded. As a result of the price paid by Christ, anyone who is willing to receive Him may be saved. "But we see Jesus, who was made a little lower than the angels for the suffering of death, crowned with glory and honour; that He by the grace of God should taste death for every man" (Hebrews 2:9).

Secondly, eternal fellowship with the Lord may be enjoyed by all who believe. Though wandering far away because of sin, the repentant soul is brought near to the heart of God. "But now in Christ Jesus ye who sometimes were far off are made nigh by the blood of Christ" (Ephesians 2:13).

Thirdly, a direct way of access to God in prayer is granted through Christ, our Mediator. "For there is one God, and one mediator between God and men, the man Christ Jesus; Who gave Himself a ransom for all, to be testified in due time" (1 Timothy 2:5-6).

Fourthly, the righteous demands of the Law are forever satisfied, delivering the believer from its bondage. This does not excuse the saint from obedience to the Law. Yet if we fail, God's forgiving grace is sufficient. "Blotting out the handwriting of ordinances that was against us, which was contrary to us, and took it out of the way, nailing it to His cross" (Colossians 2:14).

Fifthly, eternal forgiveness for sins is assured. The believer will never stand before God in judgment for sin. Christ suffered our judgment on the Cross. "In whom we have redemption through His blood, the forgiveness of sins, according to the riches of His grace" (Ephesians 1:7).

Sixthly, the believer becomes the recipient of God's righteousness. Whereas all our righteousness is "as filthy rags" at conversion, we receive the perfect righteousness of Christ. "For He hath made Him to be sin for us, who knew no sin; that we might be made the righteousness of God in Him" (2 Corinthians 5:21).

Seventhly, the anticipated hope of Heaven becomes a reality. Our Lord's word to the dying thief on the cross is His promise to us: "And he said unto Jesus, Lord, remember me when Thou comest into Thy kingdom. And Jesus said unto him, Verily I say unto thee, To day shalt thou be with Me in paradise" (Luke 23:42-43).

How marvelous are these provisions! "The *things* which are now reported unto you" are yours if you have received Christ into your heart. If you have not come to Him for salvation, turn to Him now. He invites you! And remember, this is not an invitation to a funeral, but to a marriage. For the Lord will fill your heart to overflowing with joy and peace through believing, until you meet Him face to face. Come and enjoy the blessed provision He has made for you.

9

CHRIST IS COMING

"Wherefore gird up the loins of your mind, be sober, and hope to the end for the grace that is to be brought unto you at the revelation of Jesus Christ; As obedient children, not fashioning yourselves according to the former lusts in your ignorance: But as He which hath called you is holy, so be ye holy in all manner of conversation; Because it is written, Be ye holy; for I am holy."— 1 Peter 1:13-16

It should be kept in mind that those addressed in this Epistle were suffering severe persecution for their faithful and consistent testimony for Christ. Naturally, they were disturbed and distressed by their surrounding circumstances, but Peter encourages them by a reminder of their glorious future when Christ returns to rule and reign with His saints. Until then, "Gird up the loins of your mind, be sober." That is, do not permit yourself to be encumbered by worry and fear. Williams translates this, "Tighten up the belt about your mind, be perfectly calm." Despite sorrowful and adverse conditions, the believer should rest in God's comforting peace. Not for a day, a month, or a year, but "to the end"—that is, "to the end" of this present age when Christ will return. Trust in the Lord with perfect confidence, patiently waiting "for the grace that is to be brought unto you at the revelation of Jesus Christ."

There is no hope more comforting and inspiring for the downtrodden and disheartened than the "blessed hope" of the return of our living, loving Lord. Every believer should be looking with joyous anticipation for the return of the Lord Jesus. The Second Advent of Christ is a thrilling hope. It is the key by which all modern problems are resolved and sane optimism is established. It is the vitalizing hope that transforms faith from weakness to strength, and from insufficiency to all-sufficiency.

For years Dr. A. T. Pierson was in doubt and despair concerning many obscure truths of the Bible, but he gave himself to persistent study and prayer, with the rewarding result that he discovered in the truth of the Second Coming of Christ the key which unlocked two-thirds of the Bible previously closed to him.

Indeed the belief in the Second Coming of Christ is the key that unlocks the door to balance and stability in a world torn by war and bloodshed. Confronted by a seemingly hopeless world situation, strained relationships, and tightening tensions, a great political leader in Europe was heard to confess, "I cannot see a single star of hope in the international horizon." What a defeated and futile outlook! It is obvious this man knew little of the reality of the return of Christ as unfolded in the Scriptures.

Every Bible student is assured of a "star of hope" even though the storm clouds of war and strife hover above us. "As truly as I live," God declares, "all the earth shall be filled with the glory of the Lord" (Numbers 14:21). Here is our "star of hope." The day is coming when the earth, though now overrun with hate, sorrow, and sin, shall be the dwelling place of God's righteousness, peace, and blessing. The turmoil created by restless, dissatisfied warmongers will not continue forever. "Alas for the day! for the day of the Lord is at hand, and as a destruction from the Almighty shall it come" (Joel 1:15). Christ will return to rule over the world and subdue all that oppose the truth of God.

Concerning the "blessed hope," our Lord was explicit. "If I

go . . . I will come again" (John 14:3). When the Lord ascended into Heaven, the disciples stood bewildered and perplexed as they gazed at this phenomenon. But the angels assured them that Jesus would return. "Ye men of Galilee, why stand ye gazing up into heaven? this same Jesus, which is taken up from you into heaven, shall so come in like manner as ye have seen Him go into heaven" (Acts 1:11).

Those who fully accept the scriptural truth of the return of Christ will find this anticipation a strong influence for Christian behavior in every walk of life, a spur to holy living. The direct relationship of "righteousness" to the Second Advent is mentioned repeatedly throughout the Bible. "Behold, the days come, saith the Lord, that I will raise unto David a righteous Branch, and a King shall reign and prosper, and shall execute judgment and justice in the earth" (Jeremiah 23:5). In the next verse, we are told that the name of the "King" shall be, "THE LORD OUR RIGHTEOUSNESS." In Psalm 96:13, the "King" is seen coming "to judge the earth: He shall judge the world with righteousness," David declares. In these passages, we see Jesus Christ, the personification of righteousness, coming again to judge the world righteously. But in examining another important prophecy we notice something of vital importance to those who are waiting for their Lord to return. In Psalm 85:13 God says, "Righteousness shall go before Him; and shall set us in the way of His steps." The righteousness of Christ should be manifested not only when He comes, but here and now. Every child of God should show forth the righteousness of Christ, walking "in the way of His steps." Wherever the doctrine of the return of Christ is proclaimed faithfully and believed sincerely, righteousness will be the result.

Without question, one of the foremost reasons for the worldliness evidenced in many churches is the complete disregard of the sane, scriptural presentation and acceptance of the truth of our Lord's Coming. God says, "Every man that hath this hope in him purifieth himself, even as He is pure" (1 John 3:3). It is the "blessed hope" that will impel us to obey wholeheartedly and follow our all-righteous Saviour. "If ye know that He is righteous, ye know that every one that doeth righteousness is born of Him," (1 John 2:29).

The return of Christ should have a threefold effect on the believer. It should constrain him to obey God, forsake sin (verse 14), and be holy (verse 15). Peter immediately follows the mention of the Second Advent with an admonition to be "obedient children." Obedience is not righteousness, but it is certainly the first step in that direction. What parent does not prefer obedience and detest disobedience in his children? God is no less concerned that His children obey Him. None grieves the heart of the Lord more than he who refuses to obey. It is one thing to *believe* the gospel, but quite another to *behave* it. For joy in discipleship, those who believe in Christ should obey Him.

A small boy was visiting his aunt during his summer vacation. Unable to attend church one Sunday because of illness, she sent him alone. Knowing how uncontrollable he was at times, she strongly emphasized the importance of being a "good boy." Immediately upon his return she asked, "Did you behave?"

"I surely did," he replied. "I heard the lady back of me say she never saw a child behave so."

How descriptive of many so-called believers who fail to regard behavior as closely allied with belief. Too much Christian living falls far short of God's standard of righteousness. Only as we obey God can we honor Him. He asks, "Why call ye Me, Lord, Lord, and do not the things which I say?" (Luke 6:46) "Doing" is important. His divine will for our lives must be willingly obeyed if we are to know His best.

Those who would obey God must be desirous of forsaking all known sin, "not fashioning yourselves according to the former lusts in your ignorance." All who come to Jesus Christ and are truly converted should break with the sinful habits and lusts of the old life. Before the conversion experience, we carelessly committed many sins in ignorance of God's truth. But having been delivered from this state of "ignorance," we should gladly forsake all that displeases Christ.

Though living in a carefree generation characterized by lust, believers should not bear the mark of the age. Often those who deny the claims of the Bible concerning the Second Coming are profane and exceedingly sinful. "There shall come in the last days scoffers, *walking after their own lusts,* And saying, Where is the promise of His coming? for since the fathers fell asleep, all things continue as they were from the beginning of the creation" (2 Peter 3:3, 4).

Not only do these unbelievers blaspheme the truth of the return of Christ in word, but by grossly wicked lives. How essential that such living should not be duplicated in God's people who anticipate the return of Christ. Under no circumstances should the believer stoop to the sinful lusts of the worldling. For lust is the natural inclination to run wild, to throw off all restraints. Consequently we are to break forever with the former lusts of the unconverted life and sever all practices of fleshly lusts which displease God. "For the grace of God that bringeth salvation hath appeared to all men, Teaching us that, denying ungodliness and *worldly lusts,* we should live soberly, righteously, and godly, in this present world; Looking for that blessed hope, and the glorious appearing of the great God and our Saviour Jesus Christ" (Titus 2:11-13). "Take heed to yourselves, lest at any time your hearts be overcharged with surfeiting, and drunkenness, and cares of this life, and so that day come upon you unawares" (Luke 21:34). The believer is to be controlled by the Spirit of God rather than by the old fleshly lusts. He should desire to do only what God wants, rather than please self.

Peter realized such abundant living could never be known apart from holiness. So he reaches the pinnacle of his threefold exhortation with this important theme. "As He which hath called you is holy, so be ye holy in all manner of conversation." Phillips translates it this way, "You are to be holy in every department of your lives." This is the challenge for every believer to be yielded completely to Jesus Christ. We have a high calling. "For God hath not called us unto uncleanness, but unto holiness" (1 Thessalonians 4:7).

Only as we walk with God in a life of full commitment through holiness, can we expect to attract a lost and perishing world to a mighty, redeeming Saviour. Through obedience we deepen our fellowship with God; through the forsaking of sin we enjoy victory in living. But it is through holiness we convince indifferent men and women of the satisfying reality of Christ. We act either as magnifying or diminishing glasses through which the world sees Him. How Christ appears to the world depends entirely upon each believer. Through the life of a devoted believer, the world will see a magnified Christ whose saving power has transformed and beautified. But the life of a carnal or worldly Christian will present to the world a minimized Christ who is not able to keep from sin or to satisfy with His presence. Christ must be our standard if all are to see Him honored in our lives. "Because it is written, Be ye holy; for I am holy." "For even hereunto were ye called . . . that ye should follow His steps" (1 Peter 2:21). "He that saith he abideth in Him ought himself also so to walk, even as He walked" (1 John 2:6).

Do you know what true holiness is? Some strongly affirm that God's words, "be ye holy; for I am holy," mean sinless perfection. "If we are to be like Christ, we must be perfect," they say. Actually, holiness is possession of the soul by God. It does not necessarily denote perfection; for perfection in this life is impossible to attain. But as Christ the Son was impelled to do the will of the Father in every activity of His life here on earth, so believers are to be possessed by God through complete commitment to Him. When Christ returns, we shall be made perfect. But, at this moment, our obligation is complete yieldedness to Him, permitting Him to work out His holiness through us. Complete surrender to Him is the only means by which this can be effected. It begins when we give Him top priority in every phase of living and love Him with the whole heart. Love for Christ will open the door to holiness. Therefore we must love Him more.

In the last chapter of the Gospel of John, Jesus did not ask Peter, "Do you love feeding sheep? Do you love to preach and talk to others about Me?" Nor did He ask, "Do you love sheep or do you love those to whom you preach?" The question Christ asked three times of Peter was, "Lovest thou *Me?*" This is the key to holiness. Do you love Christ with all your heart? If so, to abide by His commands in willing obedience will not be difficult. For God, with the command, gives enabling grace to fulfill it.

A Buddhist monk in Ceylon, who was acquainted with both Christianity and Buddhism, was once asked what he thought was the great difference between the two. He replied, "There is much that is good in each of them, and probably in all religions. What seems to me to be the greatest difference is that you Christians know what is right and have the power to do it; while we Buddhists know what is right but have no such power."

God says, "Greater is He that is in you, than he that is in the world" (1 John 4:4). Christ, through the Holy Spirit, gives unlimited power for holiness, but we on our part, must yield freely and completely, moment by moment, to a life of obedience and the forsaking of sin. Let us seek no other way but God's way, wholehearted commitment to the Christ who gave His all for us.

10

THE PRECIOUS BLOOD

"And if ye call on the Father, who without respect of persons judgeth according to every man's work, pass the time of your sojourning here in fear: Forasmuch as ye know that ye were not redeemed with corruptible things, as silver and gold, from your vain conversation received by tradition from your fathers; But with the precious blood of Christ, as of a lamb without blemish and without spot: Who verily was foreordained before the foundation of the world, but was manifest in these last times for you, Who by Him do believe in God, that raised Him up from the dead, and gave Him glory; that your faith and hope might be in God."—1 Peter 1:17-21

The Apostle Peter has been attempting earnestly to stimulate the courage of the downtrodden and persecuted believers with the blessed hope of our Lord's Coming. He further emphasizes the fact that not only should this hope dispel fear, and quiet restless hearts, but it should inspire the believer to live righteously for God. But who is to set the standard for righteousness? Who has the final authority on what to do and what not to do? Whose example shall we follow—the preacher's, the Sunday school teacher's, or that of other Christian friends? We must look further for the answer. If we do not, we shall fail. "And if ye call on *the Father*, who without respect of persons judgeth according to every man's work."

God, "the Father," is the judge. We must abide by His standards for righteousness as revealed in His Word. He is impartial in His judgment. He plays no favorites and has no pets. He judges righteously according to our actions. Believers may do as they please, but only as they please Him. He must reign supreme. It is not who you are, but what you are in the eyes of a Holy God. All our actions and activities must stand the test of His righteousness. Each day should be lived with but a single purpose, to glorify Him.

"Pass the time of your sojourning here in fear," that is, godly fear, with humble reverence for the Holy One, not trying to live like other Christians, but like Christ. Don't copy copies. Let the Lord be your pattern. You may be criticized; you may be marked as narrow or fanatical; but remember, God is the judge. It matters not what others may say or think about us, the question to be considered is, "What does God think?" We are to serve Him faithfully. "Not with eyeservice, as menpleasers; but as the servants of Christ, doing the will of God from the heart" (Ephesians 6:6).

So often Christians serve the Lord for the acclamation and approval of other Christians. How sad! Jesus warned against this gross evil. "When thou doest thine alms, do not sound a trumpet before thee, as the hypocrites do in the synagogues and in the streets, that they may have glory of men. Verily I say unto you, They have their reward" (Matthew 6:2). We must constantly ask, "Am I pleasing to God? Is my life what He wants it to be?" Only as we please Him can we possibly know His blessing and fruitfulness. "Whether therefore ye eat, or drink, or whatsoever ye do, do all to the glory of God" (1 Corinthians 10:31).

In verse 18, the apostle pictures the negative aspect of salvation. "Ye were not redeemed with corruptible things, as silver and gold." God's gracious provision of salvation is purely by grace and grace alone. We were hopelessly lost, dead in trespasses and sins, before God saved us. But when we received Christ, God "redeemed" us—literally, *ransomed* or *purchased* us—from the wicked one. We were made heirs of God and joint heirs with Christ. This purchase was forever. Satan cannot beg, steal, or buy us back. We are God's eternal possession, delivered from our "vain conversation received by tradition from" our fathers.

How well some of us recall the "vain conversation" that was handed down to us, the empty life which had no peace or satisfaction. This kind of life is passed on to children by unregenerate parents. Early, many children become the recipients of the worldly life which completely ignores Christ and His claim on the soul. Too many parents provide for the physical and mental welfare of their children, but completely neglect the spiritual. What a sorrowful error they shall some day realize this to be. Oh, if parents could only realize that their most important obligation to their children is to lead them to Christ. God expects parents to make adequate provision for the temporal needs of their children, but never to the exclusion of the spiritual. Tell your child about Christ. Let him see what a Christian is by observing your life in the home. Show him that the Lord Jesus is real. Other things will soon pass away, as corruptible gold and silver, but a Christian heritage passed on to the children by the parents will continue throughout eternity.

Unfortunately many parents are more interested in making money than in rearing children. They have been deluded into thinking money is the most important thing in life. Scores of examples could be cited of those who have completely missed redemption because of an insatiable desire for wealth. What a tragedy that foolish humans will barter eternity for a few dollars that often produce far more misery than happiness. How are they to be saved? Money cannot provide salvation. God could easily have studded the skies with suns of gold, stars of silver, and constellations of precious metals, but none of these could redeem fallen man. Silver and gold is not enough. Simon tried to purchase the gift of God with money, but Peter declared, "Thy money perish with thee" (Acts 8:20). How essential that everyone recognize the limitations of money. "We brought nothing into this world, and it is certain we can carry nothing out" (1 Timothy 6:7). How erroneous of man to think wealth can bring satisfaction.

A London newspaper offered a prize for the best definition of money. The prize-winning statement was: "Money is the universal passport for everywhere except Heaven, and the universal provider for everything except happiness." Someone else has said that "Money is a medium of exchange for material things but it cannot buy love, happiness, or Heaven." Paul declares, "They that will be rich fall into temptation and a snare, and into many foolish and hurtful lusts, which drown men in destruction and perdition. For the love of money is the root of all evil: which while some coveted after, they have erred from the faith, and pierced themselves through with many sorrows" (1 Timothy 6:9-10). Many have learned too late of the sorrows contiguous to money. Lest I be misunderstood, let me make it clear that there is nothing wrong with money in itself. The great temptation by which many stumble and fall is the "love of money" which is "the root of all evil." This is the age-old sin of covetousness (the itch for more), which confronts the saved as well as the unsaved. How many Christians have shrivelled spiritually because of their love for money!

The only way for a believer to enjoy continued victory over the sin of covetousness is to invest his money for God. Get rid of it as quickly as possible. Put it into the Lord's work of world-wide evangelism. If held, it will get a hold on you. Put it to work for the Lord. You will either make it a curse or a blessing. Money is what you make it.

> "Dug from the mountainside, or washed in the glen,
> Servant am I or master of men.
> Earn me, I bless you; steal me, I curse you;
> Grasp me and hold me, a fiend shall possess you.
> Lie for me, die for me, covet me, take me—
> Angel or devil, I am just what you make me."
> —Author Unknown

We are "not redeemed with corruptible things," Peter says, "but with the precious blood of Christ."

Now for the positive aspect of our salvation. Apart from the blood of Jesus Christ shed for redemption, there can be no salvation for anyone. According to the Bible this is not "*a* way," but "*the* way"—through the "precious blood." It is interesting to note that the blood is called "precious" after it was shed at Calvary. Of course, it was just as precious when Christ lived on the earth, but it is not spoken of as "precious" until after the Crucifixion. What a rebuke to the modernists who decry the term "redemption by blood." To them the blood of Christ was of far greater value before the Cross than after. "It is the example and character of Jesus that is important," they say, "and not His death." What a lie from hell! What hope can there be without the "precious blood"? Our only hope is in Christ. "In whom we have redemption through His blood" (Ephesians 1:7). He "made peace through the blood of His cross" (Colossians 1:20). Throughout eternity the blood-washed saints will sing praise "unto Him that loved us, and washed us from our sins in His own blood" (Revelation 1:5).

A Bible teacher was invited to preach in a Chicago church. Given the liberty of choosing any theme he desired, he spoke on that which was dear to his heart and ministry, "the Blood of Jesus Christ." After the service, the pastor of the church said, "We do not believe that around here. There wasn't enough blood in Christ's veins to save one man, to say nothing of the whole world." The Bible teacher replied, "It is not quantity, but quality that counts."

Christ's blood has quality. It is "precious." It is God's blood. That is why it is efficacious in redeeming from sin. It is the blood of the "Lamb without blemish and without spot." Christ is the perfect fulfillment of all the Old Testament sacrifices. He is God's eternal sacrifice, truly "the Lamb of God, which taketh away the sin of the world" (John 1:29). As the Lamb of God, He is "without blemish" in that He had no personal sin of His own. He is also "without spot." Though He freely associated with sinners, never was He defiled by their sins. He was the perfect Son of God. Even His most spiteful enemies could find no fault in Him. Boldly He challenged them with the question, "Which of you convinceth me of sin?" (John 8:46) They could only stare, speechless and silent. Jesus is the Son of God who provides salvation for all through His Blood.

> "What can wash away my sin?
> Nothing but the blood of Jesus.
> What can make me whole again?
> Nothing but the blood of Jesus.
> Oh! Precious is the flow
> That makes me white as snow
> No other fount I know,
> Nothing but the blood of Jesus."
>
> —Robert Lowry

Some consider the Cross but an accident or tragedy in Christ's life. The Cross was not an afterthought in the mind of God. Christ "verily was foreordained before the foundation of the world" to shed His blood for the sins of all. He is "the Lamb slain from the foundation of the world" (Revelation 13:8). The Cross was the pivot in God's eternal plan of redemption. Regardless of numbers or strength, wicked men could not have nailed God's Son to the cross without divine permission. Jesus in foretelling the blotting out of His life, instructed His bewildered disciples thus: "No man taketh it from Me, but I lay it down of Myself. I have power to lay it down, and I have power to take it again. This commandment have I received of My Father" (John 10:18). God not only foresaw Calvary; He arranged it.

Redemption by blood is the grand theme of the Bible. The Old Testament is composed of the Law, the Prophets, and the Writings. The heart of the Law is the Book of Leviticus, and the heart of the Book of Leviticus is chapters 16 and 17. The key to these two chapters is found in verse 11 of chapter 17: "It is the blood that maketh an atonement for the soul." Old Testament or New Testament, everything hinges on this divine truth. This is not to suggest that Calvary was built and established on Leviticus. Just the opposite. Leviticus was built upon the Cross. God has given us history in reverse. All history begins at the Cross. Either it retrogresses or progresses from the Cross.

How marvelous is the plan of God! There are no slips or failures. All has worked and shall work according to the plan. Nor is it without its purpose for each member of the human race. It "was manifest in these last times *for you*." No one is excluded. Christ died for all, but only those who receive Him are saved. It is "for you," God declares. Have you opened your heart to Christ? Have you let Him in? Don't look for another way. God "hath in these last days spoken unto us by His Son" (Hebrews 1:2).

Christ is the only way. To prove this, God "raised Him up from the dead, and gave Him glory." We readily agree, anyone could die on a cross. But God conclusively proved to the world through the Resurrection and exaltation of the Lord Jesus that His sacrifice was distinctly different. "Wherefore God also hath highly exalted Him, and given Him a name which is above every name: That at the name of Jesus every knee should bow, of things in heaven, and things in earth, and things under the earth; And that every tongue should confess that Jesus Christ is Lord, to the glory of God the Father" (Philippians 2:9-11). Hallelujah! Christ lives in the flesh at this very moment. He is coming again. All the plotting of evil minds to crucify Him was but the divine provision of redemption for you and me. Do you know Him as your Lord? If not, turn to Him. Call upon Him before it is too late. The complete price has been paid.

If you are a believer, are you living in the victory of redemption? Every need has been provided "that your faith and hope might be in God." Is your faith and hope in Him? Are you completely resting in our living Lord? Are you wholly trusting in Him who provided salvation complete and entire?

Recently, on entering a store I noticed a sign upon which these words were printed: "Complete the following limerick and win a huge cash award." By writing twenty-five words or less about the particular product mentioned, some contestant would be enriched by a large sum of money. Let me offer you a line to complete. Just one word is needed. It is a revealing word which will disclose whether you are happy or sad, peaceful or restless, victorious or defeated. Here is the sentence. You complete it: "For to me to live is ————." What is it? Money? Business? Lust? Self? No, there is but one word that makes life worth living. Paul knew the answer and could truthfully say, "For to me to live is *Christ*" (Philippians 1:21). Can you say it? Is Christ your very life at this moment? If not, throw open the door of your heart to His fullness. Give Him first place and forever know real victory.

11

GENUINE LOVE

"Seeing ye have purified your souls in obeying the truth through the Spirit unto unfeigned love of the brethren, see that ye love one another with a pure heart fervently: Being born again, not of corruptible seed, but of incorruptible, by the word of God, which liveth and abideth forever. For all flesh is as grass, and all the glory of man as the flower of grass. The grass withereth, and the flower thereof falleth away: But the word of the Lord endureth for ever. And this is the word which by the gospel is preached unto you."—1 Peter 1:22-25

The precious blood of Christ was shed on the Cross to pay the full ransom price for the sins of all who believe. Though salvation is entirely free to those who accept, it was extremely costly to God who offered up the blood of His own Son. No other price can avail. To be saved, all must come God's way.

Those who have come God's way will not fail to give evidence of it. How? There are several means. The one Peter states is by "unfeigned love of the brethren." All who become children of God by "obeying the truth through the Spirit," should manifest their new life by good works, especially through genuine love for others. The believer is saved not only to enjoy the assurance of a future heavenly home where love will pervade every motive, word, and action, but to put that same love into practice right now. "The fruit of the Spirit is love" (Galatians 5:22). All who are born of the Holy Spirit should show forth God's love.

The degree to which we respect and cherish others usually determines how closely we are walking with the Lord. Our love for God is quickly discernible by our actions toward others. In the engine room one cannot look into the boiler to see how much water it contains; but alongside the boiler there is attached a tiny glass tube that serves as a gauge. As the water stands in the tube, so it is in the boiler. When the tube is half full, the boiler is half full; when empty, the boiler is empty. Love for others is the gauge that reveals the depth of the believer's inner experience with God. It is impossible to love God without loving the brethren. When there is little love for others, love for Christ is proportionately small. But when love for the Lord Jesus is great, it will overflow and abound toward others. "If a man say, I love God, and hateth his brother, he is a liar: for he that loveth not his brother whom he hath seen, how can he love God whom he hath not seen?" (1 John 4:20)

Nothing can supersede love in practical Christianity. No sum of money given to the Lord's work, no amount of time invested in the service of Christ, not even regularity in the morning quiet hour can substitute for "unfeigned" or genuine love for the brethren in Christ. A lawyer may have no love for his clients and yet be successful and achieve. A physician may have no love for his patients and still be competent and skillful. A business man may have no love for those with whom he deals and yet be prosperous. But a Christian cannot be successful, useful, or fruitful without love. Paul declared: "If I speak with the tongues of men and of angels, and have not love, I am become sounding brass, or a clanging cymbal. And if I have the gift of prophecy, and know all mysteries and all knowledge; and if I have all faith, so as to remove mountains, but have not love, I am nothing. And if I bestow all my goods to feed the poor, and if I give my body to be burned, but have not love, it profiteth me nothing" (1 Corinthians 13:1-3, ASV).

The Lord's work suffers sadly because many Christians have much ability but little adaptability. Bible knowledge is vitally necessary, as well as clarity in expressing the truth to others; but only as our hearts overflow with sincere love for the souls of men will our work for Christ be effective. Thus the apostle implores every one of us to make certain "that ye love one another with a pure heart fervently." Actually, he is pleading with us to love *heartily* and *fervently*.

This kind of love comes from a heart so filled with Christ that there is a holy and impelling zeal to help others. It is more than talk; it puts words into action and produces. It is more than pity; it helps with a sympathetic concern. It is the kind of compassion Jesus spoke about in Matthew 25:35-36: "I was an hungred, and ye gave Me meat: I was thirsty, and ye gave Me drink: I was a stranger, and ye took Me in: Naked, and ye clothed Me: I was sick, and ye visited Me: I was in prison, and ye came unto Me." When we help others in this manner, Jesus said, we help Him. "Inasmuch as ye have done it unto one of the least of these My brethren, ye have done it unto Me" (Matthew 25:40). Our acts of kindness do not culminate with those we help. The Lord is honored and glorified. But oh, how we fail to love as our Saviour has commanded.

D. L. Moody was traveling on a train with his friend, the beloved gospel musician, D. B. Towner. The train made a brief stop in a small town and a young man, who was in a fighting mood, boarded. He was bruised and cut from a recent brawl. Recognizing Mr. Moody, he attempted to sing some of the old gospel hymns. The loud and contemptuous tones greatly incensed Mr. Moody. Soon he called the conductor and requested him to remove the young man from the car. Acquiescing, the conductor spoke gently to the young man, escorted him to the baggage car, bathed his cuts and bruises, and did all he could to make him comfortable. Hearing of this shortly afterward, Moody exclaimed to Towner, "And last night I was preaching about the good Samaritan. This morning I have my feet in the shoes of both the priest and the Levite. This is a terrible rebuke to me."

Christians have no excuse for lack of love. Regardless of what people do or say to us, we must show forth the love of God. But you say, "You don't know how I have been treated. I have stood about all I can." Wait a minute! What does God say? "Being born again" (verse 23). If you have experienced the new birth, you are a child of God. If you are not a believer, your lack of love is understandable, for then you are a child of the devil whose fruits will naturally be hatred, malice, enmity, and jealousy. It is expected that unsaved people will be inconsiderate and unkind, but not so the believer. If you have been reborn by God's Spirit, you should love and forgive at all times. Peter learned this lesson early in his discipleship. Recall when he came to Jesus and asked, "Lord, how oft shall my brother sin against me, and I forgive him? till seven times? Jesus saith unto him, I say not unto thee, Until seven times: but, Until seventy times seven" (Matthew 18:21-22). "Seventy times seven," that is four hundred and ninety. What do we do after we forgive four hundred and ninety times?

While teaching her class, a Sunday school teacher was faced with this same question. One of her more inquisitive little boys came to her and asked, "After I forgive my brother seventy times seven, what do I do next?" The teacher could not answer the question, so she sought her pastor's advice.

"Wait," he said, "till he forgives seventy times seven. Then give him the answer."

It is obvious that no one of us has forgiven to this extent. For we must measure the comparatively few times we have forgiven others against God's forgiveness of our countless sins. Only when He ceases to forgive may we withhold our forgiveness. Of course, our Lord could never stop forgiving. Even while suffering the atrocities of the cross, He cried out, "Father, forgive them; for they know not what they do" (Luke 23:34). Christians are to follow Christ. He "suffered for us, leaving us an example, that ye should follow His steps" (1 Peter 2:21). To this end He says, "When ye stand praying, *forgive*, if ye have aught against any: that your Father also which is in heaven may forgive you your trespasses. But if ye do not forgive, neither will your Father which is in heaven forgive your trespasses" (Mark 11:25-26).

Believers have been born anew by the "incorruptible" and eternal seed of "the Word of God." This seed under normal conditions will produce love. "Beloved, let us love one another: for love is of God; and every one that loveth is born of God, and knoweth God" (1 John 4:7). It is through love we can best convince others we have been reborn by God's blessed truth. Unless we reveal His love, it is questionable whether we belong to Him. "By this shall all men know that ye are My disciples, if ye have love one to another" (John 13:35). Having received new life, the result will be new love.

A young woman left her home because her father was a drunkard, but after being converted, she immediately announced her intention of returning home to do what she could to help.

"But what will you do when he finds fault with all your efforts to please him?" someone asked.

"Try a little harder."

"Yes, but when he is unreasonable and unkind, what will you do then?"

"Pray a little harder." The discourager had one more arrow.

"Suppose he would beat you as before, what then?"

"Love him a little harder." Here is genuine evidence of new life. For "we know that we have passed from death unto life, because we love the brethren. He that loveth not his brother abideth in death" (1 John 3:14).

As children of God we should cast off petty resentments and grudges. Life is short. Man withers as the grass. "All flesh is as grass, and all the glory of man as the flower of grass. The grass withereth, and the flower thereof falleth away" (verse 24). At any moment your life may be snatched from you. Don't quibble and argue. You will soon be gone and forgotten by all but a few. Maybe you were wronged; God says, "Forgive." Possibly you were treated unkindly; God says, "Forgive." Perhaps someone lied to you; God says, "Forgive." "Thou shalt not avenge, nor bear any grudge against the children of thy people, but thou shalt love thy neighbour as thyself: I am the Lord" (Leviticus 19:18).

A strong feeling of resentment harbored day after day is as dangerous as a cancerous sore. Often it is even more destructive in its effect. If you are bearing a grudge in your heart at this moment, make it right with your brother. Then you will know blessing and joy in your Christian experience. Don't say, "I'll forgive you this time but don't let it happen again." God doesn't talk like that. Let it be a clear-cut and definite forgiveness on the basis of God's love received through the new birth.

The love of God, like His Word, is eternal. He says, "the Word of the Lord endureth for ever." It is said that true love does not run smoothly. But God's love for us does, and our love for others should, as well. Some Christians are hot today and cold tomorrow. One day they are effusively friendly and the next they scarcely know you. They need a realization of God's unchanging love as revealed in His eternal Word. His promises in the Bible are not given with the possibility of His provision, but with the certainty that what he has promised, He will also perform. Our love for others should be like His eternal promises, forever changeless and sure. "Heaven and earth shall pass away: but My words shall not pass away" (Mark 13:31). In Christ, His love becomes a part of us and His Word and love shall remain forever.

"This is the word which by the gospel is preached unto you." It is God's grace that brings the good news of His love to unlovable men. If believers are to carry this message effectively to those who know not the love of God, they must abound with His love in both word and deed. It is not a loud lip but a loving life that will best convince sin-sick men and women of Christ's reality. To this end Paul beseeches us, "I therefore, the prisoner of the Lord, beseech you that ye walk worthy of the vocation wherewith ye are called, With all lowliness and meekness, with longsuffering, forbearing one another in love; Endeavoring to keep the unity of the Spirit in the bond of peace" (Ephesians 4:1-3). In closing this same chapter, Paul pleads, "Grieve not the Holy Spirit of God, whereby ye are sealed unto the day of redemption. Let all bitterness, and wrath, and anger, and clamour, and evil speaking, be put away from you, with all malice: And be ye kind one to another, tenderhearted, forgiving one another, even as God for Christ's sake hath forgiven you" (Ephesians 4:30-32).

Let us bow our heads and ask God to purge our hearts from all that would hinder His marvelous grace from effecting a mighty work of love within us and through us. Let Him remove the obstructions of unkindness, jealousy, and hatred to permit the full flow of His love's boundless stream, that we may show forth the sweet humility of Christ our Lord.

12

AS NEWBORN BABES

"Wherefore laying aside all malice, and all guile, and hypocrisies, and envies, and all evil speakings, As newborn babes, desire the sincere milk of the word, that ye may grow thereby: If so be ye have tasted that the Lord is gracious."—1 Peter 2:1-3

In the second chapter of his first Epistle, Peter uses several similes to enable us better to grasp the truth of what it means to be a Christian. While chapter one emphasized the importance of being *born* into the family of God, chapter two stresses the necessity of *growth* resulting from the new birth.

The first comparison the apostle makes is that of believers as "newborn babes." As parents expect their children to grow physically, so God expects His children to grow spiritually. All who truly have been born of the Holy Spirit are to develop into spiritual maturity.

I once met a girl who, though well advanced toward middle age, appeared to be quite young and was still greatly dependent on her parents. For many years they had tenderly cared for her as though she were but a little child. Mentally retarded, she was unable to lay aside her childhood habits and attitudes. This was a most pathetic abnormality. And yet, how much more sorrowful it is to see Christians who remain babes in Christ and never seem to grow up.

Those of us who are saved and have experienced the new life in the Lord Jesus are to become full-grown men and women for God. We should do well to duplicate the experience of the Apostle Paul who said, "When I was a child, I spake as a child, I understood as a child, I thought as a child: but when I became a man, I put away childish things" (1 Corinthians 13:11). Paul did not long remain a babe in Christ. He grew up! His faith was one of constant advance and progress. His eyes were fixed upon one goal. "But this one thing I do, forgetting those things which are behind, and reaching forth unto those things which are before, I press toward the mark for the prize of the high calling of God in Christ Jesus" (Philippians 3:13-14). How important that every believer conform unto the image of Christ by putting away those evil habits and wicked desires that stunt Christian growth.

In verse 1, Peter mentions five marks of immaturity that definitely curtail spiritual growth. The first, "malice," is so common in the lives of God's people. Peter boldly asserts, "wherefore laying aside all malice." The word "malice" connotes a spirit of ill will with a desire to get even. This sin is extremely malicious and destructive. When wronged, the malicious heart quickly but thoughtlessly asserts "I will pay back. I will get even." This should never be the attitude of the child of God. It should be remembered, the Lord fights our battles. "Say not thou, I will recompense evil; but wait on the Lord, and He shall save thee" (Proverbs 20:22). O how many of God's dear people live in spiritual defeat because of this sin of malice. Rather than forget unkindnesses by returning good for evil, they are possessed by an underlying, diabolical desire to get revenge.

The story is told that Leonardo da Vinci, while painting his great work, "The Last Supper," vowed he would get even with a bitter enemy by painting him as Judas. There was a sense of gratification in his heart as he yielded to this selfish temptation. But later, as the famed artist tried to paint the face of Christ, he was forced to give up in despair. Realizing that such a task demanded a pure heart, he put away his animosity, admitted the folly of his vindictiveness, and quickly painted out the face of his enemy. Only then, it is said, was he able to paint the face of Christ.

So long as there is a vengeful spirit, no believer can effectively serve God. He may be extremely busy for the Lord and his labors may be many, but they will be hopelessly fruitless. Only the heart which overflows with God's love for others can be useful in exalting the name of the Lord Jesus Christ. To this end God's plea to every Christian is, "Avenge not yourselves, but rather give place unto wrath: for it is written, Vengeance is mine; I will repay, saith the Lord" (Romans 12:19).

Peter further exhorts us to lay aside "all guile." This is the miserable sin of *deceitfulness*. God's people are to be true blue, stalwart men and women of the faith, honest and trustworthy at all times. "Providing for honest things, not only in the sight of the Lord, but also in the sight of men" (2 Corinthians 8:21). Under no circumstances should a child of God endanger his testimony by stooping to little tricks of deceit or falsehood.

It is said of Abraham Lincoln that he would accept no case in which the client did not have justice on his side. One time a man came to employ him. Lincoln stared at the ceiling, yet listened intently as the facts were given. Abruptly, he swung around in his chair.

"You have a pretty good case in technical law," he said, "but a pretty bad one in equity and justice. You will have to get someone else to win this case for you. I could not do it. All the time while pleading before the jury, I'd be thinking, 'Lincoln, you're a liar!' I might forget myself and say it out loud."

"A righteous man hateth lying" (Proverbs 13:5). Lying and all forms of guile grieve the heart of God. No Christian should lie or deceive, regardless of consequences to himself. If he does, he will never advance in the things of God.

"And hypocrisies," that is, *pretense*, claiming to be what we are not. This is a most suggestive sign of spiritual infancy. Frequently, in the course of my ministry, people come to consult me about their problems. Invariably, in relating their particular difficulty, someone else is involved. But how marked it is that, in nearly every case, the other person is in the wrong. The one confiding usually tries to give the impression he is right. Yet there are always two sides to any problem. No one can be wholly right.

Most of us choose to exalt self and degrade others. Why do we do it? Because of the sin of hypocrisy. We employ clever speech as a subterfuge under which to hide our own inconsistencies while enlarging upon those of others. How few of us are willing to face our own shortcomings and freely admit our failures. How different was David's earnest desire for purity of soul. He cried out to God, "Examine *me*, O Lord, and prove *me*; try *my* reins and *my* heart" (Psalm 26:2). We need this personal approach to God in confessing our own wrongdoings rather than those of someone else. A daily heart-searching is most essential if we are to be what the Lord wants us to be. He wants us without sham or hypocrisy.

We shall do well to heed the advice of the dear colored brother who reached a peak of eloquence in his sermon and shouted, "Be what you is and not what you ain't, because if you ain't what you is, you is what you ain't." Let us not try to "cover up," but "confess up" to the Lord, that we might be without hypocrisies.

Peter names "envy" as the fourth indication of spiritual infancy. The word contains the thought of *jealousy*. Not only is there an unwarranted desire for something someone else has, but a subconscious, malicious grudge toward the owner. Have you ever known a friend to get a new car, and after you saw it, you not only became envious, but sensed in your heart a feeling of resentment toward the owner? That's what Peter is speaking about here. When a young lady becomes engaged and receives a diamond, her unwed girl friends sometimes become extremely envious and are caustic in their remarks. Rather than congratulations in the spirit of Christian love, there are often such remarks as, "Well, she worked hard enough to get it."

God says, "jealousy is cruel as the grave" (Song of Solomon 8:6). Let us not be envious. Give thanks to God for any achievement or advancement your friends in Christ might receive. Say to yourself with Paul, "I have learned, in whatsoever state I am, therewith to be content" (Philippians 4:11). Be content with whatever you have and do not be concerned with the possessions of others. "But godliness with contentment is great gain" (1 Timothy 6:6).

Last but not least, Peter mentions the destructive trait of "evil speakings." Williams in his translation of this verse renders it, "all sorts of slander." This is nothing more than common ordinary gossip, which has been defined as "that which goes in both ears and comes out of the mouth greatly enlarged." Gossip greatly curtails Christian growth. How Christians need to get control of their tongues and "speak the truth in love." "Let no corrupt communication proceed out of your mouth, but that which is good to the use of edifying, that it may minister grace unto the hearers" (Ephesians 4:29).

There are so many troublemakers in the world. We who love Christ ought to let the Holy Spirit guard our lips and prompt every word that falls from them, endeavoring to edify and encourage with our speech rather than injure and hurt. We should sow seeds of peace and blessing, not division and discord.

A little girl once said to her mother, "I was a peacemaker today." The mother asked her if she had settled a quarrel for others.

"No," she replied, "I knew something and didn't tell it." How we need to start a string of such pearls each day. "Blessed are the peacemakers: for they shall be called the children of God" (Matthew 5:9).

We have considered five marks of spiritual infancy not discernible in mature saints. Let us be very personal. Do any of these traits characterize you? Has there been a failure to grow as you should into the strength and beauty of Christ? Do you see yourself described in any of the five traits? If so, get the victory through Christ immediately. Lay aside that which has been hindering. Of course you cannot do it yourself, but you can through Him. Paul declared in Philippians 4:13, "I can do all things through Christ which strengtheneth me." The victory is through the Lord Jesus. Claim it immediately. Receive it from Him. He is ready and willing to give it.

Verse 1 of 1 Peter 2 has to do wth the negative aspect of growing in God's grace, while verse 2 suggests the positive. "As newborn babes, desire the sincere milk of the word." Not only does growth come in the "laying aside" of the traits Peter mentions, but in desiring "the sincere milk of the word." As the baby cannot grow without milk, neither can a Christian without the milk of God's Word.

We are told that milk is the perfect food. So God's Word is the perfect food for the soul. There are so many weak and emaciated Christians because they are lacking in vitamin B —the Bible. Often they neglect the Word because the poisonous impurities of malice, guile, hypocrisies, envies, and evil speakings rob their appetites for it. Get the poison out of the system by laying aside the hindrances, and the "desire" will come naturally.

How necessary it is that every believer spend time daily feeding his soul upon the glories of God's Word, that he might become strong in the Lord. There are so many surface Christians because they are not taking time to go down into the deep things of God which He has provided for them in His eternal truth.

A young theological student came to me to obtain advice about a problem. He was recognized by many as a Bible scholar, though he was often criticized for being argumentative. While discussing his problem, I asked if he read much.

"Everything I can get my hands on," was the quick reply.

"How much time," I inquired, "do you spend in reading God's Word each day?"

"Not much," he answered. "I read about a chapter a day. That's about all my mind can retain." The reason for the spiritual weakness in this student's life was obvious. He had been reading and studying everything about the Bible but was starving his soul by not feeding on God's precious truth.

Nothing is more important than the Bible itself. Books and commentaries have their place, but it should be second place. It is imperative that we drink daily of the "sincere milk of the Word" if we are to expect spiritual strength for Christ. Then and only then, can we know real victory and joy in the Christian faith. Of the growing Christian it can be said, "His delight is in the law of the Lord; and in His law doth he meditate day and night" (Psalm 1:2). Though confronted by temptation and sin, he is fortified by the Word. "Thy word have I hid in mine heart, that I might not sin against thee" (Psalm 119:11). Be faithful in studying the truth and in daily drinking of the "sincere milk" of the Word.

Peter offers us a concluding thought on this subject as he says in verse 3, "If so be ye have tasted that the Lord is gracious." If Christ is in your heart, the certain result will be "laying aside" spiritual infancy as you are nourished daily by the "sincere milk," the Bible. If this is not so, Peter suggests you may never have "tasted that the Lord is gracious." You may never have been born again. Many think they are saved, but are not. They are powerless against sin; they do not love God's Word and have no will to grow strong in the Lord. If you are characterized by the five traits of spiritual immaturity, and do not love to read and study the Word of God, then you had best examine your heart. "Examine yourselves, whether ye be in the faith; prove your own selves" (2 Corinthians 13:5). Look to God at this moment. If there are any doubts, if there is the slightest trace of insecurity, say, "Lord Jesus, enter into my heart and make Thyself real." He will enable you to come to full growth and to be earnest in your desire to reveal His glory. Do you know Him? Is He your present possession? "O taste and see that the Lord is good: blessed is the man that trusteth in Him" (Psalm 34:8).

13

AS LIVELY STONES

"To whom coming, as unto a living stone, disallowed indeed of men, but chosen of God, and precious, Ye also, as lively stones, are built up a spiritual house, an holy priesthood, to offer up spiritual sacrifices, acceptable to God by Jesus Christ. Wherefore also it is contained in the scripture, Behold, I lay in Sion a chief corner stone, elect, precious: and he that believeth on Him shall not be confounded."—1 Peter 2:4-6

Peter continues the use of metaphors to describe some of the dominant characteristics of Christian living by likening believers to "lively stones." He was well qualified to speak on this subject for his surname was Cephas, meaning *a stone*. Naturally, he would be interested in delving into the statements recorded in the Old Testament which have to do with *stone*.

The phrase, "a living stone," suggests *life* and *stability*. Christ is the embodiment of both; all who have received Him as Lord are possessors of His life with its accompanying stability which enables us to face the uncertainties of our present age. How assuring it is in our constantly changing world system to have the promise of life and stability. The Lord's people can say with confidence, "He only is my rock and my salvation; He is my defence; I shall not be greatly moved" (Psalm 62:2).

Restless souls would immediately find peace and security if they would rest their troubled selves on the "Living Stone," Christ Jesus.

But in our day, as in the apostle's, Christ is "disallowed" (rejected) of men. "He came unto His own, and His own received Him not. But as many as received Him, to them gave He power to become the sons of God, even to them that believe on His name" (John 1:11-12). To this day, attitudes toward the Son of God are divided. Some reject Him. Others receive Him. To those who accept Him, He is a "savour of life unto life"; but to those who reject Him, a "savour of death unto death."

How foolish of men to reject the Son of God as Lord! Surely such a decision is without thought. When Christ was offered to the multitude for possible liberation, they cried out, "Away with this man," electing for freedom, in His stead, a murderer. This still seems to be the insensate cry of many hearts.

Why do humans choose to tread the uncertain path of shifting sands in preference to being established upon the Solid Rock, Christ? God declares in 1 Corinthians 3:11-13, "For other foundation can no man lay than that is laid, which is Jesus Christ. Now if any man build upon this foundation gold, silver, precious stones, wood, hay, stubble; Every man's work shall be made manifest: for the day shall declare it, because it shall be revealed by fire; and the fire shall try every man's work of what sort it is." Any other foundation in life but Jesus Christ will lead to ultimate judgment and perdition.

Although Christ has been rejected by many, this in no way nullifies the importance and nature of His mission. He was "chosen of God, and precious." The Father declared of Him, "Thou art My beloved Son; in Thee I am well pleased" (Luke 3:22). The Lord Jesus may be denied and rejected, but such an unreasonable and hopeless attitude does not for a moment rob Christ of His authority. In the Father's sight He is "precious" (highly valued). Unbelief cannot modify Christ's position as Saviour. Those who would seek to condemn Him are themselves condemned. "He that believeth on Him is not condemned: but he that believeth not is condemned already, because he hath not believed in the name of the only begotten Son of God" (John 3:18).

In verse 5, Peter informs us that we also are "as lively stones," better translated *living stones*. We are not "living stones" in the same sense in which Christ is *the* Living Stone, for we read in verse 6 that He is "the chief corner stone, elect, precious." Having believed on Him as Lord, we become an integral part of His body. "I in them, and Thou in Me, that they may be made perfect in one" (John 17:23). The "living stones are built up a spiritual house." Paul says of this house, in Ephesians 2:20-21, that it is "built upon the foundation of the apostles and prophets, Jesus Christ Himself being the chief corner stone; In whom all the building fitly framed together groweth unto an holy temple in the Lord." He is speaking about the Church, the true Church, the body of Christ which is composed not of any particular denomination, but of all believers among all races in every part of the world. They are "living stones," God says, being "built up" together into a spiritual house that some day will be completed. At that time the Lord will return and "the earth shall be filled wih the knowledge of the glory of the Lord, as the waters cover the sea" (Habakkuk 2:14).

Nothing can hinder the building of this spiritual house. There have been periods in history when dictators and tyrants have been successful in effacing the visible church in some parts of the world, but not the invisible Church of which Peter speaks in this passage. Even the diabolical forces of hell itself cannot destroy Christ's Church. The Lord Jesus, in referring to Himself as the rock upon which the Church was built, declared, "Upon this rock I will build My church; and the gates of hell shall not prevail against it" (Matthew 16:18). Every born-again person is a part of the true Church of God. With unshakable confidence we may sing,

> "My hope is built on nothing less
> Than Jesus' blood and righteousness;
> I dare not trust the sweetest frame,
> But wholly lean on Jesus' name.

"On Christ, the solid Rock I stand;
All other ground is sinking sand,
All other ground is sinking sand."

But what are believers to be doing during the church age, as the building of God's "spiritual house" progresses? The Bible tells us we are to "watch." "Watch therefore: for ye know not what hour your Lord doth come." (Matthew 24:42). We are to watch for the return of the Lord Jesus.

What does it mean to watch? Consider a night watchman in a factory. Does he remain at the door throughout the night watching for a possible intruder to appear? Certainly not! His assignment is much greater. Tasks have been assigned to be done while he watches. But all the while, as he works, he does so with ear attentive to unfamiliar sounds and eye alert for unusual shadows. Though he watches, he also works. So God desires that believers work as they watch for Christ to return.

Specifically, what work should we do? Peter makes it clear that we are "to offer up spiritual sacrifices, acceptable to God by Jesus Christ." There is no little confusion, it seems, as to the meaning of these spiritual sacrifices. Some interpret them as prayers. But is prayer a sacrifice? Do you recall any time in your Christian experience when you made any sacrifices in prayer? Have you not always been the recipient of blessing, rather than the giver? As we commune with God in prayer, He pours out blessing upon blessing. Certainly, this cannot be termed a "spiritual sacrifice."

Again, Bible reading is thought of as a "spiritual sacrifice." He who daily goes to the Word to feed his soul does not sacrifice. The benefits far outnumber the few moments spent in perusal of the Sacred Writ. This is not sacrifice, but a high privilege God has committed unto all who believe in Him. What comfort, strength, and encouragement we have received from His precious Word! Indeed, this is no sacrifice.

Church attendance is sometimes spoken of as a spiritual sacrifice. But when we consider millions behind the "iron" and "bamboo" curtains, who have been forced to forsake assembling together for fellowship in Christ, it becomes obvious that worship is not a sacrifice. It is rather a wonderful blessing God has granted to those of us who live in free lands.

What then are the "spiritual sacrifices"? It is clearly evident to me that the "spiritual sacrifices" are those things we do, which directly, or indirectly, effect world-wide evangelization, that the "spiritual house" might be built up and completed to eventuate in the glorious return of Christ. We have been commissioned to go "into all the world, and preach the gospel to every creature" (Mark 16:15). How few Christians are really sacrificing time, money, and talents to reach the lost with the gospel of Jesus Christ!

Speaking at a Bible conference, I sought to impress upon the audience the importance of living one day at a time rather than attempting to live a week, a month, or a year at a time, quoting from Matthew 6:34: "Take therefore no thought for the morrow: for the morrow shall take thought for the things of itself. Sufficient unto the day is the evil thereof." I stressed the fact that most of us live in the future instead of today, while God wants us to live only one day at a time, without thought or worry about the morrow.

The following day a young missionary couple on furlough, who had attended the meeting, told me how God had spoken to their hearts and given peace through the thought of living one day at a time. They were soon to return to Africa for another term on the field and it would be necessary for them to leave their children in this country for education.

"This has been a great burden on our hearts," the young missionary father said, "for we love our children and have been wondering how we could go to the field for five years without them. But now God has spoken to us, and we are completely surrendered to His will. We realize we are to leave them, not for five years, but for just one day at a time. We are going to trust Him for each day."

How we praise God for the full surrender of these parents to offer up this spiritual sacrifice. Why are they doing it? To win lost souls to Jesus Christ. It is a tremendous price, but worth it for His sake. "He that loveth father or mother more than Me is not worthy of Me: and he that loveth son or daughter more than Me is not worthy of Me. And he that taketh not his cross, and followeth after Me, is not worthy of Me" (Matthew 10:37-38).

When one considers the sacrifices being made by missionaries in leaving not only country and friends but dearest ones, many of us in the homeland are put to shame. Scores of Christians are living lives of ease and comfort at home, making little or no sacrifice whatsoever to participate in God's program of reaching the lost for Christ. The responsibility of evangelization has not been committed to missionaries alone, who go to the fields beyond, but to all who would truly follow Christ.

On the other hand, I know of some families who are sacrificing to keep one or two missionaries out on the field. Others carelessly and indifferently give, not out of their abundance and love for Christ, but without sacrifice present their paltry offerings drawn from superfluity. When we consider the sacrifices being made by missionaries, who live in flimsy huts, endangered by disease, hindered by untold obstacles, God forbid that any of us should permit our vision to be obscured by a few transitory comforts. Christian young men and women ought to offer themselves freely as living sacrifices to carry the gospel to the ends of the earth. Every adult beyond the age of missionary endeavor should be offering his money as a spiritual sacrifice to send young people out to proclaim the gospel of Jesus Christ.

While writing this chapter, surprising news came to me in the mail. I received word from a splendid young man informing me that he had just resigned as headmaster of a Christian School to go to Japan, with his wife and four children, as a missionary. The burden of the millions without Christ in Japan had been heavy upon his heart. He could no longer work at his desk. The only satisfaction for the living consciousness within his own soul was found in giving himself to go to the field.

Oh, if more of us could hear the cry of perishing millions! If we could see the conditions in which they live, and know the heartaches they endure without Christ, I am convinced that we should likewise offer up "spiritual sacrifices" that this world might hear the truth of our wonderful Lord who lives and longs to save all men.

Peter says, "He that believeth on Him shall not be confounded." Before the lost can believe, they must hear about Him. They must be told the story of redemption. Believers are called upon by God to invest in reaching the lost with the gospel. "Lay not up for yourselves treasures upon earth, where moth and rust doth corrupt, and where thieves break through and steal: But lay up for yourselves treasures in heaven, where neither moth nor rust doth corrupt, and where thieves do not break through nor steal" (Matthew 6:20-21). Any investment made for the gospel of Jesus Christ will not be lost, but will be returned—"good measure, pressed down, and shaken together, and running over" (Luke 6:38). "Cast thy bread upon the waters: for thou shalt find it after many days" (Ecclesiastes 11:1).

Christian, can you say with a clear conscience before God, "I am doing what He wants me to do. I am daily offering up spiritual sacrifices acceptable to Jesus Christ"? Can you honestly say this before your Lord? If not, I beseech you to get on your knees and confess your sin to Him. And from this very hour, let the keyword of your life be *sacrifice*.

14

HE IS PRECIOUS

"Unto you therefore which believe He is precious: but unto them which be disobedient, the stone which the builders disallowed, the same is made the head of the corner, And a stone of stumbling, and a rock of offence, even to them which stumble at the word, being disobedient: whereunto also they were appointed. But ye are a chosen generation, a royal priesthood, an holy nation, a peculiar people; that ye should shew forth the praises of Him who hath called you out of darkness into His marvellous light: Which in time past were not a people, but are now the people of God: which had not obtained mercy, but now have obtained mercy."— 1 Peter 2:7-10

There are many advantages in following the Lord Jesus Christ. Likewise there are many disadvantages in not becoming a disciple of His. Placing the advantages alongside the disadvantages, one may readily recognize the superior value of being a believer in Christ. Peter puts this truth succinctly as he declares, "Unto you therefore which believe He is precious." It is impossible for the unbeliever to perceive the preciousness of Jesus Christ since this can only be known by those who have received Him into their hearts. "Without faith it is impossible to please Him: for he that cometh to God must believe that He is, and that He is a rewarder of them that diligently seek Him" (Hebrews 11:6). Faith in Christ is the doorway to the unsearchable riches of God.

I have yet to meet a true born-again believer who would not readily agree that Christ is precious; not only precious at the time of salvation, but throughout all the joys and sorrows of life. He is so precious in taking care of all our needs. For this reason there need be neither fear nor worry, for the Lord Jesus in His preciousness will undertake for His own. David could say, "I have been young, and now am old; yet have I not seen the righteous forsaken, nor his seed begging bread" (Psalm 37:25). Those who have received Christ will agree enthusiastically with David that the Lord never forsakes those who belong to Him.

A minister survived the entire destruction of his home. Furniture that had made home comfortable for years, a library carefully selected over his lifetime, sermon notes and studies accumulated by diligent study of the Word, personal mementos, all were destroyed. In the space of a few hours only the clothes he stood in and the contents of his pockets remained. But on the following Lord's day, as though no disaster had occurred, he stood in his pulpit to proclaim the preciousness of Christ. To his congregation it seemed as though the Lord shone forth from his face, revealing the contentment and peace that Christ alone can give. How marvelous! The consoling grace this minister experienced through our Lord's great love is for all who believe in Christ.

In contrast to this blessed truth Peter speaks of the consequences to those who refuse to believe. "Unto them which be disobedient, the stone which the builders disallowed [rejected], the same is made the head of the corner." Christ is not precious to those who rebel against Him. The horrible sin of disobedience is the root sin of mankind, it is open rebellion toward God. It had its inception in the Garden of Eden and is still freely practiced by all who have failed to enter into the preciousness of Christ by believing on Him. The Bible declares that to those, Christ becomes "the head of the corner." This means He becomes their Judge. All who do not receive Christ as Lord in this life must some day stand before Him as Judge. "Marvel not at this: for the hour is coming, in the which all that are in the graves shall hear His voice, And shall come forth; they that have done good, unto the resurrection of life; and they that have done evil, unto the resurrection of damnation" (John 5:28-29). Two resurrections are spoken of in these verses: the first, "the resurrection of life," when the bodies of believers will be raised at the Coming of Christ; the second, "the resurrection of damnation" or "judgment," when unbelievers will be resurrected to stand before Christ in judgment, to be condemned to eternal perdition.

An important phase of Christ's present ministry is that of Advocate, at the right hand of the Father, pleading the cause of those who put their trust in Him for salvation. "Wherefore He is able also to save them to the uttermost that come unto God by Him, seeing He ever liveth to make intercession for them" (Hebrews 7:25). But the day is coming when He will return as the Judge, "the head of the corner," to those who have rejected Him.

A criminal who had often been before the courts was scheduled to appear for another offense. He rejoiced when he heard that an attorney who had defended him on previous occasions was now his judge. His attitude changed, however, when the judge stated: "When I was an attorney, I defended you; but I am no longer an attorney. It is not my business now to defend, but to judge. I shall hear the evidence and then I must deal with you in keeping with the oath I have taken in the office of judge."

Today, the Lord Jesus is the Advocate, interceding for all who accept Him; but the day is coming when He will be the Judge. As Judge, He must completely fulfill His duties in keeping with the nature of His office. No one will be excused. The penalty will be meted out. There will be no exceptions.

To the unbeliever the Lord Jesus is "a stone of stumbling, and a rock of offence, even to them which stumble at the word, being disobedient." Judgment is appointed for all who neglect or reject Christ, not because God desires it, but because unbelievers choose it. He is "not willing that any should perish" (2 Peter 3:9). But if a man of his own volition chooses perdition, his way will be one of stumbling and hardship. "Good under-standing giveth favour: but the way of transgressors is hard" (Proverbs 13:15). There is no place or satisfaction apart from Christ. It is so important that we know Him as the One who is "precious" rather than "the rock of offence."

Robert Murray McCheyne, one of the most spiritual Scottish preachers of the last century, was a well reared and carefully trained youth whose outward life was without blame. He was respectable, conscientious, and well informed in every way. He knew the Bible, said his prayers, went to church, and was satis-fied with his own righteousness. He forgot, however, that in God's sight, "all our righteousnesses are as filthy rags" (Isaiah 64:6). While he was away at school, a message came telling him of the sudden death of a very godly elder brother. He hastened home for the funeral, and asked permission to go alone into the room where lay the body of his dearly loved brother.

As he stood there gazing upon the still, silent form, he asked himself the question, "If it were I, where would my soul be?" The answer to his own question came to mind sharply: "Lost forever!" Then and there he broke down, gave up all preten-tions to any self-righteousness, and found in Christ the precious-ness he had never known before. Let none of us miss the preciousness of Jesus, found only by simple faith in Him.

Peter proceeds to list four privileges that become the eternal possession of all who receive Christ. First, believers in Him "are a chosen generation." That is, they are an elect race of God, members of His body entering into all the covenant privileges made possible by His death, burial, and resurrection. As chil-dren of God, they shall never want for anything. "The Lord is my shepherd; I shall not want" (Psalm 23:1). For the believer walking in fellowship with His Lord, every provision is met for his welfare and happiness. "For the Lord God is a sun and shield: the Lord will give grace and glory: no good thing will He withhold from them that walk uprightly" (Psalm 84:11). Christ will prove Himself sufficient to all. Consequently, the child of God may claim every promise of the Word. "He is the

Rock, His work is perfect" (Deuteronomy 32:4). We are His. He cannot and will not fail us.

Peter next states that those who believe "are a royal priesthood." In Israel the offices of priest and king were always kept separate. But in Christ they become one. Every true believer is a priest with kingly lineage. Being priest-kings is not merely a privilege but a serious responsibility. As kings, we are to take God to men, revealing the righteousness of Christ in holy living, which honors the "King of kings." As priests, we are to take men to God through earnest intercession and compassionate soul-winning efforts. "Ye have not chosen Me, but I have chosen you, and ordained you, that ye should go and bring forth fruit." (John 15:16). Indeed, ours is a tremendous obligation to bring men to Christ. God has said, "The fruit of the righteous is a tree of life; and he that winneth souls is wise" (Proverbs 11:30). Regrettably, few of God's people are really concerned about winning the lost for the Lord.

Francois Huber, the great naturalist, has said, "If a wasp discovers a deposit of food, he will return to his nest and report the good news to his companions who then sally forth in great numbers to partake of the fare which has been discovered for them all." Shall we who have found Christ to be the greatest satisfaction for every need be less considerate of our fellow men?

We are also "an holy nation," a consecrated people, set apart by the Holy Spirit to reveal the glory of Christ in holiness. Holy people should by all means evidence holiness. A jewelry salesman, noticing his hands to be somewhat soiled said to himself, "Of all persons, I should have clean hands. I cannot offer diamonds, pearls, or jewels of any sort to customers with hands that are not clean." Those of us who would present the treasures of Christ to others must have clean hands. "For God hath not called us unto uncleanness, but unto holiness" (1 Thessalonians 4:7).

Fourthly, Peter states that we are "a peculiar people." This means that in a special way we are a people for God's own possession. Oh, if believers could realize the depth of truth conveyed in this expression! God is our Master. We are His, never again to live for self. "Hath not the potter power over the clay?" (Romans 9:21) How frequently Christians bring tragedy upon themselves because of self-indulgence and self-will. They ignore the importance of letting the Lord plan their lives. Child of God, you are His and you must live for Him only.

In the light of these four privileges, Peter sums up this wonderful passage by suggesting that we should "shew forth [demonstrate] the praises [perfections] of Him who hath called you out of darkness into His marvellous light." If we belong to Christ, then we must constantly reveal the perfections of Christ. "He that saith he abideth in Him ought himself also so to walk, even as He walked" (1 John 2:6). If Christ is "precious" to us, then we should manifest His preciousness to those who are groping in darkness under the load of their sin, knowing not the joy and peace in believing. We should do this because of what God has done for us through His marvelous grace and mercy. He has saved us and given us the assurance of eternal salvation. We are obligated to reveal the truth to others in the beauty of transformed lives.

Peter describes our condition before conversion, declaring we "were not a people." But having met the Saviour, we "are now the people of God." We "had not obtained mercy, but now have obtained mercy." This is a present possession—*now!* How wonderful is God's mercy toward us. There is not one of us who deserves it. "It is of the Lord's mercies that we are not consumed, because His compassions fail not. They are new every morning: great is Thy faithfulness" (Lamentations 3:22,23). It is this mercy that should prompt each believer to "shew forth" to the unsaved the perfections of the Lord Jesus who has become so "precious" to us. We are surrounded by friends and neighbors who have never heard that He is "precious." Let us, by His grace, tell them how wonderful He actually is and seek to point them to the eternal certainty we have in Him.

15

AS STRANGERS AND PILGRIMS

"Dearly beloved, I beseech you as strangers and pilgrims, abstain from fleshly lusts, which war against the soul; Having your conversation honest among the Gentiles: that, whereas they speak against you as evildoers, they may by your good works, which they shall behold, glorify God in the day of visitation."—1 Peter 2:11, 12

The power which transforms the entire personality of the one who yields himself to Christ is not only miraculous, it is marvelous. We sense something of this change in Peter's life by certain expressions he uses throughout his Epistle. Recall his hard nature, impetuous, self-willed, and unpredictable. What a contrast now, however, as he writes, "Dearly beloved, I beseech you"—literally, *I beg of you.* The rocklike will of former years is now broken, matured in the love of Christ. The braggart has learned humility. Peter has become a usable instrument in the hands of his Master. Possessed by the Spirit of God, he has been mellowed until God's love pours forth in compassionate yearning for all believers to enjoy the same experience.

He pleads with God's people as "strangers and pilgrims" to "abstain from fleshly lusts." We, who have no sure dwelling place in this world, should be in the world, but not of it. The term "worldly-minded Christian" is often used to describe some followers of Christ. Such a phrase should be just as much an anomaly as "a heavenly-minded devil." As sojourners we are exhorted to refrain from worldliness. "Love not the world, neither the things that are in the world. If any man love the world, the love of the Father is not in him. For all that is in the world, the lust of the flesh, and the lust of the eyes, and the pride of life, is not of the Father, but is of the world. And the world passeth away, and the lust thereof: but he that doeth the will of God abideth for ever" (1 John 2:15-17).

The world is filled with lust. Those who love Christ should hate all that displeases Him. Recalling the fruitlessness of his own life lived in the flesh, the apostle, now humble-hearted, pleads with every believer to get immediate victory. Lust is inordinate desire. It may result from a hunger for too much of that which is good, or any of that which is bad. "Fleshly lusts" are those that seek gratification through unrestraint of the physical nature. All of us have natural appetites which may either be controlled or allowed to become unbridled. Paul lists seventeen of the many fleshly lusts common to man in Galatians 5:19-21: "Now the works of the flesh are manifest, which are these; Adultery, fornication, uncleanness, lasciviousness, Idolatry, witchcraft, hatred, variance, emulations, wrath, strife, seditions, heresies, Envyings, murders, drunkenness, revellings, and such like: of the which I tell you before, as I have also told you in time past, that they which do such things shall not inherit the kingdom of God."

Peter pleads with us to "abstain from fleshly lusts" because they "war against the soul." The word "war" expresses the thought of an army, trained and equipped, set in full battle array, at attention, ready to launch the attack. How able sinful flesh is to break down even the mightiest fortress of best intentions to follow the Saviour. Of course, the man without Christ has no defense whatsoever against lust. Only the Lord Jesus can enable him to live victoriously. But surprisingly, though Christians have the power within to control "fleshly lusts," few of them do. They sin, curse themselves, and repent. For a short time they are uplifted, but soon they are down again. The process is repeated many times without lasting victory. They are defeated and, consequently, sad and miserable. Does God will that His children live this way? Decidedly not! He has a better way, tried and true, that cannot fail.

You will note that in this particular verse, as Peter entreats us to "abstain from fleshly lusts," he does not tell us how to do it. This is not his purpose in this portion of the Scripture. We can, however, turn to the entire counsel of God as recorded in the Word, and answer the problem. It was Peter who declared in his second Epistle "that no prophecy of the scripture is of any private interpretation" (2 Peter 1:20). From this we learn that in determining the meaning or teaching of a single verse of Scripture, we are not bound only by the verse in question; but we have the liberty to go to other portions of Scripture where light may be thrown on a difficult or puzzling passage.

It should be understood that no one, including the Christian, has human power within himself to abstain from fleshly lusts. Many have been deceived by Satan into believing that since they are Christians, they are better than other people. Believers are just as quickly aroused, when confronted by temptation, as unbelievers. The flesh is inherently sinful. Paul was a believer when he declared in Romans 7:18: "For I know that in me (that is, in my flesh,) dwelleth no good thing: for to will is present with me; but how to perform that which is good I find not. For the good that I would I do not: but the evil which I would not, that I do." How precisely this describes you and me.

But is there no hope? Ah, yes. "Walk in the Spirit, and ye shall not fulfil the lust of the flesh" (Galatians 5:16). All Christians live in the Spirit, but not all walk in the Spirit. To walk in the Spirit is to realize "ye are not your own. . . . Ye are bought with a price" (1 Corinthians 6:19-20). Therefore, constantly give allegiance to the autocracy of the Holy Spirit, which presupposes complete abandonment of one's self, in full acknowledgment of utter helplessness. "Wherefore let him that thinketh he standeth take heed lest he fall" (1 Corinthians 10:12). "It is the spirit that quickeneth; the flesh profiteth nothing" (John 6:63).

The flesh and the Holy Spirit are at enmity. There can be

no compatability between them. "For the flesh lusteth against the Spirit, and the Spirit against the flesh: and these are contrary the one to the other: so that ye cannot do the things that ye would" (Galatians 5:17). Until your life is mastered by the Spirit of God, you will be limited, not only by lack of vision and service for Christ, but also by fruitless labor. There may be a desire to serve the Lord out of loyalty, but, being controlled only by the flesh, you will lack compassion and concern to reach the lost for Christ.

What is the key to a Spirit-directed life? Surrender! It can be known no other way. We must die to self and become alive to His indwelling Person. But you say, "I have surrendered my life to the working of the Holy Spirit, and still I find myself stumbling and falling frequently." Are you sure you have surrendered your life to the Holy Spirit's ministry? Has it been a complete surrender of the heart or of the head? An honest self-examination may prove the latter to be true. A life completely committed to the Holy Spirit is not one of constant vacillation. Surely you have heard of the keeping power of God? Through the Holy Spirit He has promised to keep us during the hour of temptation. God promises that when confronted by the enemy, His people will "be strengthened with might by His Spirit in the inner man" (Ephesians 3:16). Let us depend on the Spirit of God, our unerring Guide, to direct us into victory when surrounded by Satan and his emissaries.

In the deserts of Arabia, there is a guide who carries with him a homing pigeon with a very fine cord attached to one of its legs. When in any doubt as to which path to take, the guide throws the bird into the air. Instantly it strains at the cord in an effort to fly in the homeward direction; so it leads the master unerringly. They call the guide, "the dove man."

You may be sure the Holy Spirit, the Heavenly Dove, will always direct you in the right steps if you will rely upon His leadership. God has assured us that He "is able to keep you from falling, and to present you faultless before the pr sence of His glory with exceeding joy" (Jude 24). Are you the kind of Christian who suffers constant defeat from "fleshly lusts"? Is your life one of success today and failure tomorrow? Why not remedy this contradictory existence? Bow your head in prayer, confess your utter helplessness to God, and claim His mighty and miraculous strength through the Holy Spirit. The Lord will meet you in a new way, which will result in abounding joy and peace such as you have not known before.

In verse 12 of chapter 2, Peter gives the reason why Christians should "abstain from fleshly lusts"—"Having your conversation honest among the Gentiles." He beseeches us to walk with God so we shall bear, before the unsaved, convincing testimony that Christ does give new life. The word "conversation" as used here does not refer to speech only but to the outward expression of character and conduct which is the result of the new birth. The life of the Christian should reveal Christ to others rather than turn them from Him. One reason there are so few Christians in the world is because the people of the world have seen so little of Christianity. It is impossible to convince lost men and women that Christ can save, unless we demonstrate His transforming power in our own lives.

In Luke 6:46 our Lord asks a most searching question: "And why call ye Me, Lord, Lord, and do not the things which I say?" We who have professed Christ as Lord ought to exalt that name in holy living. "For ye were sometimes darkness, but now are ye light in the Lord: walk as children of light" (Ephesians 5:8). How detrimental to the cause of Christ are inconsistent Christians who continue to walk as children of darkness.

While speaking at a Bible conference, I was invited to the home of one of the families who were attending. While the hostess was busy preparing dinner, her husband told me how he had come to know Christ several years before, although he had faithfully attended church from boyhood. Unfortunately, it had been a church where the gospel had not been proclaimed; up to the time of his conversion, he had heard nothing about salvation through Jesus Christ. While visiting in another city, he attended church one Sunday, heard the gospel, and was wonderfully converted. Old things passed away and behold all things became new. His new-found life quickly blossomed into usefulness for God. Hungering for spiritual food, he soon found another church in his home community where Christ was exalted, and became very active in its program.

As he grew in grace, this man came under deep conviction because of a custom he had followed of presenting a quart of whiskey to his former pastor each Christmas. This had not bothered him in the old life. The gift had always been graciously received, and he had felt pleased with himself. Now, however, he phoned and asked his former pastor if he might come and talk with him a few moments. After exchanging a few words of greeting, the business man readily apologized for his thoughtlessness in giving the whiskey to the pastor each year. Whereupon the preacher smiled and said, "Don't let that bother you. In fact we opened a bottle you gave me last evening after our session meeting and passed the drinks around." Shocked into speechlessness, the young Christian sat silent for a few moments. Regaining composure he asked, "What would you have done had Jesus come in?" The preacher replied without hesitation, "We would have offered Him a drink, too"

Such inconsistency seems incredible. It is such contradictions as this in the lives of those who profess to love Christ that have drawn a veil over the eyes of an unbelieving world. But, thank God, not all Christians are walking to please the flesh. In every assembly of believers, there are those who are endeavoring, by the grace of God, to be a real testimony for Christ. It is these the apostle has in mind when he says, "Whereas they speak against you as evildoers, they may by your good works, which they shall behold, glorify God."

No matter how closely you walk with the Lord, there are always those, Satanically inspired, who seek to blaspheme Christ and His followers. They laugh and ridicule because you are following Christ. This is all the more reason why we should walk so close to the Lord that the world will have no excuse to point a finger at believers. But be well-assured, if we are walking with the Lord and are falsely accused, the finger of the scoffer is also pointed at Christ. The accusation does not end with us but with Him. The Lord promises to care for His own. It is for this reason that He said, "Blessed are ye, when men shall revile you, and persecute you, and shall say all manner of evil against you falsely, for My sake. Rejoice, and be exceeding glad: for great is your reward in heaven: for so persecuted they the prophets which were before you" (Matthew 5:11-12). Criticism and ridicule are to be expected. Never let it deter you from a life of complete abandonment to your Master.

The world will easily find much for which to condemn believers without being abetted by the unchristian living of professing Christians. Thus, Peter pleads with us so to exemplify Christ in our way of life that unbelievers "may by your good works, which they shall behold, glorify God in the day of visitation." J. B. Phillips, in *Letters to Young Churches,* translates the word "visitation" as *disasters.* This is most meaningful. Believers and unbelievers alike must face the disasters of life—sickness, financial losses, poverty, death, et cetera—which result in broken hearts, shattered nerves, and distressed minds. When disasters strike, the believer has Christ to whom he may turn and find immediate help. The unbeliever is helpless. But frequently when an unbeliever, who has been under the influence of a Spirit-filled Christian, meets disasters he will turn to the Christian for help, providing him an opportunity to lead a lost soul to Christ. How willing and ready every believer should be to grasp such an opportunity for Christ.

None can escape the hallowed influence of a consecrated follower of God. How essential that every born-again believer produce the "good works" which "glorify God." "Let us walk honestly, as in the day; not in rioting and drunkenness, not in chambering and wantonness, not in strife and envying. But put ye on the Lord Jesus Christ, and make not provision for the flesh, to fulfil the lusts thereof" (Romans 13:13-14). Let us make "manifest the savour of His knowledge . . . in every place," that the beauty of His holiness may be a beacon to a lost and unbelieving world.

16

CHRISTIAN CITIZENSHIP

"Submit yourselves to every ordinance of man for the Lord's sake: whether it be to the king, as supreme; Or unto governors, as unto them that are sent by him for the punishment of evildoers, and for the praise of them that do well. For so is the will of God, that with well doing ye may put to silence the ignorance of foolish men: As free, and not using your liberty for a cloke of maliciousness, but as the servants of God. Honour all men. Love the brotherhood. Fear God. Honour the king."—1 Peter 2:13-17

We have been reminded by the apostle that we are "strangers and pilgrims" in this world, and that, consequently, we should seek to live exemplary lives as a heavenly people dwelling in the midst of a godless generation. But lest he be misunderstood, Peter is very quick to inform us that separation from worldliness does not imply the avoidance of citizenship responsibilities to the state. Thus he says, "Submit yourselves to every ordinance of man for the Lord's sake."

Every true born-again believer is obligated to be not only a faithful Christian, but a worthy citizen. Heavenly privileges do not relieve us from civil responsibilities. Believers are to respect and obey all the laws and ordinances established by the state. Whether we consider them to be right or wrong, lenient or stringent, essential or nonessential, God says, "submit yourselves to every ordinance."

118

It is noteworthy to reflect that when our Lord was on this earth He gave due deference to law and government. Though He possessed all authority and power, never did He use his position to resist or disobey His government. Actually, the governmental leaders of His day, as of any generation, were placed in positions of authority by His providence. "For promotion cometh neither from the east, nor from the west, nor from the south. But God is the judge: He putteth down one, and setteth up another" (Psalm 75:6-7). Although He controlled all governments, by virtue of the fact that He was the Son of God, He chose to obey them. On one occasion when taxes were due, you will recall, He sent Peter down to the sea to catch a fish. His instructions were: "Take up the fish that first cometh up; and when thou hast opened his mouth, thou shalt find a piece of money: that take, and give unto them for Me and thee" (Matthew 17:27). On another occasion, He commanded, "Render therefore unto Caesar the things which are Caesar's; and unto God the things that are God's" (Matthew 22:21).

Paul likewise recognized the supreme importance of paying due homage and respect to those in authority by obedience to the laws they enacted. Even though misunderstood by the civil authorities, and later imprisoned, he used his incarceration as an opportunity "for the Lord's sake." In describing one such experience to the Philippian believers, he said, "But I would ye should understand, brethren, that the things which happened unto me have fallen out rather unto the furtherance of the gospel; So that my bonds in Christ are manifest in all the palace, and in all other places" (Philippians 1:12-13).

Not only was Paul faithful during his prison days in bearing a clear-cut verbal testimony to Christ's saving grace; it is evident he became the subject of conversation throughout the palace among the governmental leaders because of the respect he paid them. Several years before his imprisonment at Rome, Paul had written to the Christians in the church at Rome urging them to submit obediently and willingly to the authorities. "Let every soul be subject unto the higher powers. For there is no power but of God: the powers that be are ordained of God"

(Romans 13:1). He added that each one who ministers the affairs of state "is the minister of God to thee for good" (Romans 13:4). Now imprisoned in Rome, he was in a position to show believers and unbelievers alike that he practiced what he preached.

Peter further declares that those who administer the affairs of the state "are sent by Him [God] for the punishment of evildoers, and for the praise of them that do well." Where would any of us be without the protection of our government? To whom could we go for refuge from evildoers? We hear much criticism of the democratic way of life. We readily acknowledge weaknesses in our government. Certainly it is not perfect. Few are favorable toward the expenditures that have skyrocketed the national debt. Someone has said, "When you think of the government debt which the next generation must pay off, it's no wonder a baby cries when it is born!" We shall not deny the graft and dishonesty practiced by some of our public officials.

But let us face the situation squarely. Is this the failure of our system of government; or is it we who are at fault in failing to elect men of spiritual integrity and moral fortitude to offices of authority? Can it not be said that much of the failure lies even among Christians who have neglected their citizenship responsibility? Abhorring corruption in the government, many Christians merely observe and then flee from it crying, "Unclean, unclean!" This is no solution. The Lord would have us bear our citizenship responsibility to remove defilement.

In spite of the existent evils in our land we cannot but agree that the United States is a wonderful country in which to live. Consider the unequalled liberties granted to all, irrespective of race, creed, or color.

During World War II, Leon Jolson, a concentration camp serial number burned into his arm, hated and hunted by Nazis and Soviets alike, fled to America's shores. In this land of free enterprise, he set up a tiny workshop in a Bronx apartment; and within five years built a seven-million-dollars-a-year business. What makes such a feat possible? This country was founded on the great truths of God's Word which grants equal liberty and freedom to all.

Our country's educational facilities are unexcelled. We have one of the finest public school systems in the world. Few of our citizens have to sign their names with an "X." Our press has freedom. Through it and radio and television, information and knowledge are brought within the common reach.

Above all, we have freedom of worship. One may worship God, the sun, or even the cow, without fear of molestation or imprisonment. The largest Protestant following of the world thrives in the religious freedom of our country. This is an unusual country. Our civil and political liberties are more extensive than those in any nation on the face of the earth.

Yet today the tragedy of moral corruption, blatant evil, and spiritual spinelessness undermines our foundations. With all the God-given privileges at our command, we have nevertheless failed to utilize them to the best advantage. One may come to this country and become a millionaire. But the exploitation of this opportunity in our nation is breeding covetousness, dishonesty, and cheating of every kind. Thousands, in their mad scramble for money, forget Jesus Christ, who alone can give peace and lasting satisfaction. With all our educational advantages, public school systems are almost without exception secularized. God and the gospel are ignored. Though we have the largest Protestant church in the world, only a small percentage of our people attend church. An even smaller percentage have actually been born again.

What is the solution for this distressing dilemma? *Revival!* "If My people, which are called by My name, shall humble themselves, and pray, and seek My face, and turn from their wicked ways; then will I hear from heaven, and will forgive their sin, and will heal their land" (2 Chronicles 7:14). By revival I do not mean card-signing or padding the rolls of churches with unsaved members. I mean a Holy-Spirit ownership of men and women all over this land of ours; men and women who will love Christ and carry Him into government, into business, into schools, into homes, and into every phase of our society. Revival can begin only in the hearts of Christians. The burden falls upon those of us who have professed Christ. We must be willing to take the step of complete surrender to Him. For only as we who know Christ experience revival, will the lost cry out to God for redemption. Be satisfied with nothing less than a life of complete commitment to Christ.

"For so is the will of God, that with well doing ye may put to silence the ignorance of foolish men." Unbelievers were extremely critical of Christians in Peter's day, regarding them with suspicion and scorn because they were accused of plotting the overthrow of the government and the dethronement of Caesar in favor of Christ. Fearing persecution and martyrdom, believers gathered secretly for worship. For this reason, they were greatly abused and misunderstood by "foolish men," unsaved men, who because of the spiritual darkness within their own souls were unsympathetic toward the cause of Christ. In an attempt to silence the false accusers Peter urges them to do all within their power to live as respectable citizens and to submit to the authorities.

There are, however, certain limits to the extent to which one may go in submitting to a government. If it opposes Christ and prohibits freedom of worship, it is indicated by Scripture that the Christian is not obliged to acquiesce. Such circumstances justly provoke refusal to comply. In the fifth chapter of Acts, we read of Peter and the apostles being haled before the high priest and the council. The question was asked, "Did not we straitly command you that ye should not teach in this name? and, behold, ye have filled Jerusalem with your doctrine, and intend to bring this man's blood upon us. Then Peter and the other apostles answered and said, We ought to obey God rather than men" (Acts 5:28-29). God is the master of the conscience. Obedience to Him must always supersede our allegiance to others.

We are "free," Peter declares in verse 16. The Christian's most cherished freedom is his deliverance from sin through the shed blood of Jesus Christ. God says, "And ye shall know the truth, and the truth shall make you free" (John 8:32). The liberating "truth" is Christ. "If the Son therefore shall make you free, ye shall be free indeed" (John 8:36). Of far greater importance than the freedom a democracy offers is the freedom experienced when sin is forgiven and the believer is united by faith to the living Christ.

Some years ago I read of a man wandering in the vicinity of the Illinois-Michigan canal. Unwittingly, he stepped into quicksands and in a matter of minutes found himself helpless, a prisoner of the rapidly freezing mire. The harder he fought, the deeper he sank. He called and shouted until he was hoarse. But no one heard; and the slime tugged relentlessly, sucking his numbed body deeper and deeper. After sixteen hours, only his head and shoulders protruded. He summoned his last strength and weakly called once more for help. This time three young hunters heard, and rushing to his aid, kept him from sinking until more help arrived. When at last the man was freed from the clutch of a horrible grave, how grateful he was. How overjoyed!

Even more important than saving the physical body from death is the rescue of the soul from eternal death! Those who have come to Christ know the joy of being liberated from sin. We were hopelessly lost, sinking in the mire of sin, but Christ saved us. "For He [God] hath made Him [Christ] to be sin for us, who knew no sin; that we might be made the righteousness of God in Him" (2 Corinthians 5:21). If you have not experienced this freedom, turn to Christ at this moment and receive the life He has for you.

If we have received Christ as Lord we are "free," but we are never to use our "Liberty for a cloke of maliciousness." Christian liberty should not be an excuse to commit evil. Though free, we are "the servants of God." This fact elicits a fourfold obligation. First, we are expected to "honor all men," saved and unsaved alike. "Bear ye one another's burdens, and so fulfil the law of Christ" (Galatians 6:2). Believers should be known for their kindness. It is inconsistent to claim to be a servant of Christ and overlook the needs of one's neighbor.

In a small country community, there lived a mean-spirited

old man. One day he died suddenly. A friend mentioned the death to another and was asked, "What was the complaint?" meaning, what was the cause of his death?

"There was no complaint," was the reply. "Everybody was satisfied." Let this never be true of us. Rather may we be "kindly affectioned one to another."

Closely allied to this obligation is our duty to "love the brotherhood." Paul in writing to the Galatians said, "As we have therefore opportunity, let us do good unto all men, especially unto them who are of the household of faith" (Galatians 6:10). We are to be kind to everyone, but we are specifically instructed to care for believers. In Christ we are bound by a common tie that nothing should break. Some Christians have been known to take the attitude that they are to love only those who love them. True Christian love does not know such favoritism. "For if ye love them which love you, what reward have ye? do not even the publicans the same?" (Matthew 5:46) It is easy to love those who are gracious and warmhearted toward us. Christian love goes far deeper. The love of Christ enables the believer to love even those who are mean and unkind to him.

Peter would also have us understand that our love is not only to be directed toward those around us, but toward the Lord. We are to "fear God," that is, to respect Him with reverential awe. Is it not true we "fear" Him only when we allow Him to be the possessor of our hearts through complete submission to His will? Paul enjoins us in Romans 6:13, "yield yourselves unto God." Weymouth translates this, "Surrender your very selves to God." This is fearing Him. When every trace of the self-life is crucified, we become mastered by the Christ-life.

> "O fill us now, Thou Living Power,
>   With energy divine,
> Thus shall our wills from hour to hour,
>   Become not ours, but Thine."
>   —Ebenezer S. Oakley

This portion of the Epistle closes with the same thought with which it began: "Honour the king." By reiteration, the apostle emphasizes the grave import of this exhortation. As children of God anticipating the joys of Heaven, let us never in the slightest measure shirk our responsibility to exalt Christ through good citizenship. "Render therefore to all their dues: tribute to whom tribute is due; custom to whom custom; fear to whom fear; honour to whom honour" (Romans 13:7).

17

ENDURING PATIENTLY

"Servants, be subject to your masters with all fear; not only to the good and gentle, but also to the froward. For this is thankworthy, if a man for conscience toward God endure grief, suffering wrongfully. For what glory is it, if, when ye be buffeted for your faults, ye shall take it patiently? but if, when ye do well, and suffer for it, ye take it patiently, this is acceptable with God. For even hereunto were ye called: because Christ also suffered for us, leaving us an example, that ye should follow His steps: Who did no sin, neither was guile found in His mouth: Who, when He was reviled, reviled not again; when He suffered, He threatened not; but committed Himself to Him that judgeth righteously."—1 Peter 2:18-23

Having considered the Christian's duties to the state, the apostle now directs our attention to the believer's proper attitude toward his employer. As in the citizenship obligation, so in one's relationship to his employer, submission is the basic requirement. "Servants, be subject to your masters with all fear."

The apostle is not thinking at this moment of slaves, but rather *household servants*, which in his day included teachers, musicians, and all free working men and women. In its broader aspect, the admonition of this passage of Scripture is most relevant to present-day business and industry. Were Christians more concerned about submitting themselves to the business interests of their employers "with all fear," that is, *with proper respect,* they would be far happier in their employment.

Of course, what Peter has to say here about employees is equally binding on the employer. The subject is not presented with all of its ramifications in this portion of Scripture. Since the apostle's specific purpose in this chapter is the emphasis of Christian growth which results in holy living, he does not discuss the employer's responsibility to the employee, though many other passages in the Bible do give us a clear-cut understanding of God's mind on every phase of the subject. For example, Paul in writing to the saints at Colosse gave pertinent advice for employers: "Masters, give unto your servants that which is just and equal; knowing that ye also have a Master in heaven" (Colossians 4:1). Christian employers, therefore, should consider the rights of their employees and at no time take advantage of them, but rather glorify the Lord in all their relationships.

In further emphasizing the duties of the Christian employee, the apostle emphasizes proper respect, "not only to the good and gentle, but also to the froward." The "froward" are those with whom it is difficult to get along. No matter how one strives to please a froward person, the task seems hopelessly futile. The froward are usually critical and often harsh in judgment. To be sure, it is irritating and disconcerting to work for such a person, but the child of God must ever be mindful of His high calling as a witness for Christ. One cannot win a person like this to the Lord by quitting and getting another job. We are to exemplify Christ under all conditions, not living for ourselves, but for Him.

Sometimes Christians become very critical of their boss or the company that employs them. What a tragic mistake! If we have prayed about the matter and the Lord has placed us in a certain place of employment, what right have we to complain? It is so easy to become a chronic grumbler. The sincere believer should be far more concerned about reforming himself than about censoring others. Putting your best foot forward doesn't mean to kick about everything. Even though things aren't just as you would have them at the office or at the plant, criticizing your employer or company policies will never remedy the situation. If you are a Christian, there is too much at stake to stoop to the influence of the sinful flesh.

Christians need to face up to this horrible sin of criticism. The Bible has much to say about it. The Lord Jesus said, "Judge not, that ye be not judged. For with what judgment ye judge, ye shall be judged: and with what measure ye mete, it shall be measured to you again. And why beholdest thou the mote that is in thy brother's eye, but considerest not the beam that is in thine own eye?" (Matthew 7:1-3) Paul, in writing to the church at Rome, said: "Therefore thou art inexcusable, O man, whosoever thou art that judgest: for wherein thou judgest another, thou condemnest thyself; for thou that judgest doest the same things" (Romans 2:1). How true it is that those who are unkind and critical of others are guilty of doing "the same things." Their lives are marked by the same inconsistencies.

Several years ago the Bridgeport, Connecticut, *Post* reported that sixty-three residents of the Roland Road area in Fairfield presented a petition to the police department demanding that reckless speeding in that area be curbed. A drive was launched by the police, and a few nights later, five drivers were arrested for reckless speeding and passing stop signs. But how astonishing it was to find that the names of all five drivers had appeared on the petition. They saw the evil of reckless speeding in others, but failed to discern it in themselves. How like so many of us today, ready to condemn and judge others. Oh, that the Lord might show us our own shortcomings as He sees them; "for the Lord seeth not as man seeth; for man looketh on the outward appearance, but the Lord looketh on the heart" (1 Samuel 16:7). A daily self-examination of one's heart is an excellent safeguard against a critical spirit. Seeing ourselves as God sees us will soon convince us of our own unworthiness and guilt and enable us to see the impropriety of a critical spirit.

During the first worship service, a newly installed pastor

invited all who wished to use their talents under his leadership
to come forward and talk with him at the close of the service.
Many came. Some could play the piano, others volunteered to
sing in the choir, some desired to teach. The outlook for the
future seemed most encouraging. One man, however, said he
could not do any of the things the others suggested but that
God had given him a special talent, the talent of criticism. He
had the ability of picking out other people's weaknesses and
mistakes and telling them how to improve. The pastor shook
his head woefully and said, "I'll tell you what you had better
do with your talent. Go and do as the man did in the Bible—
bury it! We don't need it around here."

Regrettably, in every assembly of believers, there are those
who feel they are the proud possessors of this useless and injurious talent. May God deliver us from this vicious sin, this
disease that has maimed and crippled the ability of many Christians to exalt Christ effectively.

Frequently, while doing his best in trying to please "the
froward," the Christian will be misunderstood, becoming the
target for sarcasm and false allegations. What should a believer
do under such circumstances? Should he pout and pity himself?
Should he get another job? Should he retaliate with further
unkindnesses? None of these will suffice. There is only one
answer. *Endure patiently.* This is God's answer. "For this is
thankworthy, if a man for conscience toward God endure grief,
suffering wrongfully [innocently]." If you would please the
Lord, this must be your only course of action. Peter further
says, "For what glory is it, if, when ye be buffeted for your
faults, ye shall take it patiently? but if, when ye do well, and
suffer for it, ye take it patiently, this is acceptable with God."
There is no merit in patience under the fire of criticism when
we are at fault. But if in our hearts we know we are right with
the Lord and doing His will, we should not be disturbed by
thoughtless critics. So long as you please Him, you have nothing to fear. He will undertake for you. "Shall not God avenge
His own elect?" (Luke 18:7) Never strike back. Turn the other
cheek. Jesus said, "Love your enemies, bless them that curse

you, do good to them that hate you, and pray for them which despitefully use you, and persecute you" (Matthew 5:44). Possibly others are unjust and unreasonable. Maybe you have been misunderstood. Doubtless unkind things are being said about you. "Let patience have her perfect work" (James 1:4).

Do not overlook the fact that our Lord was misunderstood, too. They called Him "a winebibber," "a deceiver," and sought to link His sanctified efforts with "the prince of devils." If the Lord Jesus was criticized, we who follow Him must expect the same. The only ones in the world who are not criticized are those who do nothing, say nothing, and, as a result, are nothing. Those who bear a consistent and faithful testimony to Jesus Christ can expect to be criticized. If one has a vision and a concern for the souls of men and surrenders himself to the Lord to reach the lost for Christ, you may be sure the Pharisees will soon appear to criticize and condemn.

In almost every case, criticism results from lack of knowledge and an incomplete understanding of the facts. Once, while in France, the famous General Smedley Butler met two soldiers carrying a large soup kettle from the kitchen.

"Here," he ordered, "let me taste that."

"But, General . . ." they demurred.

"Don't give me any 'buts,' " roared the General. "Get me a spoon!"

"Yes, sir!" replied the soldier and ran quickly for the spoon. The general took a mouthful and spat it out promptly.

"You don't call that stuff soup, do you?" he sputtered.

"No, sir," answered the soldier, "That's what I was trying to tell you. It's dishwater!" We smile, but are we not all guilty? How much less critical we should be were we to examine the motive and purposes behind the actions of others.

Just as important as refraining from criticism is a right attitude when criticized. Unwittingly, Christians fall into the error of returning evil for evil instead of enduring false accusations with patience. They become angry and breed hate and ill will in their unsurrendered hearts. It was John Graham who said,

"If you are in the right, you can afford to keep your temper; but if you are in the wrong, you cannot afford to lose it." God says, "Let every man be swift to hear, slow to speak, slow to wrath: For the wrath of man worketh not the righteousness of God" (James 1:19-20). Much is said about being temperamental. Usually, it's ninety-five per cent temper and five per cent mental. An angry man is not a normal man: his mouth is open, but his eyes are shut! He no longer sees as God would have him see.

Oh, how all of us need to learn the lesson of patiently enduring criticism, not retaliating, not fighting back, not becoming angry, even as God says, "Cease from anger, and forsake wrath: fret not thyself in any wise to do evil" (Psalm 37:8). "Be not hasty in thy spirit to be angry: for anger resteth in the bosom of fools" (Ecclesiastes 7:9).

Peter places the keystone on the arch of this important subject by pointing us to our supreme example. "Even hereunto were ye called," he says, "because Christ also suffered for us, leaving us an example that ye should follow in His steps." How did Christ react under bitter criticism? He "did no sin, neither was guile found in His mouth: Who, when He was reviled, reviled not again; when He suffered, He threatened not; but committed Himself to Him that judgeth righteously." Christians are expected to be like Christ.

"But," you say, "we are still human." Never forget, if you are a Christian, you are a child of God and have all power in Christ.

A man said to a Bible teacher, "I have such a bad temper, but I excuse myself because I got it from my father. He had a bad temper and I am just like him." The teacher asked, "Have you been born again?"

"Yes, certainly."

"Were you born of God?"

"Yes."

"Is God your Father?"

"Yes."

"What kind of temper did you get when you were born again?"

We still possess traits of the old nature, but we are also "partakers of the divine nature" if we have received Christ as Lord (2 Peter 1:4). Because of this fact, it is possible to control the tongue. Peter says of our Lord, "Neither was guile found in His mouth." What an inspiration for every believer to be without guile in speech. "The tongue is a little member, and boasteth great things. Behold, how great a matter a little fire kindleth!" (James 3:5) Someone has wisely observed, "The thing most frequently opened by mistake is the human mouth." If the child of God retaliates with a sharp and caustic reply, when confronted by allegations, he is often remorseful for days afterward. But it is too late, the words can never be recalled. The injury is done, even though forgiveness may be granted by the Lord and the injured person. For this reason we should speak in a way that will please and honor Christ. May God deliver us from being critical, harsh, and unkind. Let us pray daily the words of the Psalmist, "Set a watch, O Lord, before my mouth; keep the door of my lips" (Psalm 141:3).

Consider the attitude of our Lord as He faced the sufferings of the Cross. He was falsely accused and beaten until the flesh hung from His back in strips. A crown of thorns was pressed upon His head, and His hands and feet were pierced with nails. He hung on the cross, tortured by excruciating pain, until He cried out, "It is finished." Yet no complaint was heard from His lips. Not the slightest hatred was shown. Rather, He prayed, "Father, forgive them; for they know not what they do" (Luke 23:34).

Hear Peter's pronouncement again, "Even hereunto were ye called." Ours is a serious obligation. God grant that we may hold high the standard and exemplify Christ's spirit of forgiveness and love.

Have you been critical, harsh, or unkind? Are you easily provoked to barbed speech that wounds and destroys like a poisoned arrow? Let God do a work in your heart at this moment. We cannot overcome these evils, but He can. Trust Him. He will give you victory. David knew the secret: "In my distress I cried unto the Lord, and He heard me" (Psalm 120:1). If you confess your guilt to God, He will give you victory and strengthen you against future temptations.

18

REDEMPTION

"Who His own self bare our sins in His own body on the tree, that we, being dead to sins, should live unto righteousness: by whose stripes ye were healed. For ye were as sheep going astray; but are now returned unto the Shepherd and Bishop of your souls."—1 Peter 2:24-25

While upholding the Lord Jesus as the believer's supreme example in faith and practice, Peter, impassioned by God's love, directs our attention to a subject dear to his heart, redemption. In these two brief verses, this cardinal doctrine of Christian truth seems to be presented clearly and concisely in three aspects: its price, its purpose, and its provision.

The eternal price for our redemption has been paid through the sacrifice of Christ on the cross. No other payment could possibly appease the wrath of a holy and righteous God. "Who His own self bare our sins in His own body on the tree." Oh, what love, what mercy, that God should send His beloved Son to die for sinful rebels. This is the greatest manifestation of compassion ever known. "Herein is love, not that we loved God, but that He loved us, and sent His Son to be the propitiation for our sins" (1 John 4:10). Foreseeing our sinfulness and utter unworthiness, Christ, because of His unfathomable love, willingly forsook the splendor and magnificence of Heaven and deigned to come to earth's shame to die the ignominious death of the Cross. What profound humiliation, that Christ "made Himself of no reputation, and took upon Him the form of a servant, and was made in the likeness of men: And being found in fashion as a man, He humbled Himself, and became obedient unto death, even the death of the cross" (Philippians 2:7-8).

Occasionally we are asked to prove the deity of Jesus. How do we know Jesus is divine as well as human? Alexander Maclaren once gave a conclusive answer to this question: "What Christ does, is the best answer to the question as to what He is." The fact that the Lord Jesus was willing to die, the righteous for the unrighteous, the holy for the unholy, the innocent for the guilty, is proof enough for me that He is the Son of God. "For when we were yet without strength, in due time Christ died for the ungodly. For scarcely for a righteous man will one die: yet peradventure for a good man some would even dare to die. But God commendeth His love toward us, in that, while we were yet sinners, Christ died for us" (Romans 5:6-8). Such love is incredible to the human mind, but not to the mind of God. In creation God revealed His might and skill, but in redemption He opens His heart to us and His eternal love pours forth in the price He paid for our redemption.

Lady Kinnaird used to tell a touching incident about the Prince of Wales. The prince was invited to visit thirty-six men severely wounded in World War I, who were in a hospital on the outskirts of London. He graciously accepted the invitation, and upon arrival was shown through the main ward. He shook hands with some, spoke encouraging words to many, and sympathized with all. Then looking around he said, "I thought there were thirty-six; but I have seen only thirty." It was explained that six of the very worst cases were in a special ward not usually visited.

"I must see them," said the prince. He was guided to the bruised and maimed physical wrecks.

"But there are only five," the prince exclaimed. "Where is

the other man?" He was told that that poor man was so badly mutilated that he was kept in a room alone and that it would be wiser not to see him.

"I must see him, too," the prince insisted. Taken into a little room, the Prince of Wales saw an unforgettable sight. There lay what remained of a brave soldier. He was blind, deaf, legless, armless, and disfigured almost beyond recognition as a man. Standing silent for a moment, immeasurably touched, the prince stooped down, kissed the veteran's scarred brow and with a break in his voice exclaimed, "Wounded for me!"

This pitiable victim of the horrors of war died for his country in the cause of freedom. Christ died for the entire world for the purpose of redemption. If you have received Him as your Lord, you too can exclaim, "Wounded for me!" The entire price for sin has been paid once and for all. "Neither by the blood of goats and calves, but by His own blood He entered in once into the holy place, having obtained eternal redemption for us" (Hebrews 9:12).

Knowing the rebellious nature of sinful man, we are inclined to wonder why God should even consider paying such a price for our redemption. What was the purpose behind it? Why did Christ die? Peter proffers an answer. "That we, being dead to sins, should live unto righteousness." The righteousness Peter speaks about is more than forbearance from doing evil. It presents a broader obligation of serving God in divine acts of well-doing which emanate from the Christ-nature within. The believer was identified with the Saviour in His crucifixion, burial, and Resurrection. Having been raised with Christ, the child of God is enabled through the Holy Spirit to walk in newness of life, seeking to honor the Lord not only by a holy life, but also in good deeds. The shackles of sin's power having been destroyed by believing on the Lord Jesus, the child of God is energized for a life of usefulness. But, being the possessor of both the old sinful nature and the new Christ-nature, there must be the constant, daily choice to follow Christ and to do His will. "As ye have therefore received Christ Jesus the Lord, so walk ye in Him" (Colossians 2:6).

We are to live no longer for self, but for Christ. We are to put away the old habits and lusts of the flesh in order to carry out God's will in doing all that is good. "Knowing this, that our old man is crucified with Him, that the body of sin might be destroyed, that henceforth we should not serve sin" (Romans 6:6). When we consider what the Lord Jesus endured for us, it should be a joy, never a burden, to forsake all compromise with sin to follow Him wholly. We sing, "Jesus paid it all, all to Him I owe." Have you noticed the two "alls"? The last is often overlooked: "*all* to Him I owe." He paid the entire price for our sins. Consequently we owe Him ourselves, complete, with no reservations for self, and a readiness to serve Him whatever the cost.

One muggy summer day in the early 1700's a young German count strolled leisurely into the Düsseldorf Art Gallery. Studying the paintings one by one, none seemed to impress him as much as Stenberg's portrayal of the Crucifixion of Christ. In deep admiration he stood before this magnificent work, gazing with reverence at every detail. Then his eye moved to the inscription below the painting. He read it over again and again: "This have I done for thee; what hast thou done for Me?" When he left the art gallery he carried with him a new purpose in life. The count went out with such an impelling zeal to serve the Lord Jesus Christ, that soon all of Europe was to feel its impact. The inspired nobleman was Nikolaus Ludwig, Count von Zinzendorf and justice of Dresden, who became the distinguished leader of the Moravian Church. He saw Europe begin to burn for God in one of the greatest revivals of all time as the Moravians organized into one of the most sweeping world-wide missionary efforts since the days of the disciples. Their influence spread swiftly. Even John and Charles Wesley attributed their assurance of salvation in Christ to the help received from a Moravian missionary. Zinzendorf met many obstacles, but he stood firm for his convictions. Though perpetually sniped at from every angle by friends and foes alike, he at one time shouted, "I have one passion! It is Christ and Christ alone!" His entire life personified that motto.

How do you explain Zinzendorf's life of abundant fruitfulness for God? There is but one answer: he saw in the painting of the Crucifixion that Christ's death had a purpose—not only that we turn from sin, but also that we pour every energy and effort into service for the Lord. When one experiences the true meaning of Calvary, as did Zinzendorf, he will no longer live for self, but for Christ. "He died for all, that they which live should not henceforth live unto themselves, but unto Him which died for them, and rose again" (2 Corinthians 5:15). If you have been to Calvary, you will be actuated by an impassioned concern to do everything within human power to impart the good news of redemption to the entire world. After the Cross the Lord Jesus declared to those who had experienced His righteousness, "All power is given unto Me in heaven and in earth. *Go ye therefore, and teach all nations*" (Matthew 28.18-19).

A colporteur in northern India entered a small town and gathered a group of natives around him to tell the story of Christ's birth as revealed in the Scriptures. After the reading was finished, one asked, "How long has it been since God's Son was born into the world?"

"About two thousand years," the missionary replied.

"Then," asked the villager, "who has been hiding this Book all this time?"

Too many professing Christians are not living "unto righteousness." They are still being rocked in the cradle of their faith's infancy, content with personal salvation, cooing foolishly to the sweet lullabies of spiritual babyhood. Meanwhile, the world reels and staggers drunkenly on toward a Christless eternity. The world needs Christ. There should be nothing of greater importance to the believer than an exhaustive effort to send the message of life to those who need salvation yet have never heard it.

Let us give attention to the provision of redemption. As the result of the sacrificial work of Christ at Calvary, God has provided salvation, restoration, and preservation. When one believes on Christ, he is the immediate possessor of salvation.

The Lord Jesus provided healing for every sin-sick soul who received Him. "By whose stripes ye were healed." The stripes mentioned here refer not only to the scourging our Lord endured before His crucifixion, but to the suffering of the Cross in its entirety—the trial, the ridicule, the anguish—all culminating in His broken heart.

Many years before our Saviour's Advent, the Prophet Isaiah foretold the sufferings of the Lord Jesus and the healing He would provide for the souls of all who believe. "Surely He hath borne our griefs, and carried our sorrows: yet we did esteem Him stricken, smitten of God, and afflicted. But He was wounded for our transgressions, He was bruised for our iniquities: the chastisement of our peace was upon Him; and with His stripes we are healed" (Isaiah 53:4-5). The price was paid in full for all sin. There is nothing one can do to obtain salvation other than receive it. Christ did it all.

This is exceedingly hard for the natural mind to accept. Some even question the thought that one should suffer for another. Yet actually, most of us have lived under such a principle. Could one's mother ever be repaid for all she has done? Not only do our mothers suffer for us to be born, but their lives have been made up of daily and continual sacrifice. Would it be possible for you fully to compensate your mother for her love, patience, and understanding? No, none of us could do it. You see, we do receive things by grace. All of us accept some things we can neither earn nor pay for. It is humanly true that one can suffer for another. So with Christ, we can be healed spiritually only through His stripes. He suffered, bled, and died. This is God's provision of salvation for us.

Peter also says, "Ye were as sheep going astray; but are now returned unto the Shepherd." Here is our restoration. Sinful by nature, we had wandered far from God. We were without love or concern for Him. But in His grace He sought us out, and by means of His great love, drew us unto Himself, redeemed us, and placed us in the family of God as His children. He "came not to call the righteous, but sinners to repentance"

(Luke 5:32). As sinful children of Adam, we were destined to eternal death, but through Christ's transforming grace, we were made new creatures in Christ. "For as in Adam all die, even so in Christ shall all be made alive" (1 Corinthians 15:22). "You hath He quickened, who were dead in trespasses and sins" (Ephesians 2:1).

But there is more. Not only are we who believe in Christ saved and restored to fellowship with God, but, through His redeeming grace, He has provided for our preservation. He is "the Shepherd and Bishop of your souls." As the Shepherd, He tenderly cares for His sheep, feeding and nurturing them throughout life. "Bishop" means *protector* or *guardian*. As the "Bishop" of our souls He protects us from the onslaughts of the enemy and keeps and guides us step by step in His will. It is a marvelous comfort to know that Christ died nearly two thousand years ago to deliver us from our sins. But it is equally blessed to realize that our Saviour "ever liveth to make intercession for" us (Hebrews 7:25). Not only has the original sin, in which we all share by inheritance, been blotted out, but every present need is met by our living High Priest who pleads our case at the Father's right hand. He gently guides and directs our steps day by day so that we may say with the Psalmist, "Surely goodness and mercy shall follow me all the days of my life: and I will dwell in the house of the Lord for ever" (Psalm 23:6).

The true believer may rest in the protection of the Lord's love and care, knowing He will never fail His own. He is forever the same. He never changes. The most enduring things within our knowledge are subject to the law of change and decay. Sun, moon, stars, mountains, rocks, and trees—all are bound by this law, as is man himself. With the passing years, man becomes aware that he is not the same as he once was. He can no longer do with ease the things he once did without effort. His muscles lag and he puffs and pants to climb the hill he once climbed with youthful zest. In the span of a lifetime, also, we witness momentous changes politically, socially, economically, morally, and spiritually in the life of a nation. Circumstances have been altered radically for young and old alike in these tragic times in which we live. The young often find themselves in strange surroundings, faced with unusual trials and temptations; the old must frequently face insecurity, loneliness, and lack of respect. Yet under all conditions, the child of God may rest in the tender care of the Shepherd and Bishop of his soul. Though surrounded by change, he finds comfort, hope, and strength in the certainty of a God-planned future, for our Lord is always the same. "Jesus Christ the same yesterday, and to day, and for ever" (Hebrews 13:8). For this reason, the true follower of Christ need not fear. God's provision is all-sufficient. Believe Him, trust Him, rest in Him, and experience the gracious promises that are yours through Jesus Christ our Lord.

19

HOW TO GET A NEW HUSBAND

"Likewise, ye wives, be in subjection to your own husbands; that, if any obey not the word, they also may without the word be won by the conversation of the wives; While they behold your chaste conversation coupled with fear. Whose adorning let it not be that outward adorning of plaiting the hair, and of wearing of gold, or of putting on of apparel; But let it be the hidden man of the heart, in that which is not corruptible, even the ornament of a meek and quiet spirit, which is in the sight of God of great price."—1 Peter 3:1-4

Having considered the Christian's responsibilities to the state and also to his employer, Peter portrays next the believer's obligations in the home. His first concern is for married women who had been converted recently and, in consequence, were greatly disturbed as to what they should do about their unbelieving husbands, some of whom were extremely bitter and cruel as a result of their mates' newly-found faith.

What should a Christian wife do if her husband is unsympathetic toward the gospel? Should she leave him? Would it not be better for her to seek more congenial surroundings where the atmosphere might be more conducive to growth in grace? The scriptural answer is an emphatic *no!* Let the believing wife stay where she is and so convincingly live the gospel that her unbelieving mate will ultimately cry out,

"What must I do to be saved?" Though the husband may be an infidel of the worst sort, profane and inconsiderate, filled with bitter hatred toward Christ, the believer is exhorted to stay with him. "The woman which hath an husband that believeth not, and if he be pleased to dwell with her, let her not leave him" (1 Corinthians 7:13). Under the circumstances separation is forbidden.

Have you ever realized that it is possible for a believing wife to get a new husband? Not a different one, nor the old one made over, but the same one transformed by the miraculous saving power of Christ. If the Christian is willing to meet the conditions God presents in the Scriptures, God promises that the unsaved husband will come to Christ. It may not be until he lies in agony on his deathbed; or even after the wife has departed to be Christ. But God promises that he will come. "Believe on the Lord Jesus Christ, and *thou* shalt be saved, *and thy house*" (Acts 16:31). If the believer accepts this truth and faithfully obeys the Word of the Lord, in the providence of God the entire household will come to Christ for salvation.

If the believing wife is to be effective for the Lord Jesus, it is of prime importance that she "be in subjection" to her "own husband." This means she should adapt herself, as far as conscience permits, to her husband's desires and demands. This principle of submission had its inception in the Garden of Eden and is still in force. God said to Eve, "I will greatly multiply thy sorrow and thy conception; in sorrow thou shalt bring forth children; and thy desire shall be to thy husband, and *he shall rule over thee*" (Genesis 3:16). Our divorce courts would be less crowded and marriages would be much happier if wives would obey this God-ordained truth.

Paul, in writing to the Ephesians, said, "Wives, *submit* yourselves unto your own husbands, as unto the Lord" (Ephesians 5:22). Thousands of homes have been nothing more than centers of marital confusion and disorder because wives have assumed unwarranted authority instead of submitting patiently to the husband, whose duty it is under God to oversee the affairs of the family. It could truly be said of some women,

"Give them an inch, they take a foot and think they are rulers."

Peter states that this submission is to be "to your *own* husbands." It is not uncommon to see Christian women showing more respect and courtesy to others of the opposite sex than to their "own husbands." They are genial and gracious outside the home, but how different inside! The practice of such inconsistency will not only restrain the unsaved from believing, but will, without fail, render them even more adamant.

In addition to sincere love and respect for one's own husband, there must be holiness of life that will convince and convict. Unbelieving husbands are usually won to Christ, not by *telling* but by *showing*. It is not preaching and nagging that will draw them to Christ, but praying and living. Peter says, "If any obey not the word, they also may without the word be won by the conversation of the wives." The husbands of whom he speaks are those who are instantly incensed at the slightest suggestion of spiritual truth. Very often such husbands are extremely argumentative and anything said about Christ or salvation seems to result in further disharmony in the home.

How should the Christian wife face this problem? Should she completely ignore her husband's resistance and continue to talk about Christian truth? Though annoying to her husband, should she place gospel tracts and Christian literature around the home with the hope and prayer that he will read them? Should she heckle him for not going to church? Peter tells us this is the wrong approach altogether. Stop talking! Do not preach! Say nothing about spiritual things. Remember you are to "be in subjection" to your own husband. By constant preaching you will harden his heart. You cannot expect to win him.

Peter says your best approach is "without the word." This does not refer to the Word of God or the message of the gospel. The definite article "the" is not in the Greek. Literally, it is "without a word." If you know the gospel irritates your unsaved husband, keep quiet about it. You will never draw him to Christ by persistent urging. Someone has said, "A wife who has good horse sense never becomes a nag." How many women are driving their husbands away from the Lord Jesus because of their unscriptural handling of the problem. Solomon gave wise advise when he said, "It is better to dwell in a corner of the housetop, than with a brawling woman in a wide house" (Proverbs 21:9). It is far better to live alone in a little corner room of an attic, than to live in a mansion with a quarrelsome woman.

A man was haled before a judge for deserting his wife and received a thorough-going reprimand. The man endured patiently and then bolstered up enough courage to reply.

"Judge, if you knew that woman like I do, you wouldn't call me a deserter. I'm a refugee!"

If a husband will not listen to the gospel, how then can a wife reach him for Christ? Peter declares "by the conversation of the wives." The word "conversation" as used here does not mean *to converse* but refers to one's behavior or manner of life. When a husband resists the truth, the believing wife should not try to reach him with the preaching lip but by a practicing life.

Peter further suggests that the life of holiness exemplifying Christ should be "coupled with fear," that is, with *respect* or *honor*. One can offer no better argument for Christianity than that which can be seen in a Christian wife glorifying the Lord in a life of holiness and loving respect for her own husband. An unsaved husband cannot long resist the persuasion of Christianity when seen in the chaste manner of life and the respectful demeanor of his wife.

A wealthy society woman was invited to church one night in one of our large cities where she responded to an invitation to receive Jesus Christ into her heart. Later the pastor who led her to the Saviour visited in her home, and found that not only was her husband not a Christian, but he was a very bitter infidel. He was full of contempt for his wife's conversion, and disgustedly expressed the opinion that she would soon get over it. Six months passed and one evening the man called on the minister.

"I have read all the leading books on the evidences of

Christianity," he said, "and I can stand out against their arguments. But for the last six months I have had an open book before me, in the person of my wife, that I am not able to answer. I have come to the conclusion that I am wrong and that there must be something holy and divine about a religion that would change that woman into the loving, prayerful, singing saint she is now."

To be sure, the Lord is able to work through the life of a consecrated godly woman, if she will let Him. Of course, the Scriptures proffer no hope for believing women who knowingly have married unsaved men. The Bible clearly forbids Christians to enter relationships unequally yoking them to unbelievers. Those who willfully disobey this holy command find the penalty to be most costly. But if a wife has come to Christ since marriage, on the authority of the Word of God she has every reason to cherish hope for the salvation of her unbelieving mate.

To every Christian wife who is brokenhearted, disappointed, despairing, and sorrowful because her husband refuses to come to Christ, I offer God's promise, "Let us not be weary in well doing: for in due season we shall reap, if we faint not" (Galatians 6:9). We worship a mighty God of whom Jeremiah declared, "Ah Lord God! behold, Thou hast made the heaven and the earth by Thy great power and stretched out arm, and there is *nothing* too hard for Thee" (Jeremiah 32:17). Do not worry! Trust *Him* for the future! Let the light of the glory of Christ shine through you. Spend much time in prayer. You may rest assured the Lord will hear. Some day your unsaved husband will fall humbly at the feet of the Saviour, crying out in joyous repentance, "My Lord, and my God."

Lest we overlook the importance of holiness as the virtue God uses to attract the lost unto Himself, Peter further emphasizes the fact by a most timely comparison. "Whose adorning let it not be that outward adorning of plaiting the hair, and of wearing of gold, or of putting on of apparel." The apostle is not prohibiting the proper care of one's hair, the use of jewelry or becoming dress. He is merely making a comparison, accentuating the fact that real and lasting beauty is not achieved through the outward adorning. Outward adornment is of little importance compared to the inner adorning of the spiritual life.

The apostle is not particularly interested in *what* the adorning of the Christian should be, but *where* it should be. He says, "Let it be the hidden man of the heart, in that which is not corruptible." God is concerned about the heart. "For the Lord seeth not as man seeth; for man looketh on the outward appearance, but the Lord looketh on the heart" (1 Samuel 16:7). As He looks at some of us, He sees the outward body richly garbed, but the inner life clothed in "filthy rags." He sees others whose outward garments are worn and threadbare, but within they are all glorious. God is concerned about holiness. The greatest power in the universe next to divine power is that of a holy life. Holiness speaks in a language all its own which no argument can withstand.

What Peter has to say about the outward appearance should not be misconstrued. Doubtless he is not against proper grooming and dressing in a pleasing, Christ-glorifying manner. The Christian woman should, however, guard against flashy, revealing dress and the lavish display of finery intended only to attract attention to self. The modernism of a Christian woman's appearance often nullifies the fundamentalism of her gospel message. Decorating oneself like a Christmas tree will have little effect in reaching the lost for Christ.

On the other hand, there is danger in being careless or dowdy in one's appearance. This can be equally harmful to the cause of Christ. Vance Havner expressed it well when he said, "To be all out for God, you do not have to look all in." We may best be guided in habits of dress, as well as in all our habits, by 1 Corinthians 10:31: "Whether therefore ye eat, or drink, or *whatsoever ye do,* do all to the glory of God."

What is the adornment God especially desires for the Christian wife? "A meek and quiet spirit, which is in the sight of God of great price." J. B. Phillips translates this, "the unfading loveliness of a calm and gentle spirit." The woman who exemplifies these virtues will be the kind most effective in attracting her unsaved husband to the Lord Jesus Christ. This "calm and gentle spirit" will be obvious not only in her speech and personality, but in the way she performs the routine duties of the home which may seem boring and burdensome. Regardless of her sincerity and faithfulness in Bible reading, prayer, church attendance, and even in soul winning, unless she cheerfully cares for her family and home, it is likely her husband will see little value in Christ and Christianity. Paul stressed the importance of this truth when he wrote to Titus about Christian wives. They are "to be sober [sober-minded], to love their husbands, to love their children. To be discreet, chaste, keepers at home, good, obedient to their own husbands, *that the word of God be not blasphemed*" (Titus 2:4-5). If unsaved husbands are to refrain from blaspheming the Word of God, they must *see* Christ in their Christian mate and in all she does.

A Christian woman tells of praying for some special assignment of Christian work. She prayed and prayed, but did not seem to receive any light. Her zeal for the Lord was earnest, but she desired to do only certain forms of Christian service. No direct leading came in answer to her prayers. One day the Lord spoke to her heart in prayer and revealed her failure to care properly for her own husband and to seek to win him for Christ. She rose from her knees, concluding, "I don't know what God wants me to do, but I do know what John wants me to do." She had made the mistake of praying for Christian work while neglecting the opportunity at hand to point her husband to Christ through performance of everyday tasks. At once she changed her entire way of thinking and living so as to devote more time to John, praying that she might be more obedient and respectful as a Christian wife. She had found the mind of God in caring for her husband's needs. Certainly every Christian wife should find some kind of Christian work outside the home, but if you have an unsaved husband, your foremost duty is to do all you can, through the power of God, to win him to Christ.

Yes, you can get a *new* husband, one born anew by the Spirit of God, if you are willing to pay the price. Get serious about it. Spend hours in prayer each day. Meet the conditions outlined in the Word of God. Remember, you are God's messenger to your husband—a messenger, not in the sense of a preacher, but a messenger of thoughtfulness and kindness, whom the Holy Spirit will use to draw your unsaved mate to Christ.

In conclusion, let me ask, how is it with your heart? You profess to be a Christian wife. Is your life what it should be? Are you really "an example of the believers, in word, in conversation [behaviour], in charity, in spirit, in faith, in purity" (1 Timothy 4:12)? Perhaps your inconsistencies have contributed to the hardness of your husband's heart. Has he seen the glory of Christ in you?

A good wife makes a good husband. If a wife is exemplifying the Saviour, it will not be long before the husband will yield to the dynamics of such a positive Christian testimony. Are there certain sins in your life that ought to be put under the blood of Christ? Must Jesus say to you, "Why call ye Me Lord, Lord, and do not the things which I say?" (Luke 6:46) Can it be that your life is not fully yielded to Him? The first and the greatest need in your home is that you completely turn everythingover to the Saviour. If there have been failures, make them right with God. Surrender your very self to the Lord.

20

A GOOD HUSBAND

"For after this manner in the old time the holy women also, who trusted in God, adorned themselves, being in subjection unto their own husbands: Even as Sara obeyed Abraham, calling him lord: whose daughters ye are, as long as ye do well, and are not afraid with any amazement. Likewise, ye husbands, dwell with them according to knowledge, giving honour unto the wife, as unto the weaker vessel, and as being heirs together of the grace of life; that your prayers be not hindered."—1 Peter 3:5-7

In these verses the apostle continues to emphasize the importance of inner holiness for Christian wives as contrasted to costly and lavish outward adornment. A holy character is of far greater value than a showy appearance. "For after this manner in the old time the holy women also, who trusted in God, adorned themselves." Peter also reiterates the need of wives "being in subjection unto their own husbands." For illustration he reminds us of Sarah who "obeyed Abraham, calling him lord." Of course, having a good husband like Abraham, who obeyed God implicitly, made it pleasurable to render wholehearted deference to him, calling him "lord," or *master*.

Since the wife is to submit to the husband, it is reasonable to expect that, if the husband is to make a success of his important role, he must yield himself completely to the lordship of Christ. If there is to be any degree of happiness in the home, husbands as well as wives must know Christ experientially as their living Lord. Success in marriage is much more than finding the right person. It is being the right person. Until one enters into a personal relationship with the Son of God, he cannot be the right person, let alone a good husband. Though many men would agree with this fact, they do not practice it. They carelessly live for themselves, neglecting the Saviour who died for them.

God has ordained that the husband be the spiritual leader in the home. How many men shirk this responsibility, letting their wives be their spiritual representative, thus thoughtlessly trying to worship God by proxy. Prayer with the children, reading Bible stories to them, taking them to Sunday school and church, in fact, the entire spiritual oversight is left to the mother. If family worship is to be observed, she must arrange it. What a mistake men make in neglecting these essentials. How different it was in Abraham's life. God said of him, "For I know him, that he will command his children and his household after him, and they shall keep the way of the Lord, to do justice and judgment"(Genesis 18:19).

God has told *all* parents, not only mothers, to teach the Scriptures to their children and lead them in the way of the Lord. "And these words, which I command thee this day, shall be in thine heart: And thou shalt teach them diligently unto thy children, and shalt talk of them when thou sittest in thine house, and when thou walkest by the way, and when thou liest down, and when thou risest up" (Deuteronomy 6:6-7). Fathers are specifically entreated in Isaiah 38:19 to present spiritual truth to their children: "the father to the children shall make known Thy truth."

Walking with God is not only a woman's obligation. If a man wants the best in life, there is nothing that should demand greater precedence than a personal relationship with Jesus Christ. "For what shall it profit a man, if he shall gain the whole world, and lose his own soul? Or what shall a man give in exchange for his soul?" (Mark 8:36-37) J. Pierpont

Morgan, the well-known American financier, made his will the year before he died. It consisted of about ten thousand words and contained thirty-seven articles. There is no question as to what Mr. Morgan considered the most important clause in the will, as well as the matter of chief importance in his whole life. He had made many important business deals, some involving such vast sums of money as to disturb the financial equilibrium of the entire world.

Yet there was one transaction that evidently stood out in Mr. Morgan's mind above all others. This he revealed in the first article of his will: "I commit my soul into the hands of my Saviour, in full confidence that having redeemed it and washed it in His most precious blood He will present it faultless before the throne of my heavenly Father; and I entreat my children to maintain and defend, at all hazard, and at any cost of personal sacrifice, the blessed doctrine of the complete atonement for sin through the blood of Jesus Christ, once offered, and through that alone." Oh, that men everywhere might make such a declaration acknowledging Christ as the Lord of their lives.

Can we not agree that the desperate need of the hour is a return to the old-fashioned home, where God is honored and respected by His people who daily kneel in His divine presence for guidance and blessing? Our failure to let the Lord Jesus run our homes is gradually bringing us to the verge of ruin. Indeed, we are on the way out unless our homes come back to Him. It is almost inconceivable that in America there is now one divorce in every four marriages and that twenty billion dollars a year are spent on crime. Bewilderment, frustration, disillusionment, and disappointments sweep the world. Materialism has captured the imagination of the populace and left it bereft of hope. Our only hope is Christ in the home.

In some parts of New Guinea it is believed that when a huge weird mask, representing a distorted human face, is hung from the outside gable of the house, no harm will come to the household or to those who come to call. Of course this is a vain and ridiculous superstition. But there is a real way to secure peace and blessing and to bring security to the home. It is not accomplished by charms, nor is it known to only a few. God "hath in these last days spoken unto us by His Son" (Hebrews 1:2). Do not miss the truth. "*God hath spoken!*" He has not left us to suffer broken hearts and broken homes. He has provided the way to something far better—happiness. Do you want God's blessing for yourself and your family? Then come to Christ. It can be realized only in Him. Invite the Lord Jesus into your life and then into your home. For when He becomes the home's welcome Guest, the home will be blest.

If you know Christ personally you will be well on your way to a happy home. But there is more to be considered. The *presence* of Christ must be realized in the home. It is to this end that Peter proffers divine instruction for Christians who would be good husbands. The apostle says they are to dwell with their wives "according to knowledge." "Knowledge," as used here, has also been translated, *intelligent consideration.* Wrangling and strife, bitter and unkind words could be avoided in many a home if there were more "intelligent consideration" of the mate's problems.

Probably few of us are masters in the art of understanding others, especially those of the opposite sex. But as two people live together, their mutual understanding should deepen with time. Christian couples should be much happier after twenty-five years of marriage than after one year. Through Christ they can overlook the bad and respect the good in each other. With each passing year the light of love should burn brighter than before. The usual selfish instincts of human nature should be supplanted by thoughtfulness and consideration.

It would be safe to say that no one fully understands his mate, though some think they do. The story is told of a couple that appeared in a divorce court. The judge said to the woman, "Madam, how long were you acquainted with your husband before you were married?"

"I met my husband about eighteen months before I was married," she replied, "but never got acquainted with him until the first time I asked him for money." We smile, but how many of us are guilty. How little "intelligent consideration" is displayed in homes about monetary matters. It is the money question that often disrupts the home and leads to the divorce court.

One husband said to another, "I can't stand that wife of mine any longer. She's always asking me for money. All she thinks about is money, money, money! It gets me down."

"What does she do with it?" asked the sympathetic friend.

"I surely don't know," he said. "I never give her any."

It is only natural that financial difficulties will arise in the home, but the Christian husband and wife ought to face their problems with "intelligent consideration," committing their burden to the Lord. No problem has ever been solved by bitterness of heart and unkind words. Has not the Lord promised to supply every need for those who love Him? "But my God shall supply all your need according to His riches in glory by Christ Jesus" (Philippians 4:19).

Peter further states that the husband is to give "honour unto the wife, as unto the weaker vessel." Since it is ordained that the husband be the head of the house, he especially should regard the seriousness of this obligation. His leadership in the home should not be that of an overlord or a despot; with thoughtfulness, chivalry, and courtesy he should show respect to the wife God has given him for a helpmeet.

Woman was not created from a bone from man's head to dominate him, nor from his foot to trample on him, but from his side to be a companion and a helpmeet for him. He, on the other hand, as her leader and defender, should protect and watch over her, loving and cherishing her in the same manner in which Christ, the head of the Church, cares for each of His blood-bought children. "Husbands, love your wives, even as Christ also loved the church, and gave Himself for it" (Ephesians 5:25).

There will, of course, be times of misunderstanding. It is impossible to have two minds in perfect agreement on every point. But it must be remembered that all differences can be settled satisfactorily if considered scripturally. God says, "Husbands, love your wives, and be not bitter against them" (Colossians 3:19). "Let the husband render unto the wife due benevolence: and likewise also the wife unto the husband" (1 Corinthians 7:3). With mutual love and consideration there will be a solution for any problem which may arise.

A young Christian wife relates that in the beginning of their married life she and her husband were self-willed and obstinate. The result was frequent arguments and outbursts of temper. A clash occurred one day as they were eating lunch. There were sharp and bitter words on both sides. The husband shoved his chair back from the table and angrily rushed off to work, slamming the door behind him.

Hurrying upstairs to her room for a good cry, the young wife noticed a little card, which until then had had no special meaning for her. It had been sent to her before marriage by a pupil in her Sunday school class. She picked it up. The four words on it pierced her heart like an arrow. "What would Jesus do?" She laid the card down, but she could not dismiss the question. "What would Jesus do?" Her heart told her He would never be bitter, angry, and guilty of uncontrolled temper. She could resist no longer. Like a true child of God, she went to her knees and confessed her wrong-doing to the Lord.

When her husband returned in the evening, she met him at the door with a smile and a kiss, and was gracious and kind while serving a tasty dinner. Later in the evening she showed her husband the card and told the whole story. He, too, readily realized how foolish he had been and how he had failed as a Christian husband to respect his wife as the "weaker vessel." Together they knelt before the Lord, confessed their sin, and promised in His strength never again to permit impatience and childish resentment to rob them of joy and happiness.

What would Jesus do? Jesus would reveal love! Oh, if we would learn this marvelous lesson and act on its truth! Do not let Satan wreck your home by needless argument and discord. Practice the lesson of love—God's love. In offending our mate, we offend Christ. Our treatment of others is expressive of our treatment of the Saviour. "Inasmuch as ye have done it unto one of the least of these My brethren, ye have done it unto Me" (Matthew 25:40).

No Christian who repeatedly disobeys His Lord can know real blessing. God says to husbands, "Live joyfully with the wife whom thou lovest" (Ecclesiastes 9:9). He is concerned that homes be marked with harmony. Should there be an argument, settle it immediately, lovingly, and prayerfully. Never let it carry over until the next day. Obey God's Word. "Let not the sun go down upon your wrath" (Ephesians 4:26). Be of a forgiving spirit and a loving heart. For "if ye do not forgive, neither will your Father which is in heaven forgive your trespasses" (Mark 11:26).

Though the husband is the head of the home, Peter reminds us of the equality which should exist between Christian couples. They are "heirs" together of the grace of life. It is for this reason that only believers should be joined together in marriage. God asks, "Can two walk together, except they be agreed?" (Amos 3:3). It is difficult to find agreement in other things unless there is perfect accord in that which is basic for a successful marriage, unified faith in Christ.

The Bible pleads with every unsaved husband and wife, "Come now, and let us reason together, saith the Lord: though your sins be as scarlet they shall be as white as snow; though they be red like crimson, they shall be as wool" (Isaiah 1:18). Hear God's call! Come to Christ! Let Him transform your life that you may know lasting peace and happiness.

Peter presents a final warning to Christian married couples in this portion of Scripture. He urges them to live peacefully together that their "prayers be not hindered." Domestic strife is a common hindrance to prayer. Doubtless you have had the experience of kneeling to pray after an outburst of anger in the home. Words and phrases that often brought peace and comfort seemed cold and ineffectual. You knew the cause. Did you do as you should? Whatever keeps husband or wife from prayer ought to be dealt with at once. Never let your pride be the victor. Leave the gift at the altar and go and make the reconciliation, even though it may be costly to oneself. Allow nothing to interrupt your fellowship with the Lord Jesus.

Christianity in the home needs constant examination. It is not difficult to live as Christians when we are delivered from the daily commonplace irritations of those who know and love us best. But if our Christianity breaks down in the home, it is "sounding brass, or a tinkling cymbal," an empty, hypocritical, dead pedantry. If in the home we cannot love joyfully and unselfishly, we are not right with God. It was Hudson Taylor who said, "A light which does not shine beautifully around a family table is not fit to rush a long way off to do a great service elsewhere." Christ may be in your heart, but is He in your home? Let us extend to Him a lasting invitation to be our Guest, that our homes may be a foreshadowing of Heaven. "Except the Lord build the house, they labor in vain that build it" (Psalm 127:1).

21

CHRISTIAN KINDNESS

"Finally, be ye all of one mind, having compassion one of another, love as brethren, be pitiful, be courteous: Not rendering evil for evil, or railing for railing: but contrariwise blessing; knowing that ye are thereunto called, that ye should inherit a blessing."—1 Peter 3:8, 9

The apostle has been addressing himself to specific groups among Christians, stressing their obligations as citizens, employees, wives, and husbands. In broadening his appeal he exhorts all believers, setting forth five characteristics imperative for the development of Christian kindness. Peter suggests that the child of God who would exalt Christ in this virtue should be agreeable, loving, sympathetic, courteous, and thoughtful. Let us analyze each of these in their order.

The Christian should be *agreeable*. "Finally, be ye all of one mind." "Finally" is used here in the sense of summing up what has already been said relative to the believer's attitude toward others in the state, in his employment, and in the home. To be of "one mind" does not necessarily mean that all Christians must hold the same opinions. It should be possible for individuals and groups to have a variety of viewpoints or ideas. Yet there should be, undergirding all, a common bond of devotion to Christ and to each other which precludes division and strife. F. B. Meyer well said, "This oneness of mind does not demand the monotony of similarity, but unity in variety."

No believer must ever infringe on another's right to interpret Bible truth according to the teaching of the Holy Spirit in his own life. No one should be denied the liberty God has intended in the understanding of the Scriptures. Regrettably, most arguments about scriptural truth are the result of quibbling over views of facts rather than over facts themselves.

Though God's people may disagree, they should always disagree agreeably. "Behold, how good and how pleasant it is for brethren to dwell together in unity!" (Psalm 133:1) From its inception, the Church of Christ has experienced an increasing need for greater unity in Christ among its adherents. Those who endeavor to bring the saints closer together in Christ will reap the promised blessing, for Jesus declared, "Blessed are the peacemakers: for they shall be called the children of God" (Matthew 5:9).

Wherever I have been, I have met humble saints of God who have faithfully striven for unity among believers. Most of them would not be termed scholars in the eyes of the world, nor great leaders in the thinking of those in the church, but they manifest the love of Christ. They are so consistent, so kindly, that whatever they do, they carry in their very presence a bit of the heavenly sunshine. They are the peacemakers as opposed to the troublemakers. Concerning one of these faithful saints, who went to be with the Lord, a friend said, "Wherever she went, flowers grew in her pathway, and the air was always sweeter when she entered the room."

A similar remark was made at the funeral service of a humble country preacher who during his lifetime had pastored several very small rural churches: "He was not a wonderful speaker, but he knew how to make peace between his neighbors!" What an attribute! Not only had he learned to be agreeable, but he was used of God to lead others into the fruitful life of being of "one mind." "With all lowliness and meekness, with longsuffering, forbearing one another in love;

Endeavoring to keep the unity of the Spirit in the bond of peace" (Ephesians 4:2-3).

It is impossible to be agreeable without being *loving*. For this reason, Peter reminds us to have "compassion one of another, love as brethren." Are we not all one in Christ? Why should there ever be hatred and division among the saints? No church can progress, and no believer can grow in grace without a heart knowledge of God's love.

One tells of his attempt to drive an iron bar through a piece of timber. Though he made the hole the right size, the bar was rusty and did not fit. He hammered harder and harder until the wood began to split. Suddenly he thought of using oil. He oiled the bar and squirted some oil into the hole. Then it took only a few blows of the hammer to ease the iron into place. The oil had neither diminished the size of the bar nor enlarged the hole. It had merely relieved the friction. A few drops of oil were far more effective than many blows of the hammer.

How slow we are to learn this lesson. There are many Christians who are intensely earnest and extremely conscientious, but they have never learned the secret of using the oil of God's love. If another holds views contrary to theirs, they hammer away mercilessly, striking blow after blow until the point is won. Such action only incites friction and results in sorrow and hurt feelings. Worst of all, it hinders the Lord's work. "Be kindly affectioned one to another with brotherly love; in honour preferring one another" (Romans 12:10).

Each child of God is called to be an ambassador of love. True love is more than "being"; it is "doing" and "helping." It was D. L. Moody who said, "Faith gets the most, humility keeps the most, but love works the most."

Have you ever stopped to realize that the way Christ usually helps people is through human beings? He not only comes Himself, but He usually sends someone else. This places a serious responsibility on each of us.

When someone is struggling with a heartache or a serious temptation, he needs nothing more than the touch of God's love through the clasp of the human hand, the encouragement of a human voice, and the loving concern and interest of the human heart. "Let us love one another: for love is of God; and every one that loveth is born of God, and knoweth God. He that loveth not knoweth not God; for God is love" (1 John 4:7-8).

Peter suggests another requisite for Christian kindness, *sympathy.* "Be pitiful." How essential that the child of God should be sympathetic, prayerfully seeking to understand the problems and needs of others. Only as we get close to the Lord can we learn the secret of putting ourselves in the other person's place to the extent that we "Rejoice with them that do rejoice, and weep with them that weep" (Romans 12:15).

Sympathy involves more than mere sorrow or regret for one's circumstances. Sympathy desires to help. Matthew Henry has rightly stated that "the nature of true Christian sympathy is not only to be concerned for our friends in their troubles, but to do what we can to help them." God pleads with us to do all we can to alleviate our Christian brothers' suffering. "As we have therefore opportunity, let us do good unto all men, especially unto them who are of the household of faith" (Galatians 6:10). But oh, how rare is the kind of true Christian sympathy that will go to any limit in an earnest desire to help.

Some years ago there was a very serious flood, along the Ohio River and its tributaries in Pennsylvania, which drove many families out of their homes. Many homes were washed away in the torrential waters, everything in them lost. Flood victims took refuge in churches, schools, and city halls, while sympathetic citizens did everything possible to help in the emergency. A newspaper reporter asked some of the sufferers how they felt about it all, especially the loss of their homes, clothing, and furniture. One fourteen year old girl replied, "Oh, it's wonderful! Everyone is so kind to everyone else. It doesn't make any difference what you wear, what your father does, or to which church you belong. They are just kind. I almost wish it would happen every year."

Why should it take a flood, a war, a fire, a catastrophe to break the hard shell that so many of us wear on the outside and permit the sunshine and light of pure sympathy and kindness to shine through and warm the hearts of those around us?

God says in His Word, "Comfort ye, comfort ye My people" (Isaiah 40:1). Multiplied thousands are in need of physical, mental, and spiritual help, but so many Christians are entirely neglectful of those outside the realm of their own immediate and particular interests. The Lord has ministered to our needs repeatedly, but for what purpose? That we, in His strength, may sacrifice to help others in their adversity and sorrow. Paul wrote in 2 Corinthians 1:3-4, "Blessed be God, even the Father of our Lord Jesus Christ, the Father of mercies, and the God of all comfort; Who comforteth us in all our tribulation, that we may be able to comfort them which are in any trouble, by the comfort wherewith we ourselves are comforted of God."

We have been schooled by trial so that we may sympathize with others through the lessons we have learned. The tried heart is best qualified to care for and minister to the needs of others. But we are so forgetful to apply the knowledge we have received from the Lord to help them who sorrow. All who would truly follow Christ must be sympathetic.

The Apostle John graphically describes an incident in the life of our Lord when He was teaching in the Temple. The quietness is suddenly broken by shouts and laughter as several burly men drag forward a helpless woman. They are followed by a crude and boisterous crowd. Roughly the woman is thrust at our Saviour's feet with the accusation, "Master, this woman was taken in adultery, in the very act. Now Moses in the law commanded us, that such should be stoned: but what sayest thou?" (John 8:4-5).

There was a momentary silence as Jesus knelt and wrote on the ground with His finger, as though He did not hear them. But they continued to ask, "Master, what sayest thou?" Standing, Jesus replied, "He that is without sin among you, let him first cast a stone at her" (verse 7). Again He knelt and wrote on the ground.

Conviction gripped the hardened hearts of the woman's antagonistic accusers. One by one they slunk away until the woman was left alone in the presence of the Son of God. Turning to her Jesus asked, "Woman, where are those thine accusers? hath no man condemned thee?" She replied quietly, "No man, Lord." Jesus said unto her, "Neither do I condemn thee: go, and sin no more."

What sympathy! This is always the attitude of our wonderful Lord. Here was an immoral woman who had broken the law of God. But Jesus, who "was tempted in all points like as we are," perfectly understood the power of temptation, and in sympathy and love completely forgave this erring woman.

The brand of Christianity that fails to make us more tender and kind, more sympathetic and forbearing with others is not New Testament Christianity. God says, "Bear ye one another's burdens, and so fulfil the law of Christ" (Galatians 6:2).

A woman who was the mother of eleven children was once asked by a friend, "Aren't so many youngsters a great deal of trouble?"

"No," she answered, "no trouble. A bother sometimes, but never trouble. You see, trouble is on the heart, but bother is only on the hands." Should this not be suggestive of the attitude of believers toward others? Nothing should be a trouble to us and, as a matter of fact, not even a bother. We must help one another. For it is this kind of Christianity that speaks loudest for Christ.

"Be *courteous*," Peter says as he emphasizes another of the essential characteristics of Christian kindness. The need of courtesy might seem a trivial matter to mention to Christians. Do they not practice the rules of common politeness? Are they not mannerly in their associations with others? To see the way some Christians act and to hear them talk, one would think they knew nothing about courtesy. Often the unsaved put Christians to shame in their respect for others.

Consider the value placed upon courtesy in business where it is recognized as a most productive asset. A newspaper in one of our eastern cities reports that, according to the estimates of the local telephone company, its employees lose one hundred and twenty-five hours a day through the use of the word "please." Calls could be put through more readily and expeditiously were it not for the use of that one little word. But businessmen realize that, though a word of courtesy or an act of politeness may involve a few moments, time thus expended is not wasted. What is lost in time is made up in good will, kindly feeling, and increased patronage.

If businessmen make so great an investment in courtesy to win more business, how much more concerned Christians should be to possess and practice this attribute for the glory of the Lord. Let us not hinder the work of the Lord by curt remarks and thoughtless actions. "Grieve not the holy Spirit of God, whereby ye are sealed unto the day of redemption. Let all bitterness, and wrath, and anger, and clamour, and evil speaking, be put away from you, with all malice: And be ye kind one to another, tenderhearted, forgiving one another, even as God for Christ's sake hath forgiven you" (Ephesians 4:30-32).

The apostle further states that the child of God should not be "rendering evil for evil, or railing for railing: but contrariwise blessing." Be *thoughtful!* How we need to be considerate of others, never paying back or retaliating for unkindness. It is to be expected that some will misunderstand us and even be cruel and unchristian in their treatment of us. But this is no reason for further evil on our part.

There was an old colored brother, known for years for his Christian grace, who never had been heard to speak a harsh or unkind word. But one day he was sorely tempted when an angry and resentful neighbor hurled false accusations at him and called him names. The humble saint listened to his accuser. "Joe," he said, "if yo'all offers sumthin' to a man an' he refuses it, den who do it belong to?"

"Why it belongs to de man what offers it," Joe replied.

"Well, dem names you called me, ah refuses to accept!"

Scripture asks for more than that. Not only is the Christian to refuse to accept evil, he is to go out of his way to render "blessing." That is, he should return good for evil. "To render good for evil is godlike. To render good for good is manlike.

To render evil for evil is beastlike. To render evil for good is devil-like."

In His Sermon on the Mount, the Lord Jesus said, "Ye have heard that it hath been said, An eye for an eye, and a tooth for a tooth: But I say unto you, That ye resist not evil: but whosoever shall smite thee on thy right cheek, turn to him the other also. And if any man will sue thee at the law, and take away thy coat, let him have thy cloke also. And whosoever shall compel thee to go a mile, go with him twain" (Matthew 5:38-41).

"Knowing that ye are thereunto called, that ye should inherit a blessing." Only as we exemplify these five characteristics which Peter outlines can we enjoy the blessing God sends to kind hearts. The apostle says, "Ye are thereunto called." The Lord saved us to be agreeable, loving, sympathetic, courteous, and thoughtful. If you are a new creature in Christ, God desires that you be loving instead of hateful; generous instead of miserly; gracious instead of bitter; helpful instead of hindering; kindly instead of mean. Anything less than this falls below God's standard.

Of course, only through Christ can we achieve these goals. There must be a daily commitment to Him for strength to "walk in the light as He is in the light," practicing Christian kindness as He desires. Depend not upon yourself but upon Him. He will not fail.

22

HOW TO ENJOY LIFE

"For he that will love life, and see good days, let him refrain his tongue from evil, and his lips that they speak no guile: Let him eschew evil, and do good; let him seek peace, and ensue it. For the eyes of the Lord are over the righteous, and His ears are open unto their prayers: but the face of the Lord is against them that do evil."—1 Peter 3:10-12

Having presented the cause of Christian kindness, the apostle delineates how believers in Christ may best enjoy life. Many are deluded by the false belief that material prosperity is the means to happy living. What a sham this deceptive, worldly standard is! "They that will be rich fall into temptation and a snare, and into many foolish and harmful lusts, which drown men in destruction and perdition. For the love of money is the root of all evil: which while some coveted after, they have erred from the faith, and pierced themselves through with many sorrows" (1 Timothy 6:9-10).

The Bible teaches that the way to genuine and lasting enjoyment is found not in material prosperity but through spiritual satisfaction. In affirming this important truth, Peter quotes from Psalm 34:12-16, which suggests three requisites for spiritual satisfaction and true happiness for the believer. He who would "love life" (be well satisfied with life), "and see good days"

166

(days filled with blessing), must be careful of what he says, what he does, and what he thinks.

How necessary that Christians be careful to say the right thing at the right time. "Let him refrain his tongue from evil, and his lips that they speak no guile." He who has learned to control his tongue has made good progress on the road toward spiritual satisfaction. The manner in which we speak reveals to a large degree either the fullness or the shallowness of our spiritual life. "If any man among you seem to be religious, and bridleth not his tongue, but deceiveth his own heart, this man's religion is vain" (James 1:26). One may pretend to be spiritual, but his speech will uncover his hypocrisy.

You may recall the old-fashioned doctor, whose stock interrogation of each patient was, "May I see your tongue?" Regardless of other symptoms, the tongue was usually considered the index to the physical condition. Times have changed, and as a result of scientific research doctors have discovered more accurate methods of diagnosing physical disturbances.

But, without question, the tongue is still the index to one's spiritual condition. For what we say most clearly reveals what we are. Words are windows through which others may peer into our character. "Out of the abundance of the heart the mouth speaketh" (Matthew 12:34). How vitally important then that every Christian give constant vigilance and prayerful consideration to his speech. For who could begin to estimate the damage being wrought by an evil and unruly tongue!

There is much concern about the destructive A-bomb and H-bomb. But I have greater fear of a weapon more deadly and ruinous than either of these demons of devastation. The sad fact is that Christians are guilty of stockpiling this horrible weapon. What is it? The G-bomb! Its harmful results are rarely considered because the G-bomb is so small. It consists of only one movable part which may be defined as "a movable, muscular organ comprised of a large number of muscles covered by a mucous membrane from which project numerous papillae." The G-bomb is the gossip-bomb, and the one movable part, the tongue. Oh, what misery and sorrow has been wrought by this deadly instrument. Character has been destroyed, reputation ruined, and hearts broken. "Behold, how great a matter a little fire kindleth!" (James 3:5)

> "How like an arrow is a word,
>   At random often speeding
> To find a target never meant,
>   And set some heart a-bleeding.
>
> "Oh, pray that heaven may seal the lips,
>   E'er unkind words are spoken.
> For Heaven itself cannot recall,
>   When once that seal is broken."
> —Author Unknown

Christian, do you long to enjoy life to the fullest? Then "Put away from thee a froward mouth, and perverse lips put far from thee" (Proverbs 4:24). For, "Whoso keepeth his mouth and his tongue keepeth his soul from troubles" (Proverbs 21:23). Get the victory over caustic, cutting words and "let your speech be alway with grace, seasoned with salt" (Colossians 4:6).

Happy living consists not only in what we say but what we do. God directs us to "eschew evil, and do good." To "eschew evil" means to turn away from it. Perhaps you are like many defeated Christians who feel that this is easier said than done. They try repeatedly to overcome their besetting sin but always fail. Many even give up, acknowledging it as a hopeless task. Take courage! Do not be deceived by Satan! God never asks us to perform any task without supplying adequate means by which to do it. We read in Romans 6:6, "Knowing this, that our old man [nature] is crucified with Him [Christ], that the body of sin might be destroyed, that henceforth we should not serve sin." Here is God's assurance to the believer of clear-cut victory over sin.

The statement, "that the body of sin might be destroyed," does not mean the complete eradication of our sinful nature. The Greek verb, "to destroy," means *to render entirely idle and useless.* For the true follower of Christ, the old sinful nature is made inactive. "The body of sin" is harnessed by the power of God so that its power is invalidated and the believer is forever delivered from its bondage. Victory over sin is the believer's blessed privilege and needs only to be appropriated. For this reason, the child of God has no excuse to continue in sin.

The happy Christian will not only be careful to "eschew evil," but through the indwelling Christ he will possess an earnest desire to "do good." The Christian life consists of more than negatives. Its approach is positive as well. One of the best ways to "eschew evil" is to "do good." Too often saints miss the blessing of positive victory. Being so concerned about not sinning against the Lord, they fail to do anything for the Lord.

We sing those wonderful words, "For there is no other way to be happy in Jesus, but to trust and obey." How necessary that all who follow Christ, obey Him. Sometimes we talk so much about the precious promises of God that we neglect and ignore the commandments. Some of us have "promise boxes." Each day we draw from them precious truths, receiving inspiration to tread uncertain paths ahead. Perhaps we need some "commandment boxes" to remind us of our obligation to trust and obey the Lord. Have you ever noticed that the Bible contains far more commandments than promises? Surely this is not without meaning. God knew what we would need most. Being of the flesh, we are selfish. We choose that which pleases best and provides the most comfort.

Do you really want to enjoy life? Then heed this admonition of the Lord: "Eschew evil, and do good." For "Who shall ascend into the hill of the Lord? or who shall stand in His holy place? He that hath clean hands, and a pure heart; who hath not lifted up his soul unto vanity, nor sworn deceitfully" (Psalm 24:3-4). Happiness is unknown to those whose hands are soiled and whose hearts are tainted with sin. Jesus said, "If any man serve Me, let him follow Me" (John 12:26). To follow Christ is to seek to be like Him in holiness of life and righteousness of character. With this earnest desire in our hearts, we shall pray as Moses, "Let the beauty of the Lord our God be upon us"

(Psalm 90:17). God covets a life of obedience for each of us. But be assured it can be realized only as we keep our eyes on the Lord Jesus.

During a recess after a light snowfall, some of the children in a schoolyard were amusing themselves by trying to see who could walk the longest distance, making the straightest tracks. The older children seemed to have no difficulty, but the younger ones wavered from side to side. Of course, the secret was in the use of the eyes. The little children kept watching their feet and as a result made crooked tracks. The older children discovered that if they fixed their gaze on a tree in the distance, their feet followed without deviation. So if we turn our eyes upon Christ and follow Him, it will not be difficult to walk in a manner well pleasing to Him. The burden of eschewing evil and doing good will be lifted, and the blessing of obedience will be experienced.

"Let him seek peace, and ensue it." This statement suggests to me the inestimable value of correct thinking. For happy living the Christian must guard well his thinking. Without good thoughts there can be neither edifying speech nor holy living. For this reason God says, "Whatsoever things are true, whatsoever things are honest, whatsoever things are just, whatsoever things are pure, whatsoever things are lovely, whatsoever things are of good report; if there be any virtue, and if there be any praise, think on these things" (Philippians 4:8).

You may wonder how the idea of "correct thinking" is derived from this verse "let him seek peace, and ensue it." It is plain that to "ensue" or walk in peace is possible only as there is "perfect peace" in the mind. For as a man "thinketh in his heart, so is he" (Proverbs 23:7). It is sad that many Christians speak of "the peace of God, which passeth all understanding" though their minds are in constant turmoil, harassed by fear and worry, and devoid of rest in Him who is the Prince of Peace. They are accurately described by Paul when he says, "The way of peace have they not known" (Romans 3:17). What a pathetic picture of insecurity and uncertainty! Burdened by worry, they are distraught and depressed.

Someone has said, "Jaywalking can surely give you that run-down feeling." Many Christians are mental jaywalkers. They profess to believe the Bible and yet they permit their minds to wander among terrifying imaginations which God neither intends nor will permit to become fact. God says, "Seek peace." Do not take another step until you fall on your knees and acknowledge His enduring peace in its actual present reality. Claim this gift our Lord bequested to every child of faith. "Peace I leave with you, My peace I give unto you" (John 14:27). God has provided the peace, why not trust Him for it?

One time Oliver Cromwell's secretary was dispatched on an important mission. He spent a restless night in a seaport town, unable to sleep. Tossing on his bed, he disturbed his servant, who was sound asleep in the same room. Rousing, the servant asked his master why he could not sleep.

"I am so afraid that something will go wrong with the embassage," replied the secretary.

"May I ask a question?" queried the valet. "Did God rule the world before we were born?"

"Most assuredly," answered the secretary.

"And will He rule it again after we are dead?"

"Certainly!"

"Then, master, why not let Him rule the present, too?" The secretary accepted this logic of faith and soon joined his servant in peaceful sleep.

When will we learn to cast our burdens on the Lord and enjoy His peace? David was surrounded by temptation, trouble, and tragedy. Yet he could say, "I will both lay me down in peace, and sleep: for Thou, Lord, only makest me dwell in safety" (Psalm 4:8). Worry and anxiety should be foreign to true believers. Worry is a sure sign of unbelief and doubt of God's marvelous love and care. Oh, let us "seek peace" in our hearts and minds and "ensue it," walking in the paths of peace, ever enjoying the Lord's sustaining grace. Learn the secret of waiting on the Lord, trusting Him for all things. "God is our refuge and strength, a very present help in trouble. Therefore will not we fear, though the earth be removed, and though the mountains be carried into the midst of the sea" (Psalm 46:1-2).

We should bear in mind that we are not left to ourselves to attain to the high standards the Lord has established for His people in His Word. None of us is qualified to say the right thing, do the right thing, or think the right thing apart from the work of God's grace. We are wholly dependent on Him for constant guidance and strength. But He is ready. Peter says, "The eyes of the Lord are over the righteous, and His ears are open unto their prayers: but the face of the Lord is against them that do evil." Three facts are stated in this verse about our great God: He sees, He hears, He acts.

Whatever our need, God sees. His eyes are never closed in slumber. He is always watching over His own. "The eyes of the Lord run to and fro throughout the whole earth, to show Himself strong in behalf of them whose heart is perfect toward Him" (2 Chronicles 16:9). Though we may feel forsaken at times, He promises never to leave us nor forsake us.

Lacking funds to carry on, a certain family was forced to leave its farm home. As the last piece of furniture was being loaded into the truck, the mother stood heavyhearted, taking a last look at the old homestead with its surrounding hills, winding river, and stately trees. The youngest son, sensing her anxiety, said, "Mother, don't worry, God's sky is over us yet, and it's going right along with us." The child of God can say even more. Not only is God's sky over us, God Himself is over us! Regardless of circumstances, He is there! "The eyes of the Lord are over the righteous." He sees. Therefore He will undertake.

The apostle also says, "His ears are open unto their prayers." God hears! We have a blessed privilege. We may resort to prayer at any time with the assurance that the ear of God is turned to all who are in fellowship with Him. As a mother has her ears attuned to the cry of her child, so the Lord listens for the voice of His own. Abraham Lincoln used to say, "When I don't know which way to go, I go on my knees."

What an opportunity we have in the ministry of prayer. God

promises in Jeremiah 33:3, "Call unto Me, and I will answer thee, and show thee great and mighty things, which thou knowest not." But so often, "ye have not, because ye ask not" (James 4:2). We have a mighty God who is in no way limited by our lack of vision or perseverance. Meet the conditions and trust Him for all things. "If ye abide in Me, and My words abide in you, ye shall ask what ye will, and it shall be done unto you" (John 15:7).

Finally, there is a most solemn thought we must not overlook, the penalty for disobedience. God may find it necessary to "act" if His people habitually rebel against His will. "The face of the Lord is against them that do evil." How pathetic that many who call themselves Christians fail to do what the Lord Jesus wants them to do. Small wonder their lives seem to be but endless chains of misery and sorrow. "The face of the Lord is against them." No blessing can be theirs, no prayer power, no overflowing joy. "The way of transgressors is hard" (Proverbs 13:15). For the Christian to call Christ Lord, and then live for self, is blasphemy. To such, Christ puts the question, "Why call ye Me, Lord, Lord, and do not the things which I say?" (Luke 6:46)

Are you interested in truly enjoying life? Do you covet the supreme happiness God has intended for all His people? Then heed His voice and do His will. Be careful what you say, what you do, and what you think. Trust Him for the victory and the blessing will be yours.

23

USABLE SAINTS

"And who is he that will harm you, if ye be followers of that which is good? But and if ye suffer for righteousness' sake, happy are ye: and be not afraid of their terror, neither be troubled; But sanctify the Lord God in your hearts: and be ready always to give an answer to every man that asketh you a reason of the hope that is in you with meekness and fear: Having a good conscience; that, whereas they speak evil of you, as of evildoers, they may be ashamed that falsely accuse your good conversation in Christ. For it is better, if the will of God be so, that ye suffer for well doing, than for evil doing."—1 Peter 3:13-17

Not all Christians are working Christians. In fact, only a very small percentage of God's people are in the habit of performing some regular service for the Lord. This must be greatly displeasing to God. He earnestly desires that every follower serve Him. To do this, we must be made usable. In the verses we are to study, the apostle suggests five essentials for the believer's usefulness.

"And who is he that will harm you, if ye be followers of that which is good?" Weymouth translates the latter part of this verse, "If you show yourselves *zealous* for that which is good." A *holy zeal* is imperative for usefulness in the Lord's work. We must be "zealous for that which is good." Christians in our day seem to be fearful of the word *zeal*, even though we are exhorted in Galatians 4:18 to "be zealously affected always in a good thing." Those who have been most used by the Lord through the centuries of the Church's history, have been "zealously affected," with hearts burning to do a work for God.

Years ago a tyrannical king commanded a Christian to recant and give up Christ.

"If you don't, I will banish you," he declared.

"You cannot banish me from Christ," said the Christian, "for God says, 'I will never leave thee nor forsake thee.'"

"I will confiscate your property!" the king then angrily threatened.

"My treasures are laid up in Heaven," the Christian replied. "You cannot touch them."

"I will kill you!" the king shouted with even greater anger.

But the Christian quietly answered, "I have been dead in Christ to this world for forty years. My life is hid with Christ in God. You cannot touch it."

The king turned to some of the members of his court and said in disgust, "What can you do with such a fanatic?"

The age in which we live demands men and women with similar fanatical zeal for Christ. The world is burning with lust. The only hope is in Christ. But if the world is to hear about Him, we must have Christians wholly consecrated to God with but one supreme ambition—to make known the ever-living Christ.

Even a casual association with most churches reveals that a large percentage of our present-day disciples sadly resembles those who failed our Lord in the Garden of Gethsemane. He was tortured with the burdens of the world's sin weighing upon Him. Heavy-hearted, nearing the depths of His soul torment, he asked Peter, James, and John to watch with Him. Yet we read, "He cometh unto the disciples, and findeth them asleep" (Matthew 26:40).

Think of it! A few feet away, the Redeemer of the race was wrestling with the power of darkness, in agony too crushing to be measured in the conception of human mind. Yet those closest to Him failed to watch with their lonely Leader, even for a few moments, when their vigilant companionship would have meant so much to Him.

Is our lethargy any different today? Look at Christendom in the face of the challenge of the mighty forces of satanic darkness: soft, flabby, and drowsy, instead of zealous, strong, and forceful. To us God declares, "Awake thou that sleepest, and arise from the dead, and Christ shall give thee light" (Ephesians 5:14). We must arouse from slumber before it is too late! The enemy is fast sowing "the tares" of destruction and misery. The call is stronger than ever to saints of God, who, with hearts aflame, will be willing, if necessary, to forfeit comfort, rest, and sleep in order to spread the message of life. Let the Holy Spirit so possess your soul and overwhelm you with the zeal of God that no obstacle, regardless of its magnitude or severity, will be able to block your consecrated effort to serve the Lord.

Closely allied to the need for a *holy zeal,* is a fearless approach. "But and if ye suffer for righteousness' sake, happy are ye: and be not afraid of their terror, neither be troubled." In every age of the Church's history it has been necessary for God's people to face persecution for righteousness' sake. But in spite of the severity of the test, God says, "happy are ye," which is to say, "count it a privilege." Never should the believer grumble or complain under the fire of persecution. "Blessed are ye, when men shall revile you, and persecute you, and shall say all manner of evil against you falsely, for My sake. Rejoice, and be exceeding glad: for great is your reward in heaven: for so persecuted they the prophets which were before you" (Matthew 5:11-12). It should be an honor to suffer for Him who freely poured out His life for us. "Be not afraid" but be bold and courageous, ever seeking to exalt the name of Jesus Christ. Say with Paul, "For I am not ashamed of the gospel of Christ: for it is the power of God unto salvation to every one that believeth; to the Jew first, and also to the Greek" (Romans 1:16).

We should not be ashamed. Yet how many Christians shy away from opportunities to speak for Christ. Often their timidity is actually a fear of what people may say or think. But why should it matter what the attitude of others may be, so long as we please Christ? We are privileged to worship the Lord today because dauntless heroes of the faith, men and women in the past, were unafraid to suffer for righteousness' sake. The blood of martyrs has always been the seed of the Church.

A martyr in Switzerland was standing barefoot on the fagots, about to be burned to death. He called to the magistrate who was superintending his execution and urged him to come near. As the burly executioner came close, the Christian said in quiet confidence, "I am about to be burned to death for faith in my Lord Jesus Christ. Lay your hand on my heart. If it beats any faster than it ordinarily beats, don't believe in my Christ." What a convincing testimony to the keeping power of the Lord Jesus!

Polycarp, another great martyr, bishop of Smyrna, comes to mind. One of the first martyrs, he was the forerunner of thousands who died in faithfulness to the message of the living Christ. Hunted by godless persecutors, Polycarp was persuaded by friends to take refuge on a farm, but he was soon found and arrested. They tried every known means to get him to blaspheme the name of his Lord. But with unshakable courage, born of faith in the Son of God, he cried out, "Eighty and six years I have served my Lord and He has been my truest Friend. How then can I blaspheme Him who shed His blood to wash away my sin?" They tied him to a stake and built a fire around him, but long before his suffering body was reduced to ashes, his triumphant soul was at home with his God.

There is a desperate need in the Church of Christ today for men like Polycarp, fearless men who will stand for the Saviour at any cost, fearing God and Him alone. "Fear not them which kill the body, but are not able to kill the soul: but rather fear Him which is able to destroy both soul and body in hell" (Matthew 10:28). In Christ, we are assured of victory over fear if only we will trust Him. "For God hath not given us the spirit of fear; but of power, and of love, and of a sound mind" (2 Timothy 1:7).

But more yet is needful if we are to be used of God. There must be a *surrendered heart*. Without a doubt, here lies the crux of the whole matter. "Sanctify the Lord God in your hearts." No Christian will be zealous or fearless unless the Lord Jesus is the absolute ruler of the heart. Faithfulness and effectiveness in service depend on depth of spirituality. A mere surface experience with Christ will produce no results. To accomplish things for the Lord, one must be possessed by Him. "The love of Christ constraineth us" (2 Corinthians 5:14). Only as we are fully yielded to Him, will we be constrained by His love to serve Him.

It might be well to pause a moment and ask ourselves, "Have I sanctified the Lord in my heart? Have I given Him first place?" Sometimes our actions betray our intentions. When you see a dog following two men, it is difficult to discern which of the two is the dog's master. But let the men go separate ways, and you know immediately which of them is the dog's master. So God calls believers His way. If Christ is our Master, we shall follow Him. Those who pursue worldliness know not the blessedness of sanctifying Christ in the heart.

When the Saviour becomes the Lord of our lives, we shall desire to spend time with Him. It was Dr. J. H. Jowett who said, "There are some people who just visit Christ; there are others who abide in Him." Those who abide in Him will radiate and reflect His glory to others.

Moses had been in the Lord's presence forty days and forty nights. No one can dwell in God's presence long without a significant and noticeable transformation. The Bible says, "When he came down from the mount . . . Moses wist not that the skin of his face shone" (Exodus 34:29).

A similar experience can be ours. But we must meet the conditions. We must spend time in Christ's presence, daily submitting ourselves completely to Him. We cannot afford to waste hours and days living for selfish interests. The needs of the hour demand a full and complete commitment to Christ as Lord.

Peter further enjoins each of us to "be ready always to give an answer to every man that asketh you a reason of the hope that is in you." This is the fourth requisite for usefulness, a *ready answer.* Born-again Christians should be ready at any time to give a clear-cut testimony to the saving power of Jesus Christ. If a believer does not know how to lead another person to Christ for salvation, he should learn immediately. Soul winning is every Christian's responsibility. God never intended this ministry for preachers only. Everyone who has tasted of life eternal through Jesus Christ is appointed and ordained by God to be an evangelist.

A sincere Christian woman came to me one day and said, "Pastor, God has laid a dear woman on my heart. She needs the gospel. I have had such a burden for her. If I give you her address, will you go and speak to her about the Saviour?" I assured her I would be happy to do it, but I said, "Just a moment. You tell me God laid this woman on *your* heart? If the Lord has burdened you to speak to her about Christ, do not look for a substitute to do it. It is your responsibility and your duty."

Why is it so many of us try to sidestep this important ministry of witnessing for Christ? Some say, "I get nervous." Pray and trust God for strength. Others say, "I don't know enough about the Bible." Get busy! Study the Word! Memorize verses that can best be used to show the lost the only way to eternal life through Christ. Whenever the Lord speaks to your heart about a lost soul, let nothing interfere. Carry the gospel to that one as quickly as possible.

If you are a Christian you will normally be a soul winner. It is for this reason that I have always opposed receiving anyone into the membership of the church unless he could give convincing evidence of having experienced a real heart change through the saving power of Christ. Some feel that to be morally upright and respectable is sufficient. Such a view is a contradiction of God's Word. An unconverted man has no hope in him. God says we should be able to give "a reason of the hope" that is within us. The "reason" for this hope is the fact that Christ saved us on the grounds of His atoning death and miraculous resurrection. Only those should be received into the church who are possessors of this "hope" and who will endeavor to tell others about it. For this reason the church membership should not be considered the field, but the force. Consequently, the entire program of the church should be geared to training and challenging its force to go out into the field and to spread the gospel of Christ.

It is clear in the Scriptures that if one has really entered into a personal relationship with Christ, he will have a God-given burden for souls. Jesus said, "Come ye after Me, and I will make you to become fishers of men" (Mark 1:17). Not only a new life does the Lord Jesus put into us at the time of conversion, but a new vision. He puts the desire within us to win others to Christ.

If you are not eager to reach the lost, something is wrong. I would suggest you get alone with the Lord as soon as possible and have it out with Him. He says, "Ye that make mention of the Lord, keep not silence" (Isaiah 62:6). If you are a believer, you should be articulate for Christ. Silence may suggest the absence of a true heart experience with the Saviour. It is so easy to say, "I believe!" Do we really believe?

In a large manufacturing town, a group of infidels were busy distributing their wicked propaganda from door to door. In counterattack, a minister decided to deliver a Sunday evening sermon on the "Evidences of Christianity." He was surprised to see the champion of the infidel movement in his audience. Later, the minister called on the man urging him to believe the proofs that he had given of the truths of Christianity. The unbeliever quickly retorted, "Believe? Certainly not! Nor do you, either! Why, if I believed what you and your party profess to believe, I should scarcely be fit for business. My whole soul would be absorbed in the tremendous consequences at stake. But you and your folk are not different from other people. No, I tell you, you do not believe."

What a challenge to those who name our Saviour as Lord! Do we believe? Let us face the issue honestly. If we do believe, then we shall have a ready answer and a testimony that will convince and convert through the Holy Spirit. We shall carefully and tactfully speak forth the truth of salvation in a way that others will be humbled and see the need of receiving Christ into the heart.

From our Epistle we see that something else is needed if we are to be useful for the Lord. There must be a *convincing life.* "Having a good conscience; that, whereas they speak evil of you, as of evildoers, they may be ashamed that falsely accuse your good conversation in Christ. For it is better, if the will of God be so, that ye suffer for well doing, than for evil doing." Regardless of how close one walks with the Lord, he will be subject to criticism. But this by no means lessens responsibility. It is extremely important that the Christian do right for conscience' sake. If the heart is right with the Lord, there can be perfect peace even under severe criticism. Christians should never give the evildoer ground for criticism. Often in observing Christians who walk close to the Lord in holy living, the evildoer will be convicted of his errors and ashamed of his false accusations. Righteousness in the child of God is so important. It takes more than talk to convict the lost and lead them to Christ. They must see Him in us.

Let no Christian say, "I can't live as I should for the Lord." This is one reason why the Lord Jesus died on the Cross, that you might have everlasting victory. He "gave Himself for us, that He might redeem us from all iniquity, and purify unto Himself a peculiar people, zealous of good works" (Titus 2:14). God further says in Titus 3:8, "This is a faithful saying, and these things I will that thou affirm constantly, that they which have believed in God might be careful to maintain good works. These things are good and profitable unto men." God is concerned that our lives be so convincing for Christ that when the lost see the way we live, they will cry out, "What must I do to be saved?" It is by this means we can best lead them to our Lord.

One time while driving to a speaking engagement in a strange city, and being confused as to directions, I stopped to ask a man how to reach a certain highway. He replied something like this: "Go five blocks to the south; turn east, and go to the third stop light; go a little further, where you will meet a fork in the road; bear left; go around the circle. You can't miss it!" But I did!

In contrast, I recall another occasion. Driving through Detroit to reach the tunnel leading to Windsor, Ontario, I stopped for a red light. Opening the window of my car, I asked the man who stopped next to me how to get to the tunnel. He smiled and very pleasantly said, "Just follow me." The light changed, he pulled away and I found myself moving rapidly through the streets of Detroit. We turned right and left, went here and there, but in a matter of moments we arrived at the tunnel. I thanked the gentleman for his kindness and he continued on his way. Not only had his guidance enabled me to reach my destination quickly, but it taught me a lesson I hope I shall never forget.

All about us there are struggling souls, burdened with the cares of the day, suffering from the anxieties and the complexities of life, not knowing the way to God. They are indeed lost, in need of being directed to the only One who can give lasting peace and joy. It is not enough to "tell" them how to find Him. They may not wholly understand. We must "show" them. We should be living so close to the Lord that we can say, "Follow me," and then lead them to Him by a life of example. Paul could say, "Be ye followers of me, even as I also am of Christ" (1 Corinthians 11:1).

How about you? Are you walking with the Lord? Is your life what it should be for Christ? Are you spending precious moments witnessing for Him? You say you are a Christian. Is your soul impassioned to see men come to Christ? Does David's experience characterize your zeal to reach the lost? "My heart was hot within me, while I was musing the fire burned: then spake I with my tongue" (Psalm 39:3). As you humbly pray, ask the Lord so to inflame your heart and life with His glory and power that you will without question be a usable saint.

24

IS JESUS GOD?

"For Christ also hath once suffered for sins, the just for the unjust, that He might bring us to God, being put to death in the flesh, but quickened by the Spirit: By which also He went and preached unto the spirits in prison; Which sometime were disobedient, when once the longsuffering of God waited in the days of Noah, while the ark was a preparing, wherein few, that is, eight souls were saved by water. The like figure whereunto even baptism doth also now save us (not the putting away of the filth of the flesh, but the answer of a good conscience toward God,) by the resurrection of Jesus Christ: Who is gone into heaven, and is on the right hand of God; angels and authorities and powers being made subject unto Him."—1 Peter 3:18-22

Is Jesus God? This is a disturbing question to many. Every age has been marked by its doubters seeking a positive answer to this question. But for those who really want to know, be assured the Word of God is the most reliable source of truth. In it you will find clearly revealed "many infallible proofs" which, if considered fairly, will provide a conclusive answer, even for the most avowed skeptic. There was a time in Peter's life when he, too, was a doubter. But after conscientiously scrutinizing the life, character, and miraculous powers of our Lord, all incredulity was silenced and he became a staunch believer. From his divinely guided pen, consider, the four indubitable proofs of Christ's deity: His *death,* His *appearances,* His *Resurrection,* and His *position.*

Our Lord's *death* was remarkably different from any other because of the finality of its accomplishment. "For Christ also hath *once* suffered for sins." His atoning death forever eliminated the need for further sacrifice for sin. The price was fully paid once and for all by His shed blood. This fact is stated by the Holy Spirit no less than three times in the tenth chapter of Hebrews. Frequently repetition is utilized in the Scriptures to draw attention to some important truth. "We are sanctified through the offering of the body of Jesus Christ *once for all.* . . . But this man, after He had offered one sacrifice for sins *for ever,* sat down on the right hand of God. . . . For by *one offering* He hath perfected *for ever* them that are sanctified" (Hebrews 10:10,12,14). God's Word is unmistakably clear. The only satisfactory expiation for sin is the voluntary sacrifice of Christ on the Cross 1900 years ago.

Christ's death was also unique in that it was representative in its nature. The Lord Jesus died, "the just for the unjust." Sinful humanity deserved to die, but in His substitutionary sacrifice, He paid the entire price. "But we see Jesus, who was made a little lower than the angels for the suffering of death, crowned with glory and honor; that He by the grace of God should taste death for every man" (Hebrews 2:9). There are no exceptions. Christ died for all. He is "the Lamb of God, which taketh away the sin of the world" (John 1:29). He suffered the righteous for the unrighteous; the holy for the unholy; the true for the false; the pure for the impure; the strong for the weak; the innocent for the guilty; the king for the subject; the prince for the pauper; the shepherd for the sheep; the prophet for the people. To us it seems incredible that the sinless Son of God should suffer such loss for condemned sinners, but He did. Why? That all might be saved and have eternal life.

A twenty-year-old American soldier stationed in Japan was court-martialed for killing two Japanese civilians. He was brought to trial, found guilty, and later sentenced to death.

Having seen the account in one of our United States papers, a fifty-five-year-old man in New Jersey wrote to the soldier's parents and offered to die in the place of the young man.

"Perhaps you will think me a crank," he wrote, "but honestly, I am disgusted with this life. Perhaps you can arrange with our government that I be destroyed instead of your son."

Offers of this nature have been made in the past for other condemned men but have not been accepted. Evidently no legal provision has been made for this type of substitution in the United States. But rest assured, God made such a provision before the creation of the world, foreseeing our condemnation for sin. Christ did not present His life a sacrifice for us because He was disgusted with life. It was eternally decreed in the purposes of the Father, Son, and Holy Spirit that Christ would be "the Lamb slain from the foundation of the world" (Revelation 13:8).

Christ's death was different also because of the purpose it achieved: "That He might bring us to God." Because of his innate sinfulness, man is out of fellowship with God and hopelessly lost. For this reason Christ was born into the world, that He might provide a way for fallen humanity to reach God. This was the paramount purpose of His death: "Christ Jesus came into the world to save sinners" (1 Timothy 1:15). "For the Son of man is come to seek and to save that which was lost" (Luke 19:10). "Neither is there salvation in any other: for there is none other name under heaven given among men, whereby we must be saved" (Acts 4:12). The only way to eternal salvation has been provided in the person of God's Son. The entire provision has been made. There is nothing to be done but to believe and accept it.

But some will not believe until they reason out everything. They will not accept until every trace of uncertainty is banished. How contrary to God's thinking. He does not require understanding on our part for salvation. Why should we demand it? Why should the dependent creature expect the Creator to tell all He knows? If God is willing to save us by simple faith in Christ's sacrifice, we should be willing to believe Him. But we must come by faith. "Without faith it is impossible to please Him" (Hebrews 11:6).

After a hot and dusty drive, a businessman registered at a hotel in the South. He noticed a drinking fountain with a sign above it, "Stoop and Drink." He eagerly stepped to the fountain anticipating a cool, refreshing drink. Upon reaching it, he put out his hand to turn on the water, but found no handle. He looked for a button to press or a foot pedal to step on, but found none. Confused, he tried to reason out the perplexing situation. He was thirsty and the sign over the fountain plainly said, "Stoop and Drink." Was it a joke? Then suddenly the meaning of the sign became clear. He simply bent to the fountain and cool water flowed instantly to his lips. Refreshed, he examined the fountain and discovered a hidden electric eye so placed that when a certain beam of light was intercepted, a switch was thrown which opened the faucet and permitted the water to flow.

There is another fountain where men are invited to drink in a similar way. It is the fountain of the Water of Life. Jesus said, "But whosoever drinketh of the water that I shall give him shall never thirst; but the water that I shall give him shall be in him a well of water springing up into everlasting life" (John 4:14). Some refuse to drink from this fountain of life because they cannot fully comprehend how it works. Others, like the traveler, are trying to do something themselves, looking for a handle to turn, a button to press, or some other way. There is nothing to do but "Stoop and Drink!" All is ready. God has provided everything in the person of His Son Jesus Christ. "Christ died for our sins" (1 Corinthians 15:3). There is no reason for anyone to be lost. Men may offer excuses, but they are not reasons. God says, "Whosoever shall call upon the name of the Lord shall be saved" (Romans 10:13).

Unquestionably, Christ's unique *death* presents unequivocal evidence of His deity. But consider what transpired after His death: our Lord's *appearances*. Those who crucified the Lord Jesus did so in the hope that this would be the end. To their chagrin it immediately expanded the sphere of His activity.

Though His body was placed in the tomb, where it remained until the third day, Peter suggests that His spirit departed when He died on the cross to fulfill a specific mission. "Being put to death in the flesh, but quickened by the Spirit: By which also He went and preached unto the spirits in prison; which sometime were disobedient, when once the longsuffering of God waited in the days of Noah, while the ark was a preparing, wherein few, that is, eight souls were saved by water."

From these verses we gather that the Saviour descended into Hades, often called *hell* in the Scriptures. This is what is meant by the statement in the Apostle's Creed, "He descended into hell." Paul corroborated Peter's account of this incident in Ephesians 4:9-10: "Now that He ascended, what is it but that He also descended first into the lower parts of the earth? He that descended is the same also that ascended up far above all heavens, that He might fill all things." After His appearance to the souls of the dead who are being detained in the place of waiting until the Great White Throne Judgment, it seems from other passages that the Lord next appeared to the souls of departed saints in Paradise. You will recall He had promised the repentant thief crucified by His side, "To day shalt thou be with Me in paradise" (Luke 23:43).

Doubtless many questions have already come to your mind. Why did Christ descend into Hades? What did he preach about? Indeed this entire passage is shrouded in mystery. For centuries Bible students have sought to understand its meaning. One thing is certain. We must not add anything to that which is written, as some have done.

What does the passage mean? Let me begin by telling you what it does not mean. It does not mean ultimate salvation for all. There is no suggestion of a second chance for those who failed to receive or did not have an opportunity to receive salvation by grace during their physical existence. Nor does it offer substantiation for purgatory with the prospect of meriting Heaven. God states that Jesus "preached unto the spirits in prison." No more is said. Let us not try to read into the passage the possibility of repentance on the part of the wicked, or a special commitment of salvation to them. They are forever lost and eternally condemned to the unquenchable fires of hell.

What then did Jesus preach about to "the spirits in prison"? I reply at once, "I do not know." Like others, I too have prayed over the passage, seeking some spiritual insight into its meaning. As the result, this is what I think it means. It is my conviction that our Lord appeared to the disembodied spirits of all unbelievers of the Old Testament dispensation in hell, who were there because they carelessly disregarded the warning of the prophets and had ignored the message of grace, failing to prepare for impending judgment. In life they gave little or no thought to God's eternal truth. Like those of Noah's day, they ate and drank, married and gave in marriage, but had no time for the Lord. They laughed and scoffed at God's truth. But I am sure when the Lord Jesus appeared to them, no one laughed, for there is no humor in hell.

It would appear that Christ descended to hell as a witness to every unbeliever bound in the chains of eternal darkness, to silence forever the remonstrations of their wicked hearts by both showing and telling them that what God had spoken throughout the ages past was truth. "Heaven and earth shall pass away, but My words shall not pass away" (Matthew 24:35).

The condemned souls in hell must have recalled immediately the scores of opportunities they had in life but had neglected or rejected. What a horrible state, to be forever haunted by the memory of rejecting God's way of Life. Even the eternal fires of hell will not be able to destroy the memory. How important that the unsaved consider God's claims and come to Christ immediately. For if they reject Him now, they will never forget it in hell. I believe the never-to-be-forgotten word in hell is *remember!* It is impossible to forget.

The Lord Jesus told in Luke 16:23-25 of a certain rich man who "in hell . . . lift up his eyes, being in torments, and seeth Abraham afar off, and Lazarus in his bosom. And he cried and said, Father Abraham, have mercy on me, and send Lazarus, that he may dip the tip of his finger in water, and cool my tongue; for I am tormented in this flame. But Abraham said, Son, *remember*"! What terrible thoughts must have crowded his mind. If only he had taken time for the Lord! If only he had come God's way.

This should be a clarion to every living soul to remember and repent before it is too late; to believe, and to accept Christ as Lord, lest He be met as Judge. "Therefore we ought to give the more earnest heed to the things which we have heard, lest at any time we should let them slip. For if the word spoken by angels was stedfast, and every transgression and disobedience received a just recompense of reward; How shall we escape, if we neglect so great salvation; which at the first began to be spoken by the Lord, and was confirmed unto us by them that heard Him; God also bearing them witness, both with signs and wonders, and with divers miracles, and gifts of the Holy Ghost, according to His own will?" (Hebrews 2:1-4)

The *appearances* of Christ attest His deity. But Peter further mentions the *Resurrection* from the dead, which probably is the most outstanding proof. "The like figure whereunto even baptism doth also now save us (not the putting away of the filth of the flesh, but the answer of a good conscience toward God,) by the resurrection of Jesus Christ." There is a continuous and present realization and manifestation of His Resurrection being experienced in new life and power in all who put faith and trust in Him. Jesus must have been God. Were He merely a man, it would no longer be possible to receive new life and power from Him, with all its accompanying blessings.

Christ's enemies tried their best to get rid of Him. They bullied Him. They threatened Him. They set traps for Him. They assaulted Him. They contrived His betrayal. They condemned Him. They watched Him crucified. They laughed at His torture. They buried Him. They were satisfied! This, they thought, was the end! But He came back again. On the third day His Spirit entered His body and He arose from the dead—not a ghost, not an apparition, but Jesus, the Son of God.

Even today men still try to get rid of Him. But as then, so now, they cannot. He is not wanted in politics. He is not wanted in business. He is not wanted in the factory. He is not wanted in pleasure. He is not wanted in the school. He is not wanted in the home. This age tries its best to expel Him from every walk of life. But it cannot. He is here! Christ is risen! He is God!

When one receives the living Christ into his heart as the Son of God, the immediate result is new life. It is this experience Peter has in mind when he says, "eight souls were saved by water" and "even baptism doth also now save us." He is not suggesting that water baptism produces this transformation. He is drawing an analogy from Noah's experience. It is not the water that saved Noah and his family but the ark resting upon the water. It is not water baptism that saves anyone but the ark of the New Testament, Christ Himself. Water baptism is a testimony to the fact that the believer has entered into a covenant relationship with Christ. It is an outward sign of an inward act.

It is Holy Spirit baptism and not water that can produce "a good conscience toward God." When one believes on Christ, he is immediately baptized into the family of God. "For by one Spirit are we all baptized into one body, whether we be Jews or Gentiles, whether we be bond or free; and have been all made to drink into one Spirit" (1 Corinthians 12:13). It is only through this baptism that we can pass from the old life to the new, as did Noah.

In the closing verse of the chapter, Peter suggests the fourth witness to Christ's deity, *His position.* "Who is gone into heaven, and is on the right hand of God; angels and authorities and powers being made subject unto Him." Christ's position is one of supreme authority. He is indeed the ruler of the universe. "His name shall endure for ever: His name shall be continued as long as the sun: and men shall be blessed in Him: all nations shall call Him blessed" (Psalm 72:17).

Christ is at God's right hand, the place of special strength and honor. He is the executor of God's will, the place of highest honor in the universe, "Far above all principality, and power, and might, and dominion, and every name that is named. . . . And [God] hath put all things under His feet, and gave Him to be the head over all things to the church" (Ephesians 1:21-22).

The Lord Jesus has not as yet fully exerted His power by virtue of His position. But some day He will come again to rule and reign over the earth. Then kings, authorities, and powers will kneel humbly before Him, acknowledging Him as Lord of Lords and King of Kings.

Jesus is God! There is no other God but Him. "For it pleased the Father that in Him [Christ] should all fulness dwell" (Colossians 1:19). Oh, that helpless, struggling, sinful men and women would recognize Him as God by humbling themselves in His sight, realizing His mighty power through the conversion experience. If you do not know Him, turn to Him now. He is the only way to real life, eternal life. Believe His words: "I am the way, the truth, and the life: no man cometh unto the Father, but by Me" (John 14:6).

25

THE COST OF DISCIPLESHIP

"Forasmuch then as Christ hath suffered for us in the flesh, arm yourselves likewise with the same mind: for he that hath suffered in the flesh hath ceased from sin; That he no longer should live the rest of his time in the flesh to the lusts of men, but to the will of God. For the time past of our life may suffice us to have wrought the will of the Gentiles, when we walked in lasciviousness, lusts, excess of wine, revellings, banquetings, and abominable idolatries; Wherein they think it strange that ye run not with them to the same excess of riot, speaking evil of you: Who shall give account to Him that is ready to judge the quick and the dead. For for this cause was the gospel preached also to them that are dead, that they might be judged according to men in the flesh, but live according to God in the spirit."—1 Peter 4:1-6

Anyone who thinks the Chirstian life is a road of flowery ease, glistening in the sunshine of comfort, is sadly in error. Indeed the Christian life is a happy one, but it is not without its hardships and obstacles. In fact, it is an extremely costly life.

Peter continues his message of instruction and encouragement to a persecuted people by emphasizing the fact that *suffering* must be *faced*. Those who would be cross-bearers for Christ cannot escape the offense of the Cross. "Let us go forth therefore unto Him without the camp, bearing His reproach" (Hebrews 13:13). Christ endured untold agony throughout

His life and ministry, culminating in the excruciating sufferings of the Cross. Those who have believed on Him for salvation are expected to follow Him through manifold sufferings and afflictions. The followers can expect no less than their Master. Jesus declared, "Verily, verily, I say unto you, The servant is not greater than his lord" (John 13:16). Because He suffered, we must suffer too. There is no easy way. Rugged and thorny paths will be our lot. Other paths may appeal to the flesh, but if these are followed they will lead to the gratification of selfish desires, which always endeavor to escape the much-needed ministry of suffering.

"Forasmuch then as Christ hath suffered for us in the flesh, arm yourselves likewise with the same mind." What are you to do when surrounded by the trials of life? "Arm yourselves!" Fortify yourselves with God's marvelous promises. Determine through His grace and strength never to know defeat. Satan will tempt and distress you. With all of his diabolical subtlety, he will sow the seeds of discouragement and dissatisfaction. If we trust ourselves, we shall fail. If we clothe ourselves with God's armor, we shall be able to withstand all the attacks of the evil one. "Put on the whole armour of God, that ye may be able to stand against the wiles of the devil. For we wrestle not against flesh and .blood, but against principalities, against powers, against the rulers of the darkness of this world, against spiritual wickedness in high places" (Ephesians 6:11-12).

Those who love the Saviour are not fighting *for* victory, but *in* a victory already won through Christ's redemptive sacrifice. Consequently, though suffering is a necessity for Christian maturity, the believer should live a day at a time, trusting the Lord, assured He will never fail or forsake His own. How wonderful is His promise, "Cast thy burden upon the Lord, and He shall sustain thee: He shall never suffer the righteous to be moved" (Psalm 55:22). He constantly watches over us and will faithfully protect and defend us from the hands of our worst foe, the devil. "For the Lord God is a sun and shield: the Lord will give grace and glory: no good thing will He withhold from them that walk uprightly" (Psalm 84:11). There should be no room for fear or alarm in the surrendered heart. We must rely fully on the Lord, never turning to faithless devices of the flesh, which at best produce only a false security. Rest in God's precious work and wait until He moves. "Wait on the Lord: be of good courage, and He shall strengthen thine heart: wait, I say, on the Lord" (Psalm 27:14).

It is difficult to understand why God permits so many perplexing trials to darken the paths of those He loves. But be assured, there are numerous lessons to be learned in suffering that could never be acquired any other way. Though God's dealings often seem harsh and cruel, they are always for His glory and our good. He makes no mistakes. His ways are never without purpose.

Consider the mother eagle's treatment of her young; she too might appear cruel and harsh. But what she does is most necessary for the future of the eaglet. The greatest responsibility the mother eagle has toward her young is to teach them to fly. She feeds and shelters them, protecting them from sun, storm, and enemies. But these things are only secondary. Above all else, the eagle has an innate desire to instruct her offspring to spread his wings, and wing his way from lower to higher heights, to soar upward above the clouds into the vast expanse of sun and blue, and to be what God intended an eagle to be, the king of birds.

How does the mother eagle achieve this purpose? First, she stirs up the nest, rousing the eaglet from his lethargy, comfort, and state of dependence. Next, she topples him over the edge of the nest, forcing him to save himself by spreading his wings in flight. Quickly she hovers about him, encouraging him by her example and cries. From time to time she spreads her wings beneath him, bringing him up higher for a fresh flight. Finally sensing his weariness, she carries him back to the nest for rest and refreshment under her comforting and protecting wings.

In a similar way God providentially cares for His own. It is this fact that explains many otherwise confusing acts of His mercy. How disturbed and anxious we have been over trials which stirred us up and tore us loose from lives of peace and tranquility. How we have wondered at the seeming ruthlessness of providence which permitted us to fall headlong from sure places into the uncertainties of seemingly empty space. But looking back now, we understand that every experience was in God's love and for the fulfillment of His high and noble purposes. In spite of the anguish, we soon recognized His presence and heard His voice of comfort. Though weary, we knew His strong wings were beneath us.

Our God is a great God. Why should we be discouraged? Let us fully trust Him. May we surrender our lives so completely to Him that we shall know with unquestionable certainty that He who *can* do all things, *will* do them if we depend on Him.

Sometimes even Christians become disgusted with life and no longer wish to live. "I wish I could die," they cry in hopeless despair. Why does life become such a burden to some of God's own? Because they have not yet learned to roll their burdens on the Lord and to walk with Him, trusting Him for all He is willing to do. Those who completely rely on Him will readily realize every trial to be a blessing in disguise. "For whom the Lord loveth He chasteneth, and scourgeth every son whom He receiveth. . . . Now no chastening for the present seemeth to be joyous, but grievous: nevertheless afterward it yieldeth the peaceable fruit of righteousness unto them which are exercised thereby" (Hebrews 12:6,11). Look for "the peaceable fruit of righteousness" which God has promised in the hour of affliction. If you trust and believe Him, you will see the fruit, the blessing intended for you, though it be temporarily obscured in the trial.

Discipleship is not only costly because *suffering* must be *faced,* but because *sins* must be *forsaken.* Unquestionably, much of the believer's suffering is to bring him face to face with his sinfulness, provoking repentance. Few of us would hear the still, small voice were it not preceded by the angel of sorrow. Is it not true that most of the revivals we have known in our hearts have been the result of some sorrow or affliction? Repeatedly we have emerged from the gloom of physical illness with the sunshine of God's love flooding our hearts with renewed determination to walk closer than ever to the side of our wonderful Lord. "For he that hath suffered in the flesh hath ceased from sin." Not only did we renounce certain sins, but in humble commitment to Christ we vowed to let Him rule and reign within us. All of this was God's plan. His greatest desire for us was being effected that we might please Him and, above all else, do His blessed will. "That he no longer should live the rest of his time in his flesh to the lusts of men, but to the will of God."

How many Christians there have been who started out well, but ended up in total disgrace and failure because of neglect or a refusal to do God's will. The Lord often permits the trials of life to deliver us from such pitfalls. Christians who do not follow the will of God must suffer the price. Often this is learned through the most tragic circumstances. Do not neglect the Lord. Beware of the appeal of the flesh to rob you of happiness. There can be no real satisfaction in life unless we yield our wills completely to Christ, following in the chosen path He has prepared, rather than the way of human ingenuity.

The only place of real and lasting happiness is that spoken of by Abraham's servant: "I being in the way, the Lord led me" (Genesis 24:27). As long as you are walking along God's way, there can be no mistakes or failures. Misery and disappointment are never known to those whose wills are buried in His will. Do you want God's will for your life? I do not mean simply in some things, or in the so-called big things, but in all things. This is God's supreme desire for you. As long as you follow Him, this goal will be realized with its accompanying joyfulness and fruitfulness.

I shall never forget the young man who knocked on my cabin door late one night after an evening meeting at a youth conference. When I opened the door he quickly informed me of his spiritual distress. Though a professing Christian for most of his life, the message of the evening had enabled him to realize he was not living in the center of God's will. He was a defeated Christian, his heart devoid of joy and satisfaction.

Without any hesitation he admitted that for many months he had been resisting the Lord. I explained to him that our God is a forgiving God who desires to give immediate victory, and sought to make clear that all he needed to do was to confess his sin to the Lord and appropriate the victory made possible through Christ's death and Resurrection. At first he was reticent, feeling God would not forgive. But soon, by faith, he claimed the simple promise of God's Word and received the victory in Christ.

The next day when I met the young man it was obvious that he was rejoicing in the newly-found victory. Weeks after the conference closed he said, while visiting in our home, "I am the happiest boy on the earth." Oh, what wonderful joy there is for those who desire to walk in the center of God's will. "Thanks be to God, which giveth us the victory through our Lord Jesus Christ" (1 Corinthians 15:57).

Could it be that you are out of fellowship with the Lord? He who puts things, plans, or persons before Christ cannot be happy. True happiness can only be known by walking with the Lord daily. Only then can we know the great blessing of living in the center of His wonderful will. Dependent on His shepherding care, we shall hear His voice saying, "This is the way, walk ye in it, when ye turn to the right hand, and when ye turn to the left" (Isaiah 30:21).

Of extreme importance in living in the center of God's will is the necessity of breaking with all known sin. Lust, deceit, hate, gossip, covetousness—all must go. These and other sins may have marked the believer's past, but they should never characterize the present. "For the time past of our life may suffice us to have wrought the will of the Gentiles, when we walked in lasciviousness, lusts, excess of wine, revellings, banquetings, and abominable idolatries." These and other sins of the flesh are abominable to the Lord. There is no power in unconsecrated fleshly living. "For they that are after the flesh do mind the things of the flesh; but they that are after the Spirit the things of the Spirit. For to be carnally minded is death; but to be spiritually minded is life and peace. Because the carnal mind is enmity against God: for it is not subject to the law of God, neither indeed can be. So then they that are in the flesh cannot please God" (Romans 8:5-8). Make certain that all sin is forsaken and that you follow Christ closely.

Indeed it is costly to be a follower of Christ. But it is wonderful! Sometimes discipleship even costs us friendships. Unsaved friends and even loved ones often make a travesty of the believer's faithful witness to the Saviour. This is to be expected. "Wherein they think it strange that ye run not with them to the same excess of riot, speaking evil of you." We must not be disturbed. *Scoffing* must be *forgotten.* This may not be easy, but it is part of the cost of discipleship.

Scoffers may accuse us of acting queer, and even make fun of our consecrated efforts to serve Christ. We shall be considered peculiar because of refusal to take cocktails or to listen to smutty, suggestive stories. Unkind and evil things will be said about us. Forget it! All this must be accepted in the realm of discipleship. Anyone who takes a positive stand for Christ and sincerely bears witness to His saving grace will be criticized. Nevertheless, stand! Let no one deter you from faithful service.

Once, after a message, I was approached by a young mother who had been a Christian only a few years. Having been converted since her marriage, she was greatly burdened for her husband's salvation. She came to me extremely disturbed because her husband, as well as his family and her own family, constantly made light of her faith in Christ and criticized her unjustly because she refused to have a part in their worldly practices. She was much comforted when I informed her that such attitudes were to be expected. Out-and-out believers in Christ will always be criticized by the ungodly. The Lord has told us, "If the world hate you, ye know it hated Me before it hated you. If ye were of the world, the world would love his own: but because ye are not of the world, but I have chosen you out of the world, therefore the world hateth you" (John 15:18-19). Those who love Christ and denounce the world, standing against its evil practices, will be hated by the world.

Of course, not all Christians are hated by the world. The reason is that they love the world more than they love Christ. For those who surrender all, to live for the Saviour, ridicule must be expected.

How few of God's people are willing to take a stand in the face of ridicule and persecution. It is so easy to drift with the crowd, to fit into one's environment. Those who love Christ will pay the price of hardship. It would have been very easy for Moses to yield to sin and relax himself in the comforts of Pharaoh's court. But this was not for God's man. "By faith Moses, when he was come to years, refused to be called the son of Pharaoh's daughter; Choosing rather to suffer affliction with the people of God, than to enjoy the pleasures of sin for a season; Esteeming the reproach of Christ greater riches than the treasures in Egypt" (Hebrews 11:24-26). Let us never be ashamed of the fact that we belong to Christ. We must let the unsaved know where we stand, refusing to drift along with the worldly crowd, living and walking with God's own people, doing His will and pleasing Him.

Be assured the Lord will have the final word with those who ridicule the people of God. For these "shall give account to Him that is ready to judge the quick and the dead." Judgment is impending. Some day all unbelievers will stand before God in judgment. "It is appointed unto men once to die, but after this the judgment" (Hebrews 9:27). The ungodly may criticize followers of Christ, but God declares, "Therefore thou art inexcusable, O man, whosoever thou art that judgest: for wherein thou judgest another, thou condemnest thyself; for thou that judgest doest the same things. But we are sure that the judgment of God is according to truth against them which commit such things" (Romans 2:1-2).

God rarely speaks about judgment without giving an invitation to the unsaved to respond to His love. "For this cause was the gospel preached also to them that are dead, that they might be judged according to men in the flesh, but live according to God in the spirit." It seems that the "dead" of whom Peter writes are the unsaved who are "dead in trespasses and sin."

As in Peter's day, so now the gospel is being proclaimed to them. They will be "judged according to men in the flesh." That is, even if they believe, they will suffer physical death, which is the judgment upon all flesh. But if they are willing to trust in Christ, they will "live according to God in the spirit." They will live eternally as possessors of life through Christ.

God longs that all have this life. Jesus came "that they might have life, and that they might have it more abundantly" (John 10:10). Do you know Him personally, or is He just a name to you? Is He the Lord of your life? Have you committed yourself to Him? If not, come to Him now. Let nothing keep Him out of your life. Heed His Word and believe. "Come now, and let us reason together, saith the Lord: though your sins be as scarlet, they shall be as white as snow; though they be red like crimson, they shall be as wool" (Isaiah 1:18).

26

CLOSE TO THE END

"But the end of all things is at hand: be ye therefore sober, and watch unto prayer. And above all things have fervent charity among yourselves: for charity shall cover the multitude of sins. Use hospitality one to another without grudging. As every man hath received the gift, even so minister the same one to another, as good stewards of the manifold grace of God. If any man speak, let him speak as the oracles of God; if any man minister, let him do it as of the ability which God giveth: that God in all things may be glorified through Jesus Christ, to whom be praise and dominion for ever and ever. Amen."—1 Peter 4:7-11

Divinely inspired, Peter declares, "the end of all things is at hand." Though penned almost two thousand years ago, this statement is by no means out of date. In fact, existing conditions in the world today suggest strongly that the fulfillment of this prophecy is very near. It could be said that Peter's statement is headline news, right up to the minute. Every newspaper in the world could well make this its top news item and be wholly accurate, for it has to do with the return of Christ, which appears to be near at hand.

There have been many days of outstanding importance in the history of the world. It was a momentous day when God created the heavens and the earth, and all things therein. It was a cataclysmic day when God cleansed the world of corruption and sinfulness by a flood. It was a significant day when the Saviour was born into the world to provide life and liberty for hopeless souls. It was a solemn and memorable day when, grown to manhood, the Saviour hung on the cross to shed His atoning blood to provide the only remedy for man's sin. It was a victorious day when for all time He conquered death by His Resurrection. It was a notable day when He ascended on high to His place of authority at the right hand of the Father. But the day of days is yet to come, when He shall return with power and glory to rule the world in righteousness. It is my personal conviction that all history now points to one event: the visible, bodily, premillennial return of Jesus Christ to reign as Lord of Lords and King of Kings over all the kingdoms and powers of the earth.

Time cannot nullify prophecy. The promise given to the disciples by the angels at our Lord's ascension is still genuine and true, "Ye men of Galilee, why stand ye gazing up into heaven? this same Jesus, which is taken up from you into heaven, shall so come in the manner as ye have seen Him go into heaven" (Acts 1:11). There can be no doubt as to the meaning of this text. Christ will come back again in the same form in which He left.

We need to remind ourselves again that Peter is writing to persecuted believers who have been suffering unmercifully at the hands of ruthless and godless men. He seeks to inject hope into their downcast spirits by reminding them that "the end of all things is at hand." It is obvious that he meant that all undeserved persecution on the earth, resulting from sin and wickedness, would cease with Christ's return.

Peter as well as the other New Testament writers not only believed Christ *could* return in their day; they wholeheartedly *expected* Him. Because of his avowed anticipation of our Lord's Second Advent, the apostle emphasizes some of the duties of believers who share the scriptural view of the "blessed hope."

During our Lord's sojourning in this world, He spoke of certain signs that would presage His coming again. Peter considers several of these signs in relationship to the Christian's obligation while waiting for the Lord Jesus to come again.

Please do not misunderstand. In speaking of signs we are by no means setting a date for Christ's return. I personally believe He is coming soon. My understanding of prophetic truth suggests this very emphatically. Beyond that we must not trespass. Anyone who endeavors to set times or dates for the return of our Lord, presumptuously makes himself greater than Christ and more authoritative than the Word of God. Our Lord clearly stated, "But of that day and hour knoweth no man, no, not the angels of heaven, but my Father only" (Matthew 24:36). "It is not for you to know the times or the seasons, which the Father hath put in His own power" (Acts 1:7).

On the other hand, our Lord reproved the ecclesiastical authorities of His day for ignoring important prophetical signs. "Ye hypocrites, ye can discern the face of the sky; but can ye not discern the signs of the times?" (Matthew 16:3) We must not be guilty of this same error. Let us "search the Scriptures" to see what God has said about the future.

First of all, Peter deals with the *fear* sign. The Lord Jesus foretold the sense of fear and tension that would dominate the world prior to His Second Coming. "And there shall be signs in the sun, and in the moon, and in the stars; and upon the earth distress of nations, with perplexity; the sea and the waves roaring; Men's hearts failing them for fear, and for looking after those things which are coming on the earth: for the powers of heaven shall be shaken. And then shall they see the Son of man coming in a cloud with power and great glory. And when these things begin to come to pass, then look up, and lift up your heads; for your redemption draweth nigh" (Luke 21:25-28).

Because of the torment of fear characterizing the last days, man is groping in every direction for a possible solution. More and more his search for security seems hopeless and vain. He has devised the United Nations in the cherished hope that it might somehow effect a miracle to banish arms and warfare and produce good will and peace among all men. But like its predecessor, the League of Nations, the United Nations has proved itself impotent to perform such a miracle. It never will! For this is not God's plan for peace.

The only peace the world can ever know is that to be realized when the Prince of Peace, Christ Jesus, returns. Any attempt of man to produce a just and lasting peace will be as futile and ineffectual as the building of the tower of Babel. Of course, the United Nations has merit. It has already proved to be a valuable instrument for bringing the nations of the world closer together for a clear understanding of mutual problems and perplexities. But beyond this there is no answer but Christ.

What about fear? Is the believer to be alarmed and troubled by the uncertainties of the age? God's answer is, "Be ye therefore sober." That is, be sober-minded. Have a sound mind. Do not allow yourself to be distraught and disturbed by fear of any kind. "Be ye also patient; stablish your hearts: for the coming of the Lord draweth nigh" (James 5:8). Trust in the Lord. Rest in Him. Do not become overwrought by atomic scares. Never forget, the God who created this world is still on the throne. He will never allow mere puny man to blow His world apart. The hymn writer has given us an assuring truth:

> "This is my Father's world;
> Oh, let me ne'er forget
> Though the wrong seem oft so strong,
> God is the ruler yet."

Peter further urges God's people to "watch unto prayer." This suggests the sign of *prayerlessness*. Just as the disciples were commissioned to watch and pray until our Lord returned from the agony of the Garden of Gethsemane, so the Lord has enjoined His Church to be faithful in this same ministry of intercession until He returns from Heaven. "Take ye heed, watch and pray: for ye know not when the time is" (Mark 13:33). Like the slumbering disciples in the garden, instead of praying and watching, many in the Church of Christ are sleeping. While the enemy hoodwinks the world into thinking the Bible is a book of fables, salvation is unnecessary, and the Church is useless and meaningless, inconsistent Christians are failing to call on God for the mighty power to resist the powers of Satan.

Probably prayerlessness has maimed the power of the Church more than any other sin. Yet we call ourselves New Testament churches. Are we abiding by the New Testament in respect to prayer? From the Book of Acts we note that the New Testament Church discovered itself through prayer. While about one hundred and twenty believers were assembled in one place at one time, where they had been in constant fellowship for ten days, doing little else than praying, the Spirit of God fell upon them in unprecedented power, later scattering them in every direction to proclaim the unsearchable riches of Christ. Those people believed and practiced prayer.

Few churches really believe in prayer today. Many abandoned the midweek prayer service years ago. Most of those trying to preserve it cannot get more than a "corporal's guard" out to pray. A few centuries ago, repentant souls would come frequently at the conclusion of services, tearfully seeking salvation. Men and women used to pray for souls. Entire nights were spent in expectant prayer before services on the Lord's day. Saints of God, burdened for lost souls, would gather to cry together to the living God to save men.

Doubtless you have heard of the old Fulton Street prayer meetings in New York where scores of businessmen would unite during their lunch hour to pray. They brought unsaved business associates who, in the midst of the prayer meeting, would become so convicted by the Holy Spirit that they would cry out to God for salvation. We do not hear much about this kind of praying any more. In fact, we hear very little about prayer at all because few Christians are concerned enough. This is another mark of the end of the age. Prayerlessness! Oh, Christians, do not be deceived by the devil. "Watch unto prayer."

Another sign of Christ's return is the increasing intensity of the sin of *hatred*. Certainly little need be said about wars, strife, and division existent in this present evil age. By His divine foreknowledge our Lord spoke of coming division and strife between nations to be evident in the last days, all of which results from the sin of hate. "And ye shall hear of wars and rumours of wars: see that ye be not troubled: for all these things must come to pass, but the end is not yet. For nation shall rise against nation, and kingdom against kingdom: and there shall be famines, and pestilences, and earthquakes, in divers places. All these are the beginning of sorrows" (Matthew 24:6-8).

An even worse tragedy is that this same spirit of hatred has found its way into the Church of Christ. As a solution for the evil, Peter pleads, "Above all things have fervent charity [deep love] among yourselves." The Church should be marked by "deep love" among the believers, rather than by hatred. This kind of love is forgiving love which God implants in the heart of the believer through the Holy Spirit. When offended, this love will not permit the true Christian to bear a grudge, for it will "cover the multitude of sins." That is, it will veil over the offense from the eye of the offended, enabling him to forgive completely, leaving no ill feeling in his heart toward the offender.

The forgiveness the Lord expects His people to practice should not be born of a sense of compulsion. Rather it should be "without grudging." "Grudging" as used here means to forgive merely because God commands it in the Bible, not because of a hospitable desire truly to forgive. I have known Christians to say regarding someone with whom they have experienced a strained relationship, "I love them, but I don't like them." They love only out of duty, because the Bible teaches that love is obligatory. Such a spirit is not satisfactory to God. Possessors of God's love forgive in such a way as to be kindly and considerate in every possible dealing with the offender. Through the Lord's strength Christians are enabled not only to forgive, but to forget. To harbor resentment is not true forgiveness. May our blessed Lord give us grace to love even as He has loved us, that hatred shall find no place in our hearts.

Next the apostle considers the *selfishness* sign. All of us are aware of the devastating sin of selfishness. Everyone seems to be suffering to some degree from this dreaded malady. God has told us that this evil will be easily recognizable in the days just prior to our Lord's return. "This know also, that in the last days perilous times shall come. For men shall be lovers of their own selves" (2 Timothy 3:1-2). The sin of selfishness is one of the commonest sins of all time. So often the Lord is almost wholly excluded as we speak of *my* business, *my* home, *my* family, or *my* church as though we are owners. It should always be remembered that all we have has come from God's hand. God gives, but He never gives away. He gives that we may be conscientious stewards of the trust committed unto us. This should in no way tend to selfishness or pride. Everything belongs to Him.

Because they are so selfish, men in business often lie, deceive, and cheat to achieve coveted goals. Our penitentiaries are crowded with people who have given little thought to the rights of others and have considered only their own selfish interests. A sad feature is that the tentacles of this sin have gotten such a hold on the hearts of some Christians that they have lost all sight of their high calling in Christ. Their selfish pride permits few considerations for others and their needs. They live for one person alone—*self.* They are vividly portrayed in the man who daily prayed, "Lord, bless me and my wife, my son John and his wife, us four and no more. Amen." To such Peter writes, "As every man hath received the gift, even so minister the same one to another, as good stewards of the manifold grace of God." The "gift" we have received in Christ is His marvelous grace.

Since He has showered His all-availing grace upon us, we should unreservedly reveal it in our attitudes towards others, ministering the grace of God, with no thoughts of self.

Another of the important signs of the end is *apostasy*. Paul, in speaking of "the day of Christ" which will be the day when the Lord Jesus returns, says, "That day shall not come, except there come a falling away first" (2 Thessalonians 2:3). He bears out this same truth in 1 Timothy 4:1: "Now the Spirit speaketh expressly, that in the latter times some shall depart from the faith, giving heed to seducing spirits, and doctrines of devils." Also in 2 Peter 3:3, Peter warns, "Knowing this first, that there shall come in the last days scoffers, walking after their own lusts."

These scoffers are infesting the Church of Jesus Christ as never before. Not so long ago they were on the outside doing their scoffing and laughing at the children of God. Now they have "crept in unawares," as Jude reminds us (Jude 4), seeking by subtle teaching to turn away the hearts of the people of God from the truth. The Word of God is being discredited and its authority and inspiration derided. To this end, Peter declares, "If any man speak, let him speak as the oracles of God."

Those who stand behind the sacred desk are to declare the entire message of God as revealed in His eternal Word. This leaves no room for excuses or apologies as to what God has said. "The law of the Lord is perfect, converting the soul: the testimony of the Lord is sure, making wise the simple" (Psalm 19:7).

God has promised to bless and honor His word whenever it is proclaimed in truth. He has said nothing about blessing our illustrations or jokes, but He has emphatically declared, "So shall My word be that goeth forth out of My mouth: it shall not return unto Me void, but it shall accomplish that which I please, and it shall prosper in the thing whereto I sent it" (Isaiah 55:11). Consequently, we must in faithfulness hold forth His infallible and unchangeable Word. If men and women are to be saved, they will be reached only through the Word of God. "So then faith cometh by hearing, and hearing by the word of God" (Romans 10:17).

In addition to the faithful proclamation of the truth of the Scriptures, Peter emphasizes the necessity of undeviating dependence on the power of God. "If any man minister, let him do it as of the ability which God giveth." No one can preach God's Word effectively in human strength. If you are blessed by a sermon, praise the Lord, not the preacher. God's messages are the result not of human ingenuity, but of divine direction. "Not by might, nor by power, but by My spirit, saith the Lord of hosts" (Zechariah 4:6). How frequently men stand in the pulpits in the strength of their scholarship and facile speech, excluding Christ while parading mere human wisdom.

A friend tells of attending a morning service in a large, beautiful church and hearing Dr. Silver-Tongue and him glorified. But in the evening, he attended another church and heard Jesus Christ, and Him crucified.

God is not looking for great orators. He is not especially interested in pulpit eloquence. He is concerned about a manifestation of His power. For what reason? "That God in all things may be glorified through Jesus Christ, to whom be praise and dominion for ever and ever." To this Peter shouts, "Amen." Those who love Christ will affirm his "Amen." So be it, Lord!

What could be more important for any believer than to glorify God through Jesus Christ? Everything we do and all we say should be to this end. Let nothing interfere with this high and noble purpose. For some day soon our living Lord will return. Then "the earth shall be filled with the knowledge of the glory of the Lord, as the waters cover the sea" (Habakkuk 2:14).

How vital that we enjoy a foretaste of the "glory of the Lord" right now in the closeness of walking with Him. The question is, are we right with Him? Are we living in fellowship with Him? Are we anxious to see Him? Can we pray as did John: "Even so, come, Lord Jesus" (Revelation 22:20)?

Is there anything between us and our Lord? If so, let us confess it immediately. Let nothing bar the joy of His glory in our lives. May we fully commit everything to Him at once, that we may be ready and rejoicing in the hope of His return.

27

WORTHWHILE ADVICE

"Beloved, think it not strange concerning the fiery trial which is to try you, as though some strange thing happened unto you: But rejoice, inasmuch as ye are partakers of Christ's sufferings; that, when His glory shall be revealed, ye may be glad also with exceeding joy. If ye be reproached for the name of Christ, happy are ye; for the spirit of glory and of God resteth upon you: on their part He is evil spoken of, but on your part He is glorified. But let none of you suffer as a murderer, or as a thief, or as an evildoer, or as a busybody in other men's matters. Yet if any man suffer as a Christian, let him not be ashamed; but let him glorify God on this behalf."—1 Peter 4:12-16

Having endured numerous hardships and afflictions as a servant of the Lord Jesus Christ, Peter was well qualified to write on the subject of suffering. After offering encouragement to the persecuted believers by reminding them of the "blessed hope," he proceeds by proffering worthwhile advice for those confronted by the trials of life.

How should the believer react when he finds himself thrust suddenly into some "fiery trial"? The apostle first replies to this question by telling us what our attitude should not be: "Beloved, think it not strange concerning the fiery trial which is to try you, as though some strange thing happened unto you." One who is truly born of God's Spirit should never be shocked or dismayed by adversity; it is not possible for anything to enter the believer's life without the sanction of our Heavenly Father. How necessary when trial comes that the believer reassure himself from God's Word that it is the Lord's doing. God makes no mistakes. Nor can He fail His own. Trials are to be expected. For this reason every follower of Christ is commanded to "endure hardness, as a good soldier of Jesus Christ" (2 Timothy 2:3).

It is so easy to fall into the common fault of self-pity, even questioning God's infallible providence. In his positive approach to the subject of trial, Peter suggests a workable solution to such temptations: "Rejoice, inasmuch as ye are partakers of Christ's sufferings; that, when His glory shall be revealed, ye may be glad also with exceeding joy." Do not feel sorry for yourself. Rejoice! It is a privilege for the servant to suffer for his Master. But even more, rejoice in the fact that your Master lives. "His glory shall be revealed." He is not the great "I was," but "I Am." Were He but dust and ashes in a Syrian tomb, complaining would be in order. He lives and someday He will reveal His glory to all, when He returns. But be sure His glory is being manifested in His own at this moment, producing the "exceeding joy" as they rely on Him for His tender care and unfailing grace.

Because we worship the Living Christ, and cherish the hope of His soon return, there should be no room for doubt in our minds, even when surrounded by trial. The true believer must never ask God, "Why?" Even though sorely tried, may our faith never become so weak and small that we question God's unerring providence. Rejoice! Trust! Believe! Our Lord has not promised that all our questions will be answered now. Jesus said in John 13:7, "What I do thou knowest not now; but thou shalt know hereafter." There is coming a day, "hereafter," when we shall "know even as we are known," but not now. Until God's time we must "walk by faith" and rely implicitly on Him.

So often we hear Christians lamenting, "Why, oh why, did this happen to me?" Why did this little child come in contact with the deadly virus? Why could he not fight it off? Why was the road wet? Why was he on that curve at that particular moment? Why did he meet that girl who has brought so much misery into his life?

There are scores of events in your life about which you could ask, "Why?" But I wonder if it would really console us if all our "why's" were answered. Suppose we did have a scientific, philosophical explanation for all these perplexing questions, would that be the solution? I am sure it would not. A child is not comforted by being told why his toy broke, or why he pinched his finger in the door. He is consoled by the fact of his mother's presence and her expression of love and sympathy. Indeed it is true, we are all little children at heart, and God often permits trials as a medium for a further illustration of His marvelous and unsurpassable care for His own.

Are not all Christians familiar with God's love and care? Why must we suffer so many trials and afflictions? Simply because we forget very quickly. It is so easy to become preoccupied with "things" to the extent that we get our eyes off the Lord. Repeatedly He must remind us that material things are merely transitory. He is eternal. Our constant temptation is to fix our sight on things we see, completely disregarding the unseen.

Recall John the Baptist's imprisonment at the height of his ministry, as recorded in Matthew 11. It seems obvious that he had become so occupied with his work for the Lord that He was forgetting that which was of supreme importance, fellowship with the Lord Himself. How do we know? The question he sent to the Lord Jesus reveals it. John had been with Christ and had seen Him perform miracles. When thrown into prison he turned his thoughts to himself.

Most of us praise the Lord for His goodness while all, as we see it, goes well. But when faced with discomfort and affliction, we feel God has forsaken us.

Probably John began to question the reason for his dilemma. "Why should I suffer like this? I have been serving God. Why does He allow this?" Suddenly he calls two of his disciples and rushes them off to Jesus to ask, "Art thou He that should come, or do we look for another?" (Matthew 11:3) Formerly John had boldly declared of Jesus, "Behold the Lamb of God, which taketh away the sin of the world" (John 1:29). But it is different now. Like most of us, John misinterpreted the purpose of trial.

Jesus promptly sent John's disciples back to him with the message, "Go and show John *again* those things which ye do hear and see: The blind receive their sight, and the lame walk, the lepers are cleansed, and the deaf hear, the dead are raised up, and the poor have the gospel preached to them. And blessed is he, whosoever shall not be offended in Me" (Matthew 11:4-6).

Our Lord was endeavoring to convey to John the lesson we need so badly, that the Christ who was in yesterday is also the same Christ of today and tomorrow. He changes not! Trials are not a sign of His failure or neglect, though we cannot understand why a particular trial has befallen us. We must never forget, "It is the glory of God to conceal a thing" (Proverbs 25:2). He knows best. Leave the purpose with Him while you unreservedly rely on His promises.

God says in Psalm 125:2, "As the mountains are round about Jerusalem, so the Lord is round about His people from henceforth even for ever." After thousands of years the mountains still stand "round about Jerusalem." It is forever assuring to know that even if the mountains were to crumble to dust, their Creator would still care for His people. David declared, "O Lord God of hosts, who is a strong Lord like unto Thee? or to Thy faithfulness round about Thee?" (Psalm 89:8) No, let us never be surprised at trials. Let us never pity ourselves, but rejoice, inasmuch as we know our wonderful Lord lives to undertake for every care of those who love Him.

Peter provided additional encouragement by suggesting that however grievous and painful the affliction may be, the sincere follower of Christ may find repose and rejoice in the fact that "the spirit of glory and of God resteth upon you." This is to say, God is with you. Let the Holy Spirit indelibly write this simple truth on your mind. The Lord will never leave you. Even though you may forsake Him hundreds of times, His love will not waver.

False comforters will seek to discourage. You will be "reproached for the name of Christ." They will try to persuade you to forget about God, since by allowing such a tragedy, He seemingly has forgotten you. Some will even say, as did Job's wife, "Curse God, and die" (Job 2:9). Never listen to such diabolical nonsense. What do unbelievers know about the providence of God? Peter tells us, "On their part He is evil spoken of." Do not permit them to discourage you. Fix your eyes on the Lord and keep them there. You belong to Him. "The spirit of glory and of God resteth upon you."

A story is told of an atheist whose pumpkin crop was unusually good while that of a Christian neighbor was frozen. He approached the Christian, asking, "Why did your God allow your pumpkins to freeze? Mine are all right." The Christian, in humility realizing his own need for chastening from the Lord, replied, "God is not raising pumpkins. He is raising men." Here is an important truth: God permits the fires of affliction to try us in order to make us better men and women for Himself. It is so necessary that He burn out the dross. Consequently, in acknowledgment that trials are full of purpose, we should "glory in tribulations also: knowing that tribulation worketh patience; And patience, experience; and experience, hope: And hope maketh not ashamed; because the love of God is shed abroad in our hearts by the Holy Ghost which is given unto us" (Romans 5:3-5).

Someone may ask, "What about Satan? I realize God is with me. But does not Satan bring many trials and tragedies into the believer's life?" That is quite true. Much of the sorrow we experience comes from Satan. But be sure of this: everything and everyone including the devil himself is under the jurisdiction and control of God Almighty.

Frequently the Lord uses the devil to fulfill divine purposes. But Satan is under orders. He may not trespass beyond God-placed boundaries. Satan was granted some latitude in afflicting

Job, but at the same time he was permitted to go only so far. "And the Lord said unto Satan, Behold, all that he hath is in thy power; only upon himself put not forth thine hand" (Job 1:12).

Joseph's wicked brothers were satanically inspired. But could they defeat God's purposes? Of course not. Every lie spoken, and every wicked deed, was counteracted by God's glory and resulted in Joseph's deliverance from the clutches of Satan. We have Joseph's own testimony about this: "Ye thought evil against me; but God meant it unto good" (Genesis 50:20). Though Satan thought he had ensnared Joseph, God proved otherwise. Every diabolical act of the "wicked one" is ultimately transformed by God into praise and honor.

Dr. G. Campbell Morgan said in a lecture that his friend, Dr. Samuel Chadwick, had told him this incident from his boyhood life. Like most boys he was fond of hanging around a blacksmith shop. He watched the blacksmith hold a piece of iron in the fire with the tongs, while he worked the bellows to make the iron white-hot. Then he watched the blacksmith take the iron out and lay it upon the anvil, and with a small hammer give it a slight tap. A big fellow on the other side would then strike it a terrific blow on the same spot.

One day the young Chadwick said to the blacksmith, "You don't do much good with that little hammer, do you?" The blacksmith laughed as he replied, "Not much. I only show the big fellow where to hit with the sledge hammer." Dr. Chadwick in commenting on this incident said, "I tell you, God makes the devil sweat to make saints of His people."

Nothing can enter the believer's life without the divine permission of our living Lord. Do not listen to Satan. He would have you think otherwise. The Lord may allow trial to touch our lives, but He says, "The Lord will not cast off for ever: But though He cause grief, yet will He have compassion according to the multitude of His mercies" (Lamentations 3:31-32). Because of this we may confidently affirm with David, "I have set the Lord always before me: because He is at my right hand, I shall not be moved" (Psalm 16:8).

Peter next offers a word of caution. "But let none of you suffer as a murderer, or as a thief, or as an evildoer, or as a busybody in other men's matters." Trials should provoke self-examination. Not all suffering is the result of sin in our lives, but very often it is. It is well to consider trials as a warning signal informing us that we may be disobeying the laws of God. Though God does not send trials to punish us, yet He uses them to correct us. They are remedial rather than penal.

Are you suffering some affliction at this moment? It might be well to check up. Are you a murderer? Is there any evidence of hatred in your heart toward another? Are you a thief? Have you stolen someone's reputation by false accusation? Are you an evildoer? Have you schemed and connived to deceive? Are you a busybody? Have you been guilty of interfering in the affairs of others or of gossiping? Do you want to know why you must suffer? Maybe you will find your answer in your own heart. It could be. God's desire is that the heart be kept clean. He constantly scrutinizes its condition. David declared, "O Lord, Thou hast searched me, and known me. Thou knowest my downsitting and mine uprising, Thou understandest my thought afar off" (Psalm 139:1-2).

Let us not try to play fast and loose with God. We may deceive others and even ourselves, but never God. If we refuse or neglect to judge our own sins, it is sometimes necessary for Him to use the knife; and when God operates, He uses no anesthetic, for He cannot remove the trouble and leave us asleep at the same time. Therefore the process is painful. We must be probed, roused, agitated, and disturbed, in order that we may see ourselves as He sees us.

Rather than view your trial only as a hardship to be escaped from as soon as possible, cry out to God for power to correct your faults, errors, and sins. Use it as God intended, to challenge your soul. Accept it thankfully as an opportunity to get closer to the Lord, to seek more of His presence and to commit yourself more fully to His will. Yield even your trial to Him as a delight and a blessing rather than a curse. Accept it as an auxiliary rather than a burden. It was Andrew Murray who said, "Every loss is meant to be filled up by His presence. Every sorrow is meant to make His fellowship more to us."

"Yet if any man suffer as a Christian, let him not be ashamed; but let him glorify God on this behalf." Here is the conclusion of the matter. "Suffer as a Christian." Do not grumble. Do not complain. Praise the Lord for whatever comes, for it is from His hand. You may be sure that anything coming from God's hand will not be injurious.

It is marvelous to know that because God sends the trial He understands all about it. Because He understands, He will undertake. He knows precisely how frail we are and exactly how much we can bear. Christ, who experienced all kinds of suffering Himself, is well aware of our needs. Thus we are promised in the Word, "For in that He Himself hath suffered being tempted, He is able to succour them that are tempted" (Hebrews 2:18).

Often while approaching a bridge we have noticed a sign displaying the load limit. It may have read, "Load limit 5 tons," or "Load limit 10 tons." Of course these signs are there for a definite purpose. They are a protection for life and property. Overloaded trucks that would endanger safety may not be driven over the bridge.

Though Christians carry no signs visible to others, our Lord knows the load limit of each of His own. He will never permit the load limit to be violated. If it is a matter of physical suffering or the burdens of life, His word assures us, "He knoweth our frame" (Psalm 103:14), or more literally, *our fashioning, that of which we are made and how we are put together*. He knows how much we can bear and never permits any sorrow to burden us beyond the load limit. "There hath no temptation taken you but such as is common to man: but God is faithful, who will not suffer you to be tempted above that ye are able; but will with the temptation also make a way to escape, that ye may be able to bear it" (1 Corinthians 10:13).

Though even more concerned than we about the trial, God may make us wait. Let us not try to rush Him. He who would "suffer as a Christian," glorifying God "on this behalf," must learn how to wait on the Lord. So often we pray and expect an immediate answer. We "seek" and expect to "find." But there is one factor we seldom consider in our zeal, the time factor.

In John 5 we read of a man who learned the art of waiting. For thirty-eight years he sought deliverance from his physical plague. Think of it, thirty-eight years! Somehow I feel the impotent man of John 5 learned this great lesson as he waited at Bethesda's pool. And so did others. Abraham waited a quarter of a century after the promise until Isaac was born. Moses waited half a century till the promise of God to deliver Israel became a reality. Noah waited more than a century from the promise till the flood. Let us not become overanxious. We are subject to the element of time. God is not. With Him a thousand years is but a day. All eternity is to Him but one great *today*.

Above all, let us learn the important lesson of trust, realizing every trial is designed to bring about our growth and development. Rejoice and glorify God knowing that whatever He sends is best. Regardless of the affliction, say to yourself, "Why art thou cast down, O my soul? and why art thou disquieted within me? *hope thou in God.*" (Psalm 42:11).

28

JUDGMENT

"For the time is come that judgment must begin at the house of God: and if it first begin at us, what shall the end be of them that obey not the gospel of God? And if the righteous scarcely be saved, where shall the ungodly and the sinner appear? Wherefore let them that suffer according to the will of God commit the keeping of their souls to Him in well doing, as unto a faithful Creator."—1 Peter 4:17-19

In presenting his treatise on suffering Peter now speaks of suffering as "judgment." First of all, he tells us where this judgment should begin. "For the time is come that judgment must begin at the house of God." This may seem to be a most unusual place to commence judgment. Would it not be more reasonable for God to inflict chastening first on those who frequent the taverns or the brothels or other dens of iniquity? Should He not be more concerned about the profane, the unkind, and the immoral? Are not these the ones who deserve the rod of discipline and correction? To us such a course of action seems more logical, but evidently not to God. In fact, throughout the Scriptures we frequently find God judging His own people while little seems to be done about the worldling.

In Ezekiel 8 the Lord gives the prophet a vision of the extreme wickedness and debauchery of His nation. Ezekiel was instructed not only to warn his people of condemnation to come on the land because of their sin, but to wield the sword of judgment himself. Where should he begin? The answer is found in Ezekiel 9:6: "Begin at My sanctuary." But why? With all the iniquity abounding elsewhere, why first afflict the people of God? Simply because if those who profess to be the Lord's people get right with Him, forsaking evil and yielding themselves in complete obedience to His will, the impact of such consecration will not be felt in the believing heart alone, but also among those who have not yet trusted in the Lord.

Revival has never begun among the unsaved. In fact, the term "revival" should be applied to believers only. Revival does not mean evangelism. Though the words are often used synonymously and interchangeably, there is a profound difference between them. *Evangelism* is the faithful proclamation of the gospel in an earnest attempt to reach the lost for Christ. *Revival* is a work of the Holy Spirit among Christians, convicting them of their sin and backsliding and drawing them into a life of full surrender to Christ as Lord. Revival is a spiritual awakening among those who have already come to Christ for salvation.

We need revival! It is my opinion that God's greatest desire for the Church today is revival. Certainly He is concerned that we sacrifice and labor to reach a dying world with the gospel of salvation. He longs that our hearts burn with a consuming passion to reach into every corner of the earth to pluck precious souls from the fire of unbelief. But until the saints are awakened to their own hearts' need of complete yieldness to Christ, little will be accomplished in attracting the lost to the Saviour.

One evangelist has said, "I would rather wake up five hundred Christians than convert five hundred sinners. For if five hundred Christians are really stirred, they soon will win five hundred sinners to Christ." Only as believers have a real experience with the Lord will the unsaved come to know Him. It is for this reason that Peter says, "The time is come that judgment must begin at the house of God."

Let us not stop short of God's best for us. If we expect to be fruitful, Christ must be everything to us. Unless the Lord

Jesus is the Master of our lives, we shall know little of the Holy Spirit's power. Without the energy of this power, all our efforts for the Lord will be weak and feeble. Though we may have great churches with attractive buildings, beautiful music, and eloquent sermons; and though we may have organizations, clubs, and interesting programs; these are not enough. For it is "Not by might, nor by power, but by my spirit, saith the Lord of hosts" (Zechariah 4:6). There must be a mighty manifestation of the power of God in our hearts, which can come only through a full submission to Christ.

Recall the occasion when Paul met with the congregation at Ephesus and asked that the elders give a report of progress. They bragged about their pastor, Apollos, a striking and impressive individual who could speak with spellbinding eloquence. They were also proud of the fine personnel of their congregation, naming such eminent people as Aquilla and Priscilla, who were tentmakers extraordinary. They discussed the excellent opportunity and potential for Christianity in their city.

After they finished their report, Paul ignored their boasting and asked, "Have ye received the Holy Ghost since ye believed?" (Acts 19:2) The Ephesians were chagrined. They looked at one another in embarrassment. They had considered everything but that which was of greatest importance. Immediately, they changed their course, and shortly afterward the Holy Spirit came upon the members of that church in mighty power. A revival sprang up in the city of Ephesus which shook the entire population. Books of magic were burned in the city square. Even the image-makers' entire industry was threatened as new-born Christians ceased to buy replicas of the goddess Diana.

It might be well for every professed follower of the Lord Jesus to ask himself, "Have I received the Holy Ghost since I believed? Is my life a demonstration of what God's Spirit can do through one fully committed to the will of Christ?" Let us not miss God's best. Go all the way with the Lord. "Be filled with the Spirit" (Ephesians 5:18). I am convinced that if Christians all over the world were to get on their knees, without sham and sanctimony, and were to yield completely to the fullness of the Holy Spirit, fervently claiming the promises of God's Word, the entire condition of our civilization could be changed in twenty-four hours.

But before this can be realized, there must be judgment. We reiterate: "Judgment must begin at the house of God." What is meant by "judgment"? It means personal sin in the believer must be realized and acknowledged to the Lord, followed by sincere repentance. Too often there is realization and acknowledgment, but repentance is lacking. God says in 2 Chronicles 7:14, "If My people, which are called by My name, shall humble themselves, and pray, and seek My face, and *turn from their wicked ways;* then will I hear from heaven, and will forgive their sin, and will heal their land." To "turn" from sin is to repent of it, allowing the Holy Spirit to put it out of our lives completely.

It is at this point that so many Christians fail and continue to live in defeat as they coddle and pamper their pet sin. Get the victory! Judge yourself or God must judge. As Peter has already suggested in this Epistle, God's judgment is usually severe, for He is a jealous God. He wants you to enjoy His best. He will not be satisfied with less.

Sin usually appears attractive and pleasant. Were this not so, we would not clamor after it. Regrettably, we overlook the fact that it is also very costly and ultimately painful. For this reason the child of God should learn to hate it, praying daily for constant victory. It is difficult for any of us to realize how terrible sin actually is. This is because we are still in the flesh, living in a body of sin. But as we search the Scriptures closely and realize God's estimation of sin, we shall become better qualified to recognize its devastating effects.

In the sixteenth century, while a ship anchored briefly at a seaport town of Mexico, a young cabin boy who had smallpox escaped to shore. As a result, thousands of Indians died from smallpox. Dreadful as this was, it does not begin to compare with the spread of the contagious disease of sin. The effect of sin is more deadly than the worst communicable disease. Still worse is the tragedy of sin in the hearts of those of God's people who have no concern or desire to do anything about it.

It is no wonder so many Christians exert no concerted effort to win the lost to Christ! They are cold and indifferent to the claims of God in their own hearts. How can they hope to be burdened for others? The Lord strikes at the source of the difficulty in Revelation 2:4: "Thou hast left thy first love." Can it be that you have grown cold to the things that used to thrill you? Have you drifted away from the faithful study of God's Word and from fellowship with Him in prayer? The neglect of these two important spiritual exercises will make you an easy prey to sin. Perhaps you are a slave to some sin which is robbing you of the joy and peace you once knew in Christ.

Remember, God sees all things. Suppose Christian friends had the power to look, as through a pane of glass, at the secret thoughts of your heart: could you bear their scrutiny? God sees into your heart. What does He see there? Oh, let Him have the victory. Make it right. Confess to the Lord. Judge yourselves. "For judgment *must* begin at the house of God."

Peter further says if judgment "first begin at us, what shall the end be of them that obey not the gospel of God?" He does not give the answer, but it is implied. If we who are believers do not judge our own sins, the unsaved will have no concern for the gospel because of the inconsistencies they see in us. But if we judge our sins, putting them out of our lives, it is highly probable that unbelievers will come to the Cross for salvation because they will see Christ in us.

If unbelievers do not see the effect of Christ's transforming power in us, they will continue in their unconverted and hardened condition, refusing to hear and obey the gospel of God. Has it ever occurred to you that because of some little pet sin in your life, you may be keeping someone from the joys and blessings of salvation and that this will ultimately result in their eternal separation from God? Such a possibility should provoke serious consideration.

I once called on a successful businessman who professed to be saved but refused to worship in any church, even though his wife was regular and faithful in her attendance. I urged him to come to church the following Sunday and have fellowship with the saints in the house of God.

"The saints!" he replied, "That's just the trouble! I do business with some of your so-called saints every week." After naming a list of them, some of whom were officers of the church, he said, "They may be saints on Sunday but they certainly are not saints the rest of the week! No, as long as they are members of your church, I can worship God better at home." What a sad commentary on those who profess to be saints of God in Christ! Such hypocrisy is all too common. How important that Christians be consistent, forsaking all to follow Christ.

Peter makes a further claim for consistency on the grounds of Christian faith. All we have received in Christ is entirely the gift of God. We did not earn it or buy it. We could only accept it. For this reason, Peter says the believer is "scarcely" saved. He is by no means suggesting the uncertainty of salvation for those who are truly born again. Rather it is an emphasis of a fact frequently recurring in the Scripture: salvation is of God and not of man. The word "scarcely" as used here refers to God's abundant grace and mercy which has made salvation available for all who believe. If we are saved, it is because of divine grace, not because of merit. There is a natural tendency in all of us to desire to do something to earn salvation rather than to accept Christ by faith. There is nothing we can do, however, but receive Christ.

Peter speaks of those who rebel against God's grace as "the ungodly and the sinner." You probably have realized that unbelievers are lost because they refuse to do the only two things God requires for salvation—receive and confess. They are "ungodly," that is, "against God," refusing to *receive* Christ. Christ must be received into the heart as Lord of the life. "But as many as received Him, to them gave He power to become the sons of God, even to them that believe on His name" (John 1:12). Though the provision of salvation rests with God and Him alone, the responsibility to respond to it is ours.

Because the unsaved are "sinners," it is impossible for them to be saved without admitting their sinfulness. "He that covereth his sins shall not prosper: but whoso confesseth and forsaketh them shall have mercy" (Proverbs 28:13). Those of whom Peter speaks refused to confess their sin, bearing its penalty in themselves rather than acknowledge that Christ paid the penalty in order to lift the burden from them. By continuing in such open rebellion to the plan of God, they condemn themselves to suffer the fearful consequences throughout all eternity.

If the believer is "scarcely" saved through God's mercy and grace, what hope is there for those who refuse to come to the Lord in this way? No hope! Peter asks "where shall they appear?" There is only one place they can appear: at the judgment of God. We read in Romans 2:16, "God shall judge the secrets of men by Jesus Christ according to my gospel."

What a sad, calamitous "day" it will be when the "ungodly" and "sinners," who have trod under foot the Son of God, must stand before God's throne of judgment. They will weep, beg, and plead, offering excuse after excuse. But then it will be too late. The day of grace will be past. All their cries will be useless and meaningless in the ears of God because they have rejected His Son. After giving an individual account of every sin before this all-righteous Judge, they will be condemned to eternal torment. "These shall go away into everlasting punishment" (Matthew 25:46). "And whosoever was not found written in the book of life was cast into the lake of fire" (Revelation 20:15). Should you be one who has never confessed your sinfulness and received the Saviour, hear His voice now and experience His mercy in salvation. Delay may mean irreparable tragedy.

In the concluding verse of the chapter Peter makes one more appeal to the children of God to surrender unreservedly to the Lord. "Wherefore let them that suffer according to the will of God commit the keeping of their souls to Him in well doing, as unto a faithful Creator." He entreats us to be certain we are in the center of God's will. If we are at rest in this place of blessing, we shall be prepared for any kind of suffering. I know of nothing more important for the believer than God's will in all things. Only a slight deviation from this place of confidence and satisfaction can produce misery and unhappiness.

Peter suggests, moreover, a pattern for those who would experience this kind of living by saying they should "commit the keeping of their souls" to the Lord. To "commit" should be more than a mere periodic submission. It should be daily. Though yielding yourself to God yesterday may satisfy your sinful self, God longs for a new and fresh commitment today and every day.

The verb "commit" as used here has the same meaning as our English word *deposit.* If one has a large sum of money in his home, he is concerned, fearing it might be stolen. But the moment he deposits it in the bank, his fears are over. He relaxes because he knows the bank is well equipped to protect his money. This is why the only really happy Christians are those who daily "deposit" themselves and all their possessions into the hands of the Lord. The reason Christians worry is that they fail to "deposit" themselves and all else into God's keeping. Commit yourself fully to the Lord and experience freedom from care and relief from uncertainty.

Like a deposit made in a bank, so the deposit of ourselves into God's keeping earns interest. This is the "well doing" Peter speaks about. The unyielded soul, dominated by self, will accomplish little good for the Lord and receive little blessing. Scriptural "well doing" is God at work in us and through us. "It is God which worketh in you both to will and to do of His good pleasure" (Philippians 2:13). Here is the climax, the pinnacle of truth: no longer our own selfish desires, but God at work in us. When we come into the full meaning of this, we shall need no prodding to serve the Lord. All too many Christians have never known this position of fruitfulness in Christ.

In the Old Testament the Lord presents, in a striking figure, unyielded believers who were completely devoid of spiritual power because of their indifference to the importance of complete surrender. In Jeremiah 48:11 we read, "Moab hath been at ease from his youth, and he hath settled on his lees." This figure refers to vinegar that has been allowed to stand until a scum forms over it, or to milk that has soured and turned to curds. It is a pathetic state similar to "resting at ease in Zion," the plight of the lukewarm Laodiceans. Regrettably, it is the condition of thousands of professed followers of Christ today. Many believers are "settled on their lees" and have little desire to follow Christ fully in joyous and fruitful service. Most of these saints have been so lulled by Satan's sedatives that to rouse the gift of God within them seems hopeless. Has such a spiritual stupor fallen upon us? Its only remedy is to "commit" unto Him who is "a faithful Creator."

Has your life been unfruitful, powerless, seemingly useless for God? Judge your own heart before God judges it. Commit yourself fully to Christ. Though your heart may be cold and hard, heed the voice of the Lord. "Break up your fallow ground: for it is time to seek the Lord" (Hosea 10:12). You may say, "I want to, but I cannot." Why not? Only submit to Him. He is the "faithful Creator." Let Him do it through you. Yield! He will do the rest. Believe His promise: "Faithful is He that calleth you, who also will do it" (1 Thessalonians 5:24).

29

CHURCH OFFICERS

"The elders which are among you I exhort, who am also an elder, and a witness of the sufferings of Christ, and also a partaker of the glory that shall be revealed: Feed the flock of God which is among you, taking the oversight thereof, not by constraint, but willingly; not for filthy lucre, but of a ready mind; Neither as being lords over God's heritage, but being ensamples to the flock. And when the chief Shepherd shall appear, ye shall receive a crown of glory that fadeth not away."—1 Peter 5:1-4

Though all Christians must suffer seasons of distress and grief, the Lord frequently provides comfort and relief through spiritual men. Thus Peter's swift transition from the subject of "fiery trials" to "elders." The saints to whom Peter wrote were being severely persecuted and afflicted, but he well knew that the leaders in the church could be a strong stabilizing force in keeping believers steadfast during this trying period. He calls upon the elders of the church to rally to this needed ministry. "The elders which are among you I exhort." The term "elders" is used interchangeably throughout Scripture with "overseer." Both words refer to all church officers, ministers, or laymen who have been entrusted with the oversight of the work of the local assemblies or groups of believers. Three important facts about elders are revealed in the verses we are to consider: their relationship, responsibility, and reward.

It is worthy of note that Peter identifies himself as an elder: "who also am an elder." He does this not merely to claim the privileges of his position, but to suggest that he asks no more of others than he requires of himself. Here is a most commendable sign of leadership, one to be coveted by all church officers.

The foremost requisite for an elder or overseer concerns his *relationship*. There must be a living, thriving relationship to Christ through the new birth. In consequence, there should be a continued fellowship with Christ as Lord which eliminates anything that might hinder or disrupt a harmonious relationship. Let no church officer think he can be of any value, either to God or to those of whom he has oversight, unless he lives and walks in a right relationship to Jesus Christ. Such a position invokes daily heartsearching and self-examination before God to the end that yieldedness to the will of the Master may be constant and unbroken.

Peter further states that as an elder he is "a witness of the sufferings of Christ, and also a partaker of the glory that shall be revealed." Every church officer should be "a witness of the sufferings of Christ" personally, in his own experience. This includes more than a mere head knowledge of Christ. It constitutes a miraculous heart change as suggested by the word "partaker." Peter does not say the elder is to be "a partaker" *when* the glory shall be revealed. He is to be "a partaker" now. The glory of Christ should be evidenced in him in a life of complete surrender and separation to Christ. Like Paul, he should be impassioned with the supreme desire to know Christ. "And I, brethren, when I came to you, came not with excellency of speech or of wisdom, declaring unto you the testimony of God. For I determined not to know anything among you, save Jesus Christ, and Him crucified" (1 Corinthians 2:1-2). Church leaders who have an earnest desire to put Christ first are all too rare. No one will accomplish much for the Lord until he reaches this place of entire self-abandonment and complete surrender.

Shortly before his tragic death, General Charles Gordon wrote from Khartoum, "There is not the least doubt that there is an immense, urgent field for an apostle to these countries among the black tribes. But where will you find an apostle? A man must give up everything, understand, everything, *everything!* No half or three-quarter measures will do. He must be dead to the world and have no ties of any sort and long for death when it may please God to take him. There are few, very few, such. And yet, what a field!"

In how many churches could we count beyond the fingers of our two hands, even one hand, in numbering leaders who have given up everything for Christ, completely sacrificed their lives for Him. These are the only saints who can do a lasting work for the Lord. For this reason our ability, talent, and money must be surrendered to the Lord. The world is not going to be reached by intellectual power or human ingenuity. If we are to see this present age captivated by God's power, it will be accomplished through spirit-filled men and women who have reserved nothing for self. They are the only ones able to tap the reservoir of God's grace which provides the life-giving stream for refreshment of weary souls. We must be channels only, yielded to the working power of the Holy Spirit. For "except the Lord build the house, they labour in vain that build it" (Psalm 127:1).

In spite of our efforts, excellent though they may be, if we are to see fruit, God must be at work through us, even as Paul declared, "I have planted, Apollos watered; but God gave the increase. So then neither is he that planteth any thing, neither he that watereth; but God that giveth the increase" (1 Corinthians 3:6-7). When church leaders wholly commit themselves to Christ, God can take them, educated or uneducated, intelligent or unintelligent, fill them with His Holy Spirit and use them as a source of mighty power.

Some years ago Dr. Harry Rimmer held a series of meetings in a southern state in a section of the mountains where evangelists seldom go. When the closing day of the meetings arrived, the grateful friends of the church gave him a farewell party. While they were enjoying the refreshments in country style, a man, small in stature, clad in jeans and a hickory shirt, barefoot and unkempt, came up and spoke to Dr. Rimmer. He thanked him for the sermons and said the meetings had been a rich blessing to him and that he thought he would be a better preacher and pastor because of what he had heard.

"Are you also a minister of the gospel?" Dr. Rimmer asked in surprise. The man smiled and said, "Yes, I am a preacher. I farm my own place to raise and feed my family. I am the pastor of a little country church." Dr. Rimmer was afraid he might have shown his astonishment and began to apologize; but the man stopped him.

"That's all right. I don't blame you for being a bit set back. I know I don't look like much. But Brother Rimmer, I learned a long time ago that God can strike a mighty straight blow with a pretty crooked stick!"

How true! It is not the importance of the man that counts, but God filling the man. If a man is in a right relationship to Christ, the Lord fills him and uses him.

Peter next emphasizes the elder's *responsibility*. "Feed the flock of God which is among you, taking the oversight thereof." To "feed the flock" entails more than mere provision of spiritual food. It could be better rendered *"tend* the flock"—encouraging, protecting, guiding, and leading the saints in the will of the Lord as well as building them up in the Lord. Considering this well-rounded ministry God-ordained for all church officers, we readily recognize the grave responsibility and tremendous obligation which rests on the elders of the church.

The apostle further suggests three ways Christian leaders may best fulfill their responsibility to tend the flock God has entrusted to their care. They should lead others *willingly, graciously, and attractively.*

Leadership should be "not by constraint," but "willingly." That is, a church officer should never perform his duties in a perfunctory manner, doing out of compulsion only the least necessary to get by. There should be an earnest desire to sacrifice for Christ, motivated by a sincere love to "serve the Lord with gladness" (Psalm 100:2). This seems to be the truth expressed in Ecclesiastes 9:10: "Whatsoever thy hand findeth to do, do it with thy might." Too few of God's people are possessed by this willingness to work unreservedly for the Lord. Many Christians remind us of the man who had the gold fever but he lacked the digging principle. God says in Proverbs 18:9, "He also that is slothful in his work is brother to him that is a great waster." How deplorable that there are so many lazy Christians among church leaders who are willing to glory in a title, but fail to shoulder the work leadership demands.

A mountaineer was lying on his front porch smoking a corncob pipe while his wife was digging laboriously in the front yard. A passer-by could not resist shouting: "Say, isn't that hard work for your wife?"

"Yep," he replied, "but we work in shifts."

"Oh, I see," said the passer-by. "When she gets tired you take over."

"No," drawled the mountaineer, "when she gets tired out in the garden, she shifts to the house chores."

We smile at the lackadaisical attitude of this irresponsible husband, but such an attitude in church officers is even more serious. For church officers have been elected not only by their fellows, but chosen and ordained by God to perform their tasks willingly and in a pleasing, conscientious, Christ-glorifying way.

As well as willingly, church officers should serve Christ *graciously*, "not for filthy lucre, but of a ready mind." There should be no trace of selfishness or covetousness. Sadly enough, the sin of covetousness has plagued not only the business world but has crept stealthily into the church. I have known ministers of the gospel who have refused repeatedly to accept speaking engagements unless satisfactory honorariums were guaranteed. God forbid that anyone should put a price tag on his ministry! Our Saviour did not consider for a moment the cost to Himself when He shed His own precious blood to provide eternal salvation free to all who believe. It might be well for us to ponder frequently Paul's admonition to the Colossians, "Whatsoever ye do, do it heartily, as to the Lord, and not unto men; Knowing that of the Lord ye shall receive the reward of the inheritance:

for ye serve the Lord Christ" (Colossians 3:23-24). Those who serve the Lord graciously will be blessed by Him and rewarded abundantly.

Without question, much of the blame for the mercenary and selfish spirit prevalent in our churches today can be placed on church leaders who have overlooked the sad consequences of offering seemingly innocent and harmful rewards for achievement. We give our little children prizes, picnics, banners, diplomas, and various other rewards while attempting to teach them to do things freely for the Lord. But what do we produce for future years? Christians who must be bribed to teach Sunday school classes, to sing in choirs, and to serve on committees. Should we not change our entire program? Undoubtedly, we are working backwards, not building a church of spiritual saints zealous to sacrifice for Christ but producing carnal Christians who ask, "What will I get out of it for myself?"

Frequently, people lacking in the necessary spiritual qualifications are given jobs in the church in the hope that they will become more interested in Christ. Usually such procedure produces sad results. When people lacking true fellowship with God are enlisted to undertake His work, trouble lies ahead. Such procedure is our Lord's principle in reverse. Before He commissioned Peter to feed His sheep, He asked the question, "Lovest thou Me?" (John 21:17) The only successful and productive motive for service is *love for Christ*. This must be first. There are no substitutes. Only as work is done in God's way can it be assured of His blessing. The true secret of productivity for Christ is found in Paul's word to the Corinthians, "The love of Christ constraineth us" (2 Corinthians 5:14). It is impossible to serve Christ effectively unless motivated by love for Him.

Finally, the church officer to honor Christ best must serve Him *attractively*. "Neither as being lords over God's heritage, but being ensamples to the flock." Leaders in the Lord's work should not be overbearing and arrogant, but should reveal in themselves the qualities for good leadership they desire to inculcate or instill in those they serve. Election to a church office should result in humility and respect for others. But how often it tends toward selfish pride which neglects the weaknesses and privileges of fellow believers. Such leadership will be devoid of power from above, for God declares, "Pride goeth before destruction, and an haughty spirit before a fall" (Proverbs 16:18).

The story is told of a famous but highly temperamental soloist who was rehearsing in the Metropolitan Opera House. Toscanini gave her very positive instructions just as he gave them to the members of his orchestra. This proved too much for the prima donna's vanity and she said haughtily, "I am the star of this performance!" To this Toscanini patiently replied, "Madam, in this performance, there are no stars!" He knew that unless the soloist and the orchestra were ready and willing to work together in perfect harmony, there could be no performance worth hearing, and certainly never a symphony.

If this be true in the music world, how much more needful in the church. Those who lead and those who follow must stand together on the common ground of a consecrated concern to work for the Lord Jesus, disregarding upon whom credit falls. "There are no stars." We are all one in Christ. For this reason Peter reminds us that we are not to be "lords" but "ensamples to the flock." Christ must be so revealed in us that those who work with us will be attracted to our Lord through us. Only as we follow Him in lives of complete surrender can we expect others to follow Him through our efforts. "For even hereunto were ye called: because Christ also suffered for us, leaving us an example, that ye should follow His steps" (1 Peter 2:21).

Church officers who propose to do a job for the Lord should submit themselves to a daily heart-searching to be sure all of self is crucified and that Christ is being glorified. It is not enough to rest in yesterday's experience. It must be a fresh cleansing each day in the presence of Christ. Then and only then will we be the kind of believers enabled by the Holy Spirit to attract others to the Saviour. "He that saith he abideth in Him ought himself also so to walk, even as He walked"

(1 John 2:6). "Even so hath the Lord ordained that they which preach the gospel should live of the gospel" (1 Corinthians 9:14).

Thirty years after graduation, a class of Yale University students had a reunion. One member had not met with the others since graduation. Consequently, when a dignified, gray-haired man entered the room, not one of the others recognized him. He smiled and turning to the door beckoned to his son, a young man of twenty. The moment the son entered the room, the others sprang to their feet and greeted the father by name. The boy reproduced his father.

Christians, especially church leaders, should reproduce Christ. We shall never effectively reveal Him to others until we, as "ensamples to the flock," can victoriously show Him forth.

Church officers who are faithful in carrying out the responsibility committed to them by the Lord may claim the promise of the *reward.* "And when the chief Shepherd shall appear, ye shall receive a crown of glory that fadeth not away." Though the "crown of glory" will be given to loyal and obedient servants of Christ at His return, they are not without their reward even now. There is a very definite sense in which those who are busy for Christ and diligently working for Him receive regular pay from Him. Oh, not necessarily cash pay. There are many forms of remuneration for faithful saints.

For example, consider the "pay envelope" enjoyed by a child evangelism teacher who said, "A little soul was saved in my class yesterday. One of the boys who had been there only four times brought his friend, aged nine. When the invitation was given, the new boy raised his hand, and you should have seen the joy on his face as he asked Jesus to come into his heart." What pay, to see a soul saved, rejoicing in Heaven! Could dollars and cents ever produce the joy and eternal value of leading a soul to Christ? Such reward cannot be measured in cash value.

Years ago in a little country town there lived a humble preacher of the gospel. His ministry was far from being spectacular, and few souls came to Christ. The work was often discouraging. But what a joy it was to the heart of this faithful pastor to learn later that he was responsible for winning Charles Haddon Spurgeon to Christ. Spurgeon was used of the Lord to point multitudes the world around to Christ. The humble country pastor is not without his reward. Nor will he be without even greater reward when Christ comes.

In these days when so few are really concerned about evangelism for Christ, we who love Him should pray for the same holy determination our Lord possessed as He revealed the truth to the lost. He said, "I *must* work the works of Him that sent Me, while it is day: the night cometh, when no man can work" (John 9:4). Those who faithfully perform their appointed tasks for the Lord today may look forward with joyous anticipation to a greater day of rewarding when they shall "receive a crown of glory that fadeth not away."

May we assume our responsibility for our gracious Lord, laboring *willingly, graciously,* and *attractively.* "Be ye strong therefore, and let not your hands be weak: for your work shall be rewarded" (2 Chronicles 15:7). "Cast thy bread upon the waters: for thou shalt find it after many days" (Ecclesiastes 11:1). Regardless of the cost, be true to your Lord. Sacrifice everything, that you may most effectively serve Him. "Be not now negligent: for the Lord hath chosen you to stand before Him, to serve Him, and that ye should minister unto Him" (2 Chronicles 29:11).

30

WORTH THINKING ABOUT

"Likewise, ye younger, submit yourselves unto the elder. Yea, all of you be subject one to another, and be clothed with humility: for God resisteth the proud, and giveth grace to the humble. Humble yourselves therefore under the mighty hand of God, that He may exalt you in due time: Casting all your care upon Him; for He careth for you. Be sober, be vigilant; because your adversary the devil, as a roaring lion, walketh about, seeking whom he may devour: Whom resist stedfast in the faith, knowing that the same afflictions are accomplished in your brethren that are in the world."
—1 Peter 5:5-9

In his concluding remarks, Peter does more than merely summarize. His thoughts crystallize into some very important exhortations that are well worth thinking about. He suggests that we be *humble, reliant,* and *watchful.*

How necessary that we be *humble.* The need for humility among God's blood-bought children cannot be exaggerated. The insidious sin of pride is one of the worst evils that confront us. What effective and useful witnesses for Christ we should be were our vision unobscured and our labor unhindered by haughtiness and selfish pride. Of all the besetting sins, this is the worst, the root-evil of the Adamic nature. Having its inception in Eden, pride continues with us through life, plaguing us to the grave. Most of us are like Diotrephes of whom John wrote, "who loveth to have the preeminence among them" (3 John 9). How we wince even at the thought of second place. Yet many who murmur about playing second fiddle ought to realize that it is only by God's grace that they are in the orchestra at all.

Whenever I treat the subject of pride, many who listen invariably apply the message to others only. I did, however, hear of a woman who went to her pastor after he had preached on pride and said, "You certainly hit me. I need help immediately. I am guilty of the sin of pride."

"How does it affect you?" the pastor asked sympathetically.

"Every morning," she answered, "when I awaken, I just sit in front of the mirror and admire my own beauty."

"My dear lady," replied the pastor, "that isn't pride! That is imagination!"

Unfortunately, it is all but impossible to detect pride in our own lives. It may be a constant irritation to others and yet be unknown to ourselves. For this reason we need to pray that the Lord will give us a special sensitivity to our own shortcomings that we may see ourselves as others see us and, most of all, as He sees us.

Often we wonder why we must suffer certain forms of chastisement that have fallen from above. We have examined our hearts, but have found no appreciable discrepancy. Again it evaded our detection. *Pride!* This abominable evil is not discernible by us because of our own selfish natures. We must ask God to reveal it to us daily.

Should Christians cling to that which God hates? Most certainly not! We are to be humble, respecting and honoring one another in Christ. "Likewise, ye younger, submit yourselves unto the elder." It would seem that "elder" as used here does not refer to church officers, as in verse one, but to mature saints in the faith, in contrast to new converts. The experience and discernment of the spiritual fathers should not be slighted or disregarded.

Peter does not limit the bounds of submission. "Yea, all of you be subject one to another." If Christians could learn the meaning of the scriptural concept of submission, they would never have difficulties among themselves. In thoughtfulness and kindness we are to submit one to another, showing Christian respect, courtesy, and meekness. Of course, there may be rare occasions when conscience, on the basis of moral right, forbids submission. But as a general rule, God demands the submission of Christians to each other.

Without true humility, there can be no submission. So Peter says, "Be clothed with humility." Williams' translation expresses the meaning of this statement much more clearly. "Put on the servant's apron of humility to one another." Without question, Peter had in mind the unforgettable experience of our Lord washing the disciples' feet on the eve of the Crucifixion. The Lord Jesus "riseth from supper, and laid aside His garments; and took a towel, and girded Himself. After that He poureth water into a basin, and began to wash the disciples' feet, and to wipe them with the towel wherewith He was girded" (John 13:4-5). Peter never lost sight of the lovely picture of our Lord donning the "servant's apron" to wash his feet. Those who follow Christ are to exemplify the same humility which was shown by our Lord. On that same memorable night Jesus declared, "If I then, your Lord and Master, have washed your feet; ye also ought to wash one another's feet. For I have given you an example, that ye should do as I have done to you" (John 13:14-15). How far we have deviated from this holy example of humility which was so clearly portrayed in our Lord's life.

On one occasion, our Saviour, in ministering to those who paused to listen, took a little child and setting him up before the crowd said, "Whosoever therefore shall humble himself as this little child, the same is greatest in the kingdom of heaven" (Matthew 18:4). Much can be learned from the sweetness of a child's life. One priceless lesson is that of humility. But most of us revolt at the thought of reverting to childhood characteristics. Who wants to be like a "little child"? A child often goes unnoticed and unknown. We want to be somebody, to be exalted. In our quest for importance, we overlook the essential test of our faith, humility. It is obvious that we have become a generation of tired, fussy, would-be Christian experts with few examples of humility among us. Maybe we know too much. We have heard all the preachers and read all the books. It is practically impossible for us to become as little children. We want to be brilliant scholars, profound philosophers, and deep-thinking theologians, but childlike? Never! We shy away from even the thought of it for fear we shall be judged dull or stupid.

Is it not true, we need a new realization of our Saviour's humility? Without it we are in for trouble; "for God resisteth the proud." "Resisteth" embodies the thought of being set in battle array. God must judge pride for He hates it. He says of those tainted with pride, "These are a smoke in My nose, a fire that burneth all the day" (Isaiah 65:5). Can there be peace or blessing under such circumstances? Pride provokes the wrath and fury of God. Blinded by pride, Pharaoh and his army perished in the engulfing waters of the Red Sea, because "God resisteth the proud." The mighty Nebuchadnezzar, filled with self-praise, was punished by the Lord. He was made to crawl on the ground like a beast and eat grass until, in complete abasement and humility, he cried to God for mercy. God has always resisted the proud. He always will! Hear his warning. "O thou that dwellest in the clefts of the rock, that holdest the height of the hill: though thou shouldst make thy nest as high as the eagle, I will bring thee down from thence, saith the Lord" (Jeremiah 49:16). "Woe unto them that are wise in their own eyes, and prudent in their own sight!" (Isaiah 5:21)

On the other hand, how much more joyous and rewarding is the Lord's promise to those who practice His humility. He "giveth grace to the humble." There is an uninterrupted flow of God's unremitting favor into the lives of those who obey God in respect to humility. "What doth the Lord require of thee, but to do justly, and to love mercy, and to walk *humbly* with thy God?" (Micah 6:8) Those who "walk humbly" with the Lord will not lack His blessing. "Humble yourselves therefore under the mighty hand of God, that He may exalt you in due time." The Lord will do the exalting if we do the humbling. "Whosoever exalteth himself shall be abased; and he that humbleth himself shall be exalted" (Luke 14:11). It is not necessary for the believer to parade his own importance. He need not sound his own trumpet. God never fails to reward faithfulness. "Humble yourselves in the sight of the Lord, and He shall lift you up" (James 4:10).

Peter leaves pride to speak of another sin which is equally destructive, care. Christians should be *reliant*. "Casting all your care upon Him; for He careth for you." How few Christians really take this verse to heart. How do I know? Just by looking at their anxious, careworn faces. Their furrowed brows publish the story of their troubled hearts. They remonstrate, "What can you expect when I have suffered such trials in life?" Is anyone of us exempt from the chastenings and disciplines of life? "Man is born unto trouble, as the sparks fly upward" (Job 5:7). God's people are no exception, "For whom the Lord loveth He chasteneth" (Hebrews 12:6). Strokes from His rod are to be expected. Even the worst trial is thousands of times better than we deserve. Trial should never be used as an excuse for anxious care. Care works havoc in the soul and diverts attention from duty and obligation to groundless imaginations that rarely become reality. By needless perplexity and useless fear, we cross bridges before we come to them and sin against God.

Oh, how devastating is this sin of care! Not only is care a sin against God, it is a sin against ourselves. A fearful heart is often the index to death at an early age. Discontent and unhappiness in Christians can often be traced to worn and weary minds torn by care. Few die from honest toil and labor, but millions perish under the slavemaster's lash of worry.

Be assured, true believers have a perfect right to call upon God for strength equal to the tasks of the day. "As thy days, so shall thy strength be" (Deuteronomy 33:25). But there is not one of us who has the prerogative to ask God for even an ounce of strength for tomorrow. When tomorrow dawns, the Lord's grace and provision will be abundantly sufficient. "Take therefore no thought for the morrow: for the morrow shall take thought for the things of itself" (Matthew 6:34). What peace we could experience if only we could master the simple lesson of taking no thought for tomorrow.

Care has never accomplished one thing for any of us. It never will! Care is like a rocking chair. It gives us something to do, but we get nowhere! We should realize that no matter how well-meaning the purpose of care may be, it is not only useless but extremely detrimental.

Occasionally, we find ourselves disturbed and depressed, even in trying to do the Lord's work. Could anything be further from what God desires? God cannot work through anxious hearts. Whenever a Christian reaches this state, he should stop at once and ask himself, "Whose work is it?" If it's God's work, never forget the burden of it is His, too. You are not the important person. Christ is! He is at work through us. What should we do then when things do not go well? Go to Him! Anything less than this is disobedience. "Commit thy works unto the Lord, and thy thoughts shall be established" (Proverbs 16:3).

Are not many of us like the man who came to Martin Luther one time, saying: "Everything goes against me. None of my wishes come true. My hopes go wrong. My plans never work out."

"My dear friend, that is your own fault," replied Luther. "Pray and mean, 'Thy will be done,' and you will be satisfied." If we should really resign our wills to do God's choice in all things, we should have nothing left to worry about. Care would vanish and peace would reign.

Without question, the Lord would have every Christian settle the question of care for all time. Why not decide at this moment to make your life one of trusting rather than trying? Never again carry your troubles. Cast them on Him! If you have been guilty of the sin of fruitless care, bow your head and confess it and claim God's gracious forgiveness. Vow never again to insult His wisdom and goodness by faithless worry. From this moment, resolve to cast *all* your care on Him. How much more enjoyable life will be!

Let us not misunderstand. Trials will still be a part of our lot. Problems will confront us in the same old way. But our response should be different. When Satan sows seeds of care in your mind, never let them take root! If you do, you will be defeated once more. Just hand them over to the Lord. Christ's shoulders are broad. He who bore the load of the world's sin can bear anything, even *"all your* care." His love is the answer. Love knows no limits. Love "beareth all things, believeth all things, hopeth all things, endureth all things" (1 Corinthians 13:7).

In writing of the sins of pride and care, Peter is constrained to warn us of our "adversary the devil" who "as a roaring lion, walketh about, seeking whom he may devour." Christians must stay on guard and be *watchful.* "Be sober, be vigilant." Our enemy, the devil, is not only crafty and clever, but over-poweringly strong. "We wrestle not against flesh and blood, but against principalities, against powers, against the rulers of the darkness of this world, against spiritual wickedness in high places" (Ephesians 6:12).

Of course, Satan must cringe before God's superior power, but he is not deterred from plaguing and deceiving the saints. He hates our Saviour, though he cannot hurt Him. He mustered all his evil forces against Christ on Calvary, but he failed miserably and completely. Now he roars out his hate against the followers of Christ. He stops at nothing. No church or child of God is free from his wiles. We must we watchful lest he attack us unawares.

Occasionally I have heard people say they believe in Christ but cannot believe in a personal devil. Such statements are a strong warning to me to be more vigilant and aware that the devil in his subtlety not only destroys property, happiness, and peace throughout the world, but he is highly successful in shielding his identity. Indeed, he is the master in the sly art of deception. Even the clergy have been fooled by his chicanery.

Several years ago a survey was conducted in which questionnaires were sent to fifteen hundred ministers. Among the questions this one appeared: "Do you believe in a personal devil?" Fifty per cent of the ministers gave a negative reply. The devil may hoodwink ministers and laymen alike into thinking he does not exist, but God warns us to beware "Lest Satan should get an advantage of us: for we are not ignorant of his devices" (2 Corinthians 2:11).

What tactics should we employ to withstand such a mighty foe? Be assured we cannot face him in human strength. "Whom resist stedfast in the faith." We must trust the Lord! Do not attempt to fight the battle yourself. Let the Lord do it. Face the devil squarely "in the faith."

Peter was a long while learning this simple truth. Early in His earthly ministry our Lord recognized Peter's lack of dependence on divine power. "Simon, Simon, behold, Satan hath desired to have you, that he may sift you as wheat: But I have prayed for thee, that thy faith fail not" (Luke 22:31-32). How marvelous that our Lord's watchful eye is never turned from His own. He watches over us and "ever liveth to make intercession for us," providing an escape from the devil's attacks. "There hath no temptation taken you but such as is common to man: but God is faithful, who will not suffer you to be tempted above that ye are able; but will with the temptation also make a way to escape, that ye may be able to bear it" (1 Corinthians 10:13).

When tempted by the devil, get in touch with headquarters at once. Let there not be the slightest trace of self-dependency. "Wherefore let him that thinketh he standeth take heed lest he fall" (1 Corinthians 10:12). Call upon the name of the Lord. Don't wait! Satan is never weaker than when the saint is on his knees. "Watch and pray, that ye enter not into temptation: the spirit indeed is willing, but the flesh is weak" (Matthew 26:41).

No one is free from the devil's snares. "The same afflictions are accomplished in your brethren that are in the world." In every corner of the earth Christians are sorely tested and tempted. But though the kinds of temptations may be sundry and varied, the remedy is always the same, our mighty Christ.

The story is told of the Christian professor who lived a life of such purity and serenity in the presence of his students, that they were overwhelmed by his challenging example. They resolved to ask the elderly saint the secret of his holy life and abundant peace. One day they came to him and explained that they were harassed by many temptations which appealed to the flesh so strongly that they were distraught. They asked, "Do not the temptations that harass our souls appeal to you? Do they never come knocking at the door of your heart?" The man of God listened and smiling, replied, "Yes, I do know something of the things of which you speak. The temptations that trouble you do come making their appeal to me. But when these temptations knock at the door of my heart, I always answer, 'The place is occupied'!"

Here is the real secret of victory, a heart filled with Christ. Whether it be pride, care, or even the devil himself, there will be no room if we are fully yielded to the Lord Jesus. "Our help is in the name of the Lord" (Psalm 124:8). Trust Him for all He desires to do for you. He will not fail!

31

THE GOD OF ALL GRACE

"But the God of all grace, who hath called us unto His eternal glory by Christ Jesus, after that ye have suffered a while, make you perfect, stablish, strengthen, settle you. To Him be glory and dominion for ever and ever. Amen. By Silvanus, a faithful brother unto you, as I suppose, I have written briefly, exhorting, and testifying that this is the true grace of God wherein ye stand. The church that is at Babylon, elected together with you, saluteth you; so doth Marcus my son. Greet ye one another with a kiss of charity. Peace be with you all that are in Christ Jesus. Amen."
1 Peter 5:10-14

Peter has been emphasizing the importance of watchfulness and vigilance as a safeguard against the Christian's mighty adversary. But lest we overestimate the power of the wicked one, he hastens to remind us of our invincible Lord, "the God of all grace" who enables His willing disciples to overcome the subtle attacks of the devil. For this reason we are not to look about with fear and dismay but to look up with the assurance of hope and victory. The believer may say with confidence, "I will lift up mine eyes unto the hills, from whence cometh my help. My help cometh from the Lord, which made heaven and earth. He will not suffer thy foot to be moved: He that keepeth thee will not slumber" (Psalm 121:1-3) God has promised to "preserve thee from all evil: He shall preserve thy soul. The Lord shall preserve thy going out and thy coming in from this time forth, and even for evermore" (Psalm 121:7-8)

How wonderfully descriptive of our great Jehovah is the phrase "the God of all grace." He supplies grace not only for some of the exigencies of life, but for *all* of them. Whatever the need may be, sickness, sorrow, or stress, His marvelous promise holds good. "My grace is sufficient for thee" (2 Corinthians 12:9). Those who have believed these words have found them to be altogether true.

Often we are guilty of doubting God in our heart. Consequently, we miss the blessing of His abundant provision of grace. Has He not proved Himself to us over and over? Why do we not believe His Word and trust Him completely? Does not a loving parent respond instantly to the cry of his child in distress? We may be sure our Heavenly Father is no less concerned about His children. Divine love elicits far greater concern than human love. "If ye then, being evil, know how to give good gifts unto your children, how much more shall your Father which is in heaven give good things to them that ask Him?" (Matthew 7:11) The devil is ever present to sow the seeds of doubt, but we must trust the Lord and believe His Word.

An elderly saint was telling a friend about a miraculous answer to prayer.

"How do you explain it?" asked the surprised friend.

"I don't," she answered. "I just took the Lord at His Word and He took me at mine." That is all God expects of any of us. Just take Him at His word. Do not doubt Him for a moment for He is "the God of *all* grace."

> "Go to the deep of God's promise
> And claim whatsoever you will.
> The blessing of God will not fail thee,
> His Word He will surely fulfill."

Perhaps one reason we do not believe God's promise of grace more firmly is our personal unworthiness. We feel so undeserving in comparison to His goodness and love, and rightly so in view of our sinfulness. But, praise God, He has never apportioned His grace on the basis of our worthiness. We need to remind ourselves constantly of 2 Corinthians 3:5: "Not that we are sufficient of ourselves to think anything as of ourselves; but our sufficiency is of God." May we never lose sight of the fact that "our sufficiency is of *God.*"

Have you ever considered what wealth is ours as children of God? We were made partakers of possessions the moment we placed our faith in Jesus Christ for salvation. He "hath called us unto His *eternal glory* by Christ Jesus." As joint heirs with the Lord Jesus Christ we share forever the "eternal glory" of God. In His high priestly prayer, the Lord Jesus prayed, "The glory which Thou gavest Me I have given them" (John 17:22). Having received Christ into our lives, we have every right to claim the privileges of His "eternal glory."

You are wondering, perhaps, what is meant by the "eternal glory." It is far more than the hope of never-ending life in the presence of Christ, though this in itself would be sufficient to elicit praise from the heart of believers for all eternity. The "eternal glory" to which every believer is called includes all that is ours as the result of Christ's redemptive work. Someone has very ably listed some of these possessions.

> "A love that cannot be fathomed
> A life that cannot die.
> A righteousness that cannot be tarnished,
> A peace that cannot be understood.
> A rest that cannot be disturbed,
> A joy that cannot be diminished.
> A hope that cannot be disappointed,
> A light that cannot be darkened,
> A happiness that cannot be interrupted,
> A strength that cannot be enfeebled,
> A purity that cannot be defiled,
> A beauty that cannot be marred,
> A wisdom that cannot be baffled,
> Resources that cannot be exhausted."

Do not riches such as these exceed the wealth of multimillionaires? What earthly affluence can be compared to the heavenly treasures we possess as coheirs with Christ? Yet with all this boundless provision, too many Christians live as spiritual paupers. Why do we fail to believe God and permit our lives to be undermined by doubt when God has made such ample provision for us?

Our possessions in the "eternal glory" are not left to mere speculation, for the Lord has given us a deed of trust, the Bible. The precious Word abounds in promises of His enduring faithfulness and love.

A certain farmer was heavily in debt. He promised his creditor that he would repay him when the apple crop came in.

"But," asked the creditor, "how do you know you will have a good apple crop?"

"Because there are blossoms on the trees," replied the farmer. That was enough for him. He had learned to expect tomorrow's fruit because of the promising blossoms of today! How essential for Christians to learn that God's promises today shall surely come to fruit in His tomorrow. Therefore, being heirs by promise to His "eternal glory," let us claim all the possessions! "Commit thy way unto the Lord; trust also in Him; and He shall bring it to pass" (Psalm 37:5).

With the believer's possessions in mind, Peter reverts to the subject he mentions so frequently in this Epistle, suffering. He never considers suffering unusual or useless but, on the contrary, inevitable and necessary. In his statement, "after that ye have suffered a while," Peter seems to look upon trial as a matter of course. And rightly so. Nowhere in the Bible do we find a suggestion of escape from suffering because we are believers. The saved are no more immune from disease, danger, disaster, or death than the unsaved. Thousands of God's choicest saints have been lifelong invalids. In wars, earthquakes, storms, floods, or epidemics, the godly suffer with the ungodly.

A sad calamity once befell a group of aged and godly women

who lived in a rest home. Before retiring, they had gathered for their customary evening worship. Outside a storm raged. Suddenly under the impact of a powerful blast of wind, the fifteen-foot chimney was blown down and crashed into the room where the women were assembled. Some were killed and others were severely injured. There are those, doubtless, who would question God's providence in such a catastrophe. Yet, Christianity in itself is no guarantee of security against the tragedies and ills common to mankind. If it were, I am quite certain the Christian faith would be subscribed to much more generally. Recall the incident, when many Galileans followed the Lord Jesus because they thought they would find security from hunger and want the rest of their days. They were soon disillusioned and ceased from following Christ. No, our Lord has not promised his followers a safe and easy life. He plainly declared the opposite. On the evening prior to His own suffering and death on the cross, He forewarned His disciples, "In the world ye shall have tribulation" (John 16:33).

Those who accept Christ as their Lord must be prepared to tread the path of suffering and self-sacrifice. Our Lord also said, "Whosoever doth not bear his cross, and come after Me, cannot be My disciple" (Luke 14:27). We are not to pray for easy lives, but to be stronger men. Pray not for tasks equal to your powers, but for powers equal to your tasks. Dr. F. B. Meyer has written aptly, "No cross, no crown; no Gethsemane, no empty grave; no cup of sorrow, no chalice of joy."

Suffering may be our lot, but let us not look only to the affliction and weep in self-pity. Let us look to the Lord and rejoice in triumph. "Trust in Him at all times; ye people, pour out your heart before Him: God is a refuge for us" (Psalm 62:8). David poured out his heart before the Lord and could say with assurance, "For in the time of trouble He shall hide me in His pavilion: in the secret of His tabernacle shall He hide me; He shall set me up upon a rock" (Psalm 27:5).

Peter reminds us that the trials and afflictions of life are only for "a while." Not many of our trials, comparatively speaking, are for long periods of time. For most of us weeks and months of joy supersede the few hours and days of suffering we must bear. We have so much for which to praise God! "Weeping may endure for a night, but joy cometh in the morning" (Psalm 30:5). Soon all sorrow will be over. There will be no more tears. We shall meet Christ face to face. This little while, then all eternity.

God's testings are never without their purpose. Peter tells us suffering will "make you perfect, stablish, strengthen, settle you." "Perfect" as used here means *to put in adjustment*. How frequently our rebellious natures need to be adjusted to the mind of God. Suffering is often used by our Lord to do just this, until with a renewed desire to please Him, we can say with God's servant Moses: "His work is perfect . . . just and right is He" (Deuteronomy 32:4).

Suffering helps to "stablish" us by drawing our attention from the merely transitory attractions of life and directing our thoughts to things of basic worth. Made aware of the frailty of the flesh, we are impelled to put our complete reliance in our Saviour and say, "I will rejoice in the Lord, I will joy in the God of my salvation"! (Habakkuk 3:18)

Trials also "strengthen" us and prepare us for ensuing conflicts. It was only after repeated testings that Job could say, "Though He slay me, yet will I trust in Him" (Job 13:15).

Suffering will "settle you." By it we are made to realize that we rest on a firm foundation, Christ Jesus. With David we declare, "The Lord is my rock, and my fortress, and my deliverer; my God, my strength, in whom I will trust; my buckler, and the horn of my salvation, and my high tower" (Psalm 18:2).

The Apostle Peter must have been overwhelmed as he considered God's wonderful grace in providing for His people. He was moved to shout, "To Him be glory and dominion for ever and ever. Amen." When did you last take time to praise God for His goodness? It is so easy to place ourselves on the receiving end of His blessing and to neglect giving Him the honor He deserves. Thanklessness is the common sin of those who have not yet come to Christ. Of them Paul asks, "Despisest thou the riches of His goodness and forbearance and longsuffering; not knowing that the goodness of God leadeth thee to repentance?" (Romans 2:4) Nor let it be said of us who follow Christ that we are guilty of despising His goodness because no praise is heard from our lips.

A criminal, imprisoned in a tower, sought to attract the attention of a passer-by to get a message to a friend. When he saw a man coming his way, he dropped a coin. The man picked it up and went on without looking up. The prisoner dropped more coins, but the results were the same. The happy finders picked them up and hurried along without looking up. Realizing the futility of his scheme, the man in desperation dropped a stone on the head of the next passer-by, who, enraged, quickly looked up, shaking his fist and cursing the stone thrower. The prisoner apologized and explained, and soon the injured man became quiet and agreed to deliver the message.

How true to life! God pours His gracious benefits on each of us continually. His showers of blessing are ever rich in material and spiritual provision. Most of us receive them without thanks or thought of whence they came. So it is sometimes necessary for God to smite us that we may look up and turn our neglect and complacency to praise! Oh, how many painful reminders we might avoid if we would continue in praise to the Lord!

After paying tribute to Silvanus, the messenger, whom Peter regarded as a "faithful brother," Peter outlines his threefold purpose in writing his brief Epistle. First, he seeks to encourage the saints by "exhorting, and testifying" and giving helpful and practical advice from his own personal experience in fellowship with the Lord. Next, he faithfully unfolds the message of "the true grace of God" to sustain and strengthen the saints during their time of severe affliction. Finally, he wishes to exhort them to "stand" firm for Christ.

Little is known about "the church that is in Babylon." Possibly Peter had made a recent visit there prior to writing his Epistle. Along with greetings from the believers of the Babylonian church, he also bears salutations from John Mark, the writer of the second Gospel. Peter had been instrumental in leading Mark to Christ. This may explain his reference to him as "my son." Peter further reminds the saints of the need for continuing Christian charitableness. "Greet ye one another with a kiss of charity." The kiss, as an expression of love, was the usual greeting among the early Christians. If the apostle were writing to us in our day, he would probably urge us to "give the handclasp of love one to another."

The letter concludes with a benediction: "Peace be with you all that are in Christ Jesus. Amen." No more fitting close could be given to this helpful and timely letter. Expressed in these closing words is a fact the whole world needs to hear, that true and lasting peace can be found only through a personal relationship to Christ. He is the only one who can provide an earthly life of deepest joy and an eternity of unsurpassed bliss. "Therefore being justified by faith, we have peace with God through our Lord Jesus Christ" (Romans 5:1). If you know Christ as your Lord, you should have peace. If you do not know Him, you can never hope to know real peace until you come to Him.

When a native of Hindustan made his decision to follow Christ, not only did his parents request him to leave their home, but he was bitterly despised by his former associates. One day he was asked by a fellow Christian how he endured such trial.

"How strange!" replied the young convert. "Many have sought to know how I bear my trials; yet none have asked me how I bear my joys!"

"Is Christ sufficient for your present comfort?" the friend asked.

"Yes," was the young man's answer. "I am thrice happy." He pointed upward and said, "I have Christ there." He laid his hand upon his native Bible, "I have Christ in this Book." Then placing his hand upon his heart, he said, "I have Christ here."

Do *you* have Christ in your heart? If you are not sure, if there are doubts, make certain now. Definitely and at this moment, make your decision. "Believe on the Lord Jesus Christ, and thou shalt be saved, and thy house" (Acts 16:31). You will know then the ineffable joy of living courageously day by day in His strength as He floods your heart and soul with His own peace.